RISE

A Guide to Climbing Out of Betrayal Trauma

By Misty Terrell

Hardcover: 978-0-578-85335-2
Paperback: 978-0-578-85334-5
Third paperback edition July 2024
Edited by Deborah Smith
Cover art by Brantley Ping
Layout by Misty Terrell
Photographs by Brantley Ping, Misty Terrell
Kindle Direct Publishing
www.kdp.amazon.com

Dedicated to the women who are...

Jesus talkin'
Recovery walkin'
Boundary settin'
Truth Gettin'
Myth Bustin'
Little Cussin'
Grace Seekin'
Weapon Keepin'
Faith holders
Livin' Bolder
Mountain Climbin'
Fear Defyin'
Peace-makin'
Identity Takin'

Warriors

Contents

Foreword

In early October 2017 I received a client referral from a respected colleague. He had been working diligently in marital therapy with a couple that was in the midst of addressing infidelity and betrayal. My colleague referred this client for individual therapy in order to address trauma, both childhood and adult, that he believed was significantly contributing to the client's personal and marital distress. This client was Misty Terrell.

I have been working in the mental health field for over 20 years. As a young therapist, I quickly recognized that many of the issues that bring people to therapy are only the "top layer of the cake." Very often, the initial presenting issues are only symptoms of something deeper, not the actual causes of disorder. When digging down, I noticed that many clients had experienced either one or a series of very disturbing life events at an early age that later led to dysfunctional emotional responses, poor coping mechanisms, and other distressing behaviors and symptoms. Unresolved, these disturbing life events, or traumas, provide the lens through which people interpret the world. These traumas become the filter through which the words and deeds of others pass to the heart. I have spent my career specializing in the resolution of trauma.

It was with this framework in mind that I met with Misty early that October, listened to her story, and developed a plan of action. Our plan was to first identify and resolve each layer of trauma, both childhood and adult, that impacted Misty on a personal level and then to integrate her husband, Jim, into our sessions once Misty deemed it safe and appropriate. What has transpired since is a 3+ year journey that we have taken together to address all the hurts from the past, deal effectively with the present trauma of betrayal, and restore a healthy and thriving marriage.

This book is one of the positive outcomes of this therapeutic process. Misty is specially designed by God to chronicle the process of her healing, and the healing of the marriage, and put it into a package for others. She has written from the perspective of one who has "been there and done it." Every word is sincere and honest and true. Misty will put names and descriptions to what you might be experiencing. She'll put words to your hurt and pain so that you know you are not alone. She balances using clinical terms with the raw experience and emotion of someone who knows about betrayal trauma from the inside out. Misty will also challenge some of your own beliefs and stretch you so that you too can grow emotionally and spiritually through your present crisis.

It is a rare occasion when a client willingly gives up the right of confidentiality to create a recovery guide for others. Misty has a passion for her own healing and contributing to the healing of others. God never wastes an experience. This book will be a blessing to your recovery and might inspire you to share your story to help others too.

Christopher K. Cornine, PhD

Independence, Missouri

Author Acknowledgments

Writing this book would not be possible without some very important "trail guides."

First and foremost, I thank the Lover of My Soul, Jesus. He was near me with every click of the keys on my computer. He helped me navigate through panic attacks as I prepared my heart and mind for making our story public. He inspired my writing and guided my thoughts. Every single writing session in which I carved out time in my day to devote to writing, the two of us would spend quality time together. Writing has drawn my heart to His. I have fallen head-over-heels in love with my Savior.

Secondly, thank you to my best friend, Jim. I am so incredibly proud of the man you have grown into. I wrote the "bones" of this book with no plans of ever publishing it. It was *you* who convinced me to become an author. Your willingness to share our "dirty laundry" with the world took so much courage and vulnerability. I look forward to climbing more mountains and viewing more sunsets with my favorite hiking buddy.

My amazing, kind, patient, loving, and forgiving children have been so supportive. Writing a book during Covid-19 has been quite interesting. There is a reason why many authors rent an empty beach house for a summer to write. Most authors need quiet. No interruptions. Peace. We were quarantined for months on end, all of us at home most of the time, and I was trying to write a book about the most intimate parts of my life. My kids amazed me with their maturity, patience, grace, and respect. They knew to give me space when I was in "my zone." Thank you, kids. This is your testimony, too. I'm so proud to be your mom.

No author can write without an amazing editor. I had the best there was to offer. Debby, you worked many, long hours editing a book on hard topics. You had your own life transitions to deal with in the midst of it, and yet you plugged along with joy. You have a gift. When my words were flat, somehow you made the words sing. I'm so amazed by your talent, but I'm even more amazed by your kindness, compassion, empathy, and wisdom. Thank you.

To my warrior sisters, you are the reason why this book exists. I have been surrounded by some of the bravest women I know. You are women of valor. Over-comers. Thank you for reading my book and for giving feedback. Thank you for telling me to keep writing when I wanted to quit. Thank you for affirming me and pushing me through. I love each of you so deeply, and my life is so much richer because you are in it.

To my friend, who shall rename nameless, thank you for choosing to enter the mess and never leave my side. We shed so many tears together. You remained loyal and never condemned or judged. You accepted me for who I am and truly showed me Christ through your love. Our motto, "WBTT" has made me sing in the rain. Thank you for being my friend.

Thank you to our many counselors. What a gift you are to us!

Dr. Cornine, your sensitivity to the Holy Spirit and knowledge of the brain in trauma pulled me out of a deep abyss. You gave me, Jim, our marriage and our family solid ground to begin building again. Thank you for helping us view our mountain and then break it down into sections so we didn't give up nor feel overwhelmed. You gave us hope. You never gave up on us. You weren't offended when I walked out of sessions or crossed my arms in defiance. You met us where we were and then held the lantern for us to find our way out of the dark. Thank you for showing us the Light.

Writing a book also means selling a book, and I couldn't have accomplished that on my own. Thanks to Brantley Ping for putting together the most stunning video for our website, finishing the cover of the book, and creating amazing marking material. Your creativity and attention to detail amazes us. And for the sake of old times, I couldn't finish this paragraph without first saying, "You're toast!"

To our CORE family, who has been the wind beneath our wings throughout this entire process, thank you. There were many times we thought we couldn't finish or had doubts about publishing, but you spoke truth and light into our lives. To the world we seem diverse, but under the teachings of Jesus, we are one. Jim and I love you all.

Introduction

Hello, sweet sister. Oh, how I wish I could grab your favorite coffee and come sit by your side. You need a friend. A friend who really gets the depth of pain you are experiencing right this very second. I am assuming, of course, that if you are reading this book, you have or are experiencing the heart-wrenching, hair-pulling, vomit-inducing, hormone disrupting, depression-causing realization that you have been betrayed. Betrayal can look many different ways; gossip, theft, someone getting that dream job you thought you'd get, but we are not talking about that kind of betrayal. We are talking about the most hurtful of all betrayals by the person you trusted the most: your spouse. Consider this book as me reaching across the table and taking a gentle squeeze of your hand while whispering, "Me too."

Here is my disclaimer: I am not a therapist, although I've been through a lot of therapy. I am not an expert in the area of sexual betrayal, although I have experienced it. The insight I've gained over the years is mostly from being in the trenches, not in the classroom. However, I have gained some certifications along the way to integrate my experience with education so I can do my best to provide wisdom. By the time this book is published, I will probably wish I could add more as I continue to live out my recovery and experience healing. Much of my learning has been through trial and error, an amazing support system, a closet full of books by actual experts, and some rock star counselors.

Having a background in education, I thrive on learning. After hearing of my husband's betrayal, I responded by grabbing every book I could on the topic and took bits and pieces from each one as I "personalized" my recovery process. Fast forward seven years, I now have a lot of material including journal entries, articles, conferences I have attended, recovery group failures and victories, therapy sessions and more. I felt other women would benefit from all the knowledge I had acquired if only I took the time to organize my thoughts and write them down. I love to teach and have a degree in education, so taking hard concepts and simplifying them is what I do for a living. It felt natural for me to take what I've learned and share my experiences with other women. I recently finished my certification as an advocate for women in domestic abuse relationships and my certification as a mental health coach. Therefore, you will read a lot about abuse and mental health and hopefully gain clarity on your situation.

I want to make it perfectly clear that I am on this road *with* you. I have not arrived, nor do I pretend to have it all together. We have not always handled recovery perfectly. My husband and I still have our ups and our downs. I still get triggered. He still fights old patterns. Just when I think I've finally gotten "over it", something will pop up unexpectedly and we have to revisit past hurts that bubble back up. Our children have struggled. We are still in active recovery and have been so for seven long years, rarely missing a therapy session. The climb has been hard, but the views of healing we have glimpsed along the way have been worth it.

Why Write a Book on This?

As I type these words, I'm sitting in my living room, my feet propped up on the coffee table and my laptop is open on my lap. My

11-year-old daughter is sitting in a recliner near me chatting on the phone with one of her friends. My Golden Retriever, Ralph, is curled up at my feet and I can hear my son playing with his Legos in the other room. Jim, my husband of 20 years, is working on finishing our basement and the hammering and thuds are reverberating the wall behind the sofa I sit upon. If you were to peek into our window, you would see peace. But my friend, it has not always been so. We have had to fight tooth and nail to find it. We have been relentless in our peace-making, grace-reaching, truth-seeking path and it has been a brutal fight, indeed. The thought of writing a book on sexual betrayal has my knees shaking and my fists clenching. Honestly, I cannot think of a worse topic to write a book about, can you? I might as well just slay open the deepest, most secret parts of my soul and allow the world to see how screwed up my life is, right? So why now? Why this? Why?

Two reasons: 1. Sharing our story brings healing to us and to others. 2. Because you matter deeply to God.

God sees you in your pain, and He desires for you to experience healing and freedom. He is Jehovah-Jireh, the God Who Provides, and even now, He is providing a way out of your pain.

God hasn't carried me through these wretched waters to keep it all to myself. You may need this info, just as I needed it. Maybe there is just one truth spoken that will toss you a lifesaving flotation device that will keep your head above troubled waters.

I have often been reminded that you feel alone, lost, confused, and so very sad. I know this, because I did too. The pain and questions that are constantly going through your mind have also gone through my mind, as well as many other women who are in your same shoes. Take a deep breath. You are not alone. You are not crazy.

You've been betrayed.

I know the depth of that type of betrayal. When my husband, Jim, fully disclosed to me his unfaithfulness and 25+-year porn addiction, it was an ugly, long night. I tore my clothes, pulled my hair and beat on my chest, hoping the physical sensations would lessen the pain I felt inside. I curled up on the floor and beat the jute rug with my fist, then sat back up and started the entire process over again. Rocking, reaching, ripping...rocking, reaching, ripping. Jim sat on the couch, his head in his hands, and wept. We did this literally until the sun rose the next morning, and then started all over again the next two nights.

Let me back up and give you a little history.

Pornography stole my husband at the tender age of 13. He likes to share how a 30-second image hooked him for 27 years. Our entire marriage, I never knew. As he aged, it only got worse, harder to control and harder to hide, but he couldn't stop. He tried many times. White-knuckling didn't work. It only got harder to cover his tracks.

The basis of Jim's porn use went way back before I was ever in the picture. His career in professional baseball exposed him to life "on the road" and was the perfect ground to allow his addiction to grab hold for dear life. Even on our wedding day, unbeknownst to me, his mistress of pornography was present. What resulted was a marriage that slowly drifted apart, a little at a time, over many, many years. This was not something that I knew was happening. At least, cognitively, I was unaware. My instincts knew. I knew something was "off," but couldn't put my finger on it. I was living my life and Jim was living his. Together, but certainly not united.

My husband's brain was hijacked. The "hits" had to come more frequently, and eventually led him to act out beyond the computer screen. He was a master deceiver. At the same time, I relished in my ultra-independence, another form of trauma response we will discuss later in the book. All of these dynamics were happening, and I had no idea we were in a state of true crisis.

When the truth surfaced, I was left with so many unanswered questions. I felt so lost, trying to make sense of my world gone mad. I was gasping for air. How was I so completely unaware of this? Why was it stirring up past trauma from my childhood? Why was I feeling strong distrust and hate towards all men? I began to realize that I too, had some healing to do, regardless of what choices my husband made.

Early on, I resolved that betrayal would not win. My extrovert self chose to turn inward, and in quiet determination I envisioned myself experiencing a life transforming healing through the power of Jesus. I set my mind and heart on the hope that regardless of what happened to my marriage, I could find healing. I cast that vision before me, and here I am today, writing the logistics of how that looked.

Having books to read, articles to highlight, and journals upon journals to write in, I began organizing my thoughts and my road map to healing. I found there was no "one size fits all" approach to healing. But there are some foundational aspects of recovery that I hope you will find helpful on your own journey to wholeness.

Use this book more like a textbook. Mark it up, highlight, add post-it tabs for quick reference, or doggy ear the pages if you want. Become a student of yourself. Education will be your powerhouse tool. Opening this book tells me you are committed and ready to take your healing by the bootstraps and "git 'er done." I'm so proud of you. Jesus is, too.

Jesus has known of this betrayal all along. He is so glad it is finally out, because now He can come in and do His redemptive work in you and hopefully, your spouse too. Your discovery of betrayal is God's grace poured out on your life as He is bringing everything into the Light. You deserve to know the truth and be set free. But sometimes discovery doesn't happen overnight. It is a process, and healing from betrayal trauma is definitely a process. It is similar to hiking up a mountain. You have to face the forest of grief, remove boulders that are hindering your progress, take leaps of faith, learn to trust your instincts, and more. In this book, I have broken up recovery into four main phases: Climb, Conquer, Rest, Restore. But before you begin you must do one thing: Rise.

While rising may seem obvious, easy it is not. Betrayal pushes us into a deep pit of despair. Everything in you will tell you to stay in this pit. Your body will be so tired, and you will question everything. Rising is not for the faint of heart and takes an amazing amount of courage and grit. It's okay if you do not yet see the destination clearly. This book may help you gain clarity, and the women who've walked this path before you can hold the torches to light your way. But rising is a choice. Once you have made the courageous choice to rise, you can begin phase one: climb.

The Climb

This trek may look like the largest mountain of your life. It will take sheer grit and determination to keep going and resist the urge to give up. You will need to press into the power of the Holy Spirit and trust that less burdensome days are on the horizon. This phase feels like an uphill climb with a 100lb pack on our back. Some days look like putting one foot in front of the other. You stumble, get overwhelmed, feel clumsy, feel extreme fatigue, look like a hot mess, but each day you keep showing up. You rise up and climb the mountain again. And again. And again. You learn how to be vulnerable, something that takes a great amount of courage. You pray constantly and draw your strength from Jesus, because you know you can't climb this without help. You will fight feelings of hopelessness often. During the climb, the Holy Spirit will begin to reveal what I call "stones of revelation." The stones represent the reality of your past, your present and your future. Each stone is the weight of shame-based belief systems about yourself, your life, and more. As you trek uphill in your healing process, you begin to remove these stones from your "backpack" one by one and feel it, explore it, grieve it. There are many, many stones in your pack, but over time, you will look back and see all the stones you've released, and your soul will feel lighter. You will begin to see the work has been worth it, and that keeps you motivated to keep climbing. This is also the phase in which you find your trail guides and hiking partners. There is an entire community for you, so you don't have to face this alone. It's just a matter of seeking them out. The women who've gone before you will toss you a "rope of hope" and come along beside you when you need them the most.

The Conquer

In the second phase, you see glimmers of hope as you find yourself conquering some big hurdles. Let me be clear, you are still climbing, but you begin to see occasional views that are breathtaking and awesome. There is still work to be done, but the tree's clear out a bit here and there, and you start to see some progress. Your brain fog lifts, and physically you begin to feel more like yourself. These small victories will keep you motivated to continue climbing. You may even find your joy starting to return and will slowly feel your spark come back.

You also notice perspective changes and behavioral pattern changes, in yourself and maybe even in your spouse, if he is also in recovery. These moments of clarity confirm that Jehovah-Jireh, the God Who Provides, has been paving a way out from your old circumstances, and is now providing a new way of thinking and doing.

Rest

The third phase weaves in and out of your first two phases as you prioritize rest. There are two types of rest you will experience: physical and spiritual. I've devoted an entire chapter to this topic alone. During the rest phase(s), you can breathe in God's love and find your peace return.

Restore

The last phase is restore. Isaiah 43:19 says, "Behold! I will do a new thing! Now it shall spring forth, shall you not know it? I will even make a road in the wilderness and rivers in the desert" (NKJV). This is so exciting! Your goal is to do a "new thing" in your life. This means new patterns, new ways of thinking, new concepts to grasp, and old concepts to let go of. The "restoring" phase takes you to your new you. You are on top of your mountain, and you can see the vast land of opportunity and the forest of grief far below. As far as the eye can see, you see mountain after mountain, and you realize that you can reclaim the years that were stolen from you and reclaim them!

You may even turn those years into a powerhouse of hope for others. Perhaps, for some, God did not mean for them to climb this huge mountain, conquer it, and then keep it all to themselves. Some, like myself, feel a responsibility to give back to other hurting individuals who need those ropes-of-hope tossed to them as they climb their own mountains.

Keep in mind, the healing that is taking place is for you as an individual. *Repairing the marriage isn't on the table yet.* Understanding what happened, how it affected you, how to heal, and how to find safety is what is most important.

So sister, rise. Rise into the woman of valor God created you to be. He created you with the heart of a *warrior*. This is not the end for you. Fix your eyes to the mountaintop, and watch God blow your mind. You are loved, cherished, honored, adored, valued, important, and capable. Even on your very worst days, that is how God, your Redeemer, sees you.

Climb. Conquer. Rest. Restore. Grab your compass, your hiking boots and your grit. Let's go.

THE CLIMB

"The hardest mountain to climb is the

one within."

-J. Lynn

Chapter 1: Betrayal

Betrayed. Betrayal means "an act of deliberate disloyalty." Let that sink in. Deliberate disloyalty. Let's hone in on the word, "deliberate." To be "deliberate" means to calculate. Intentional. On purpose. There is a reason why betrayal pushes us into despair. Someone we love has hurt us, harmed us, lied to us...on purpose! It is one thing when someone does it unintentionally, but when we find ourselves in a relationship where we thought there was love and trust, and then we are met with the realization that everything we built was based on lies, our lives are completely and utterly turned inside out and upside down. We question everything. Every kind gesture, every gift, every vacation and every memory of our entire marriage feels tainted by the dark cloud of betrayal. Like a thick fog, it moves in and infiltrates every area of our heart. The fog takes over our brains as we shut down, become numb, try to sort out facts from lies, and analyze every motive, every act and every word. We question who we are, why this happened, how this happened, and blame ourselves. We feel desperate to make sense of the darkness our spouses/significant others placed us in.

Did you ever read the book or see the movie "Lord of the Rings?" One of my favorite scenes is when the Fellowship of the Ring is running for their lives through a dark cave as a fiery monster known as Balrog, a demon of the ancient world, is angrily chasing after them. They all have to cross a long bridge to safety that goes over a never-ending dark abyss of nothingness. Gandolf the Gray, a wise old wizard, is the last one to make his way across the bridge as the terrible, fiery monster is quickly on his heels. He turns around, confronts the monster by yelling, "You shall not pass!" and with a determined stance, his wizardry breaks the bridge, forcing Balrog to fall into the deep abyss below. Just when you think Gandolf has escaped, in one last attempt, Balrog uses one of his long, fiery tentacles to reach up and wrap it around Gandolf's leg, pulling him down into the abyss with him.

The viewer watches in horror as Gandolf and Balrog battle it out while free-falling. That is exactly how betrayal and disclosure felt to me. Being pushed into a deep abyss, fighting the greatest battle of my life, all the while free-falling emotionally. Yet, somehow, I was expected to still perform at work, still be a mom, still serve at church, and still be a wife, daughter, sister, aunt, friend. To say I was overwhelmed is an understatement. Can you relate?

There is a reason why you feel irritable, hormonal, stressed, and tired. Betrayal causes all sorts of physical symptoms, from weight gain to weight loss, hormonal imbalances, sleep disturbances, fatigue, depression/anxiety, headaches, migraines, stomach problems, pain, heart issues and more.

You are not going crazy. You, sweet sister, have been betrayed. And all of the symptoms I just mentioned are due to trauma.

If you are anything like me in those initial days after discovery and/or disclosure, you may feel very unlike your normal self. When I think of myself during those raw, dark days, my heart gets sad. I pulled out my hair, I tore my clothes, I rocked myself on the floor next to our bed, I rolled up in fetal position and I soaked the carpet with my tears. It was raw and it was painful. Take heart and hear me out: there is hope ahead. There is life ahead. There is direction ahead. Remember, Jesus is the way, truth and life. He will present Himself to you and your situation as your way, truth and life as you pursue healing. Don't give up, even if you must give in to your situation. Stronger days are coming. This message is so important, if I could shout it at you with a megaphone I would! If I could fly an airplane and write the letters in the sky for you, I would! If I could appear to you in your dreams, I would do so in a field with bright colored daisies and blue skies, and a giant sign in rainbow colors: *STRONGER DAYS ARE COMING*! Take a minute and settle that into your heart and soul. Breathe in those words, and as you exhale, release some of your worries that whisper the lie that life is hopeless. There is a difference between "hope less" and "hopeless." Your hope is being challenged, but your hope is not gone, sweet friend. Cling to this truth, and on those days when you think all is lost, remember these words: Stronger days are coming.

As we begin this journey together, make note of the following:

1. There are many great resources for you. I will include some of my favorite resources scattered throughout the book and also in the appendix. Appendix D has some "group leader tips" for those of you using this book in your betrayal trauma recovery group.

2. Be committed to your recovery work. It is recovery *work*. Anger work. Trauma work. This process is work! It will get hard. It will be painful. It will stir up grief. Stay the course. It will be worth it.

3. Recovery work is about you. This isn't about saving your marriage or changing your spouse. Regardless of what your spouse does or does not do, you can still be in control of your healing.

4. Respect that other women are navigating through rough waters and because of that, recovery is never perfect. It is

messy and has many layers of complexity. What is right for you may not be the right path for another.

5. What you are experiencing right now is due to trauma. Therefore, we will be looking at this through a trauma-based model. We will discuss this more in detail later in the book, but it's worth mentioning up front.
6. This is a faith-based book, and I will refer to my personal relationship with God and Jesus. This is NOT a fundamentalist book. Anyone who knows me well, knows how much I loathe legalism. Regardless of your belief in God, there are still fundamental tips and tools that I believe anyone can benefit from.
7. This book is written specifically for women who have experienced sexual betrayal. However, men in recovery from sexual addiction have found this book to be a "trail guide" for them as well. It has given them a reality check into fully understanding how their addiction has affected their wives. Men have told me that learning about some of the detailed approaches we took in order to create safety and trust has proven beneficial and helpful.
8. At the end of each chapter, I will gently push you further with optional recovery "heartwork challenges." (I wasn't a teacher for 14 years for nothing!) You can use this book as a group study, a personal study, or as a complimentary book to your support group.
9. Buy a good highlighter, journal, and sticky note tabs to mark pages and excerpts that stand out to you. If you read something that resonates, consider placing a sticky note tab

on the page and label it for a quick reference point should you want to revisit it again.

10. Give yourself loads of grace during this season. Everything will feel overwhelming. Consider letting go of other responsibilities or events so all your energy can go towards what matters-you.

11. I encourage you to take the time to read the Q & A. I asked Jim, my husband, three to six questions in response to the topic covered. Hearing what a man in recovery sounds like might prove to be helpful as you gain clarity on your situation and feel empowered to make the right choices unique to you. (Keep in mind, we believe their actions not words, and his words were backed up by his actions.)

12. I want to acknowledge that betrayal and addiction occur in *both* genders. For the sake of simplicity, I will reference gender terms specific to my target audience. Women will be labeled as the spouse who has experienced betrayal, and men will be labeled as the sex addict/addict in recovery, but take note that I understand those roles can be reversed.

The Struggle to Rise

Right now, your brain is in a trauma-response state. We will be digging into the implications of that throughout this entire book. To ease the overwhelming flooding of emotions you may be experiencing right now, you and I are going to take this process one step at a time, and the first step is to rise up. You may find it exceedingly difficult to move into that posture. Let me explain in two words why: trauma brain.

Betrayal trauma occurs when a person's relational trust has been significantly violated. It isn't necessarily caused by one isolated event, but it can be. In my experience, the "trauma" aspect of betrayal came from learning about years and years of lying, manipulation, gaslighting, and more. These cycles took its toll on my body and the discovery of betrayal resulted in a physiological response in my brain that professional's term as "complex trauma" or "complex PTSD".

Rising into the recovery process when your brain is in full blown trauma can be challenging on many different levels. One of the areas that immensely bothered me initially was my lack of ability to focus. I would open my Bible or a book I was interested in and just stare at the pages, as I felt completely overwhelmed and inadequate to soak in God's loving truths that I knew I so desperately needed and wanted. I felt overwhelmed, fuzzy-brained, and disconnected. Guess what? This is normal! Let me offer some encouragement to you if you find your heart is available to God but your brain is not.

In those first few months after Jim's disclosure of his betrayal, my brain literally shut down. It was everything I could do to remember personal hygiene. How can I read recovery material or my Bible when I can hardly crawl out of bed each day? God, in His deep and abiding love, offered me an awesome analogy one day that poured out grace upon my hurting heart.

We live on 14 acres. Our home is modest, with a huge front porch that I spend many precious hours on. Our porch faces a five-acre field of tall prairie grass that bends in the wind like a golden sea. When my kids were younger, I loved sitting on the porch to watch them play in the tall grass. My memories can still hear their giggles as they chased our Golden Retriever, Ralph. Sometimes the grass would be so tall I could only see the tops of their sun-kissed heads and the tip of our Golden Retriever's tail. They loved that time to wander under my watchful eye. I did not pressure them to return, but rather, I took great delight in allowing them the freedom to just be. To explore. To discover. If they needed me, I was near. But in those precious moments, we all valued space. Space to learn and space to grow. If they called me, I answered. But I did not worry because I knew that they could find their way home. They never worried either, because they knew I was on the front porch and that made them feel safe to explore. Now, imagine that you are that precious child in the field. God is not threatened by or disappointed in your need for space and time. God's grace extends far beyond time and distance. God is available to you and understands what is happening. You are experiencing trauma, and trauma physiologically affects the brain. My heart was there, but my brain simply wasn't. I wanted to read my Bible, but my body and brain could barely function. It was a very strange place to be. Give yourself some slack. Breathe. Rest. Grieve. Accept. It's okay. Most of the women I work with in betrayal trauma have experienced some form of a faith crisis. This is normal. If you are a woman who desires to read the Bible or go to church, but find yourself unable to do so, let me offer some encouragement.

For starters, it's okay. Give yourself permission to question, doubt, be angry, or any other emotions/thoughts that are swirling around in your head and heart. This is part of the process.

Here is a tip to keep the communication with God going, even if you find yourself unable to be in God's Word every single day: simply talk to God. The thoughts swirling in your head and the intense range of feelings in your heart, tell God! You can do this silently in your head, out loud, or write it in a journal. This discipline is what kept me from drowning in those early days. Even though I didn't pick up my Bible every single day, or hardly ever, in God's pure creativity and love for me, found ways to speak to me anyway. I started telling God the truth of how I felt ("Hey God, I'm really struggling today and feel so overwhelmed. Thank you for being patient with me. I'm so angry and hurt. I'm angry at You, too. Please help me to press into my anger instead of stuffing it. It's so hard! Teach me about my anger, and help me worth through it. I feel too weak to do this by myself. Please help me."). That is an example of a prayer on a good day. Here's an example of a prayer I journaled on a bad day. "God, I'm so effing angry at You. I hate my life. Some days I hate You, too. Why has every man in my life betrayed me? What is wrong with me? My life is effed up!" (I used the real "f" word in my journal.) If you were to flip through my pages, you'd see and read it all. I just openly admitted to you that I cussed God out and you know what? Something amazing happened! I wasn't met with condemnation. God probably responded with, "Well, it's about time!" When we get honest with our pain, honest with our feelings, and quit denying our situation, multiple things happen simultaneously.

First, honesty invites God into our pain to partner with us and do the redemptive work. This is huge, because this mountain of pain is so ginormous, you'll need lots of help from multiple sources. I quit praying, "God, help me not to feel angry." Feelings are neither right nor wrong. They just are. God wants to enter in our feelings *with* us so we are transformed and healed.

Second, honesty draws us closer to God's heart. This was impactful to me because my version of grace was skewed. As we learn how to be truly vulnerable with God, it opens our heart to better understand His heart and thus, better understand our own.

Third, honesty opens the door of opportunity for God to reveal Himself to us in ways we never imagined. Psalm 86:15 says, "But you, Lord, are a compassionate and gracious God, slow to anger, abounding in love and faithfulness" (NIV). God is this way towards you, right now, right in your pain and hurt and anger and grief. Let God hear it all. Cuss words, hate, sobbing, and more, hold nothing back. It is time to finally get real.

Here is an extra dose of God's goodness and love towards us. God chooses many ways to speak to you if you just pay attention. Consider how God spoke to people before the Bible was written. God will use nature, dreams, other people, and circumstances to speak truth to your heart. Let's not put God in a box!

In my early days of recovery, there were choices I made and stood firm upon that I know pushed me through those really dark days. I feel like those early days are about finding healthy coping mechanisms. Here are some things that helped me, but find your own, too!

- Practiced spirituality. This can look a hundred different ways, but I truly believe incorporating spiritual disciplines into my life really helped me cope. For example, I talked to God throughout my day, in my car driving around, when my eyes opened in the morning, when I closed my eyes at night and off and on in the moments between. Pave your own way and find your own spiritual disciplines to incorporate, if that is something you feel compelled to do. I believed a Higher Power desired to partner with me in my healing process. I also started dreaming a lot during sleep, so I began journaling my dreams. It was amazing. Reflect on expanding your definition of "spiritual disciplines" that are way outside the textbook "reading my Bible and praying."
- I didn't isolate myself. Trauma works hard to convince your brain that you need to be alone to stay safe. Make a

concerted effort to stay connected with others who are safe. (Chapter 6)

- I practiced gratitude. Gratitude does so much more than just lift our spirits. Science has now proven through detailed research that gratitude retrains and rewires the traumatized brain. But during trauma, gratefulness will not come naturally. This will be a discipline to practice. Keep in mind, I was never grateful for betrayal, addiction, rejection or abandonment. Let's not lean towards toxic positivity, but find real, small, concrete things to be grateful for.
- I gave myself permission to feel all the feels. With Jesus as a trail guide, we are completely free to feel, and we will discuss later the importance of feeling. Suppressing our emotions will stall our efforts, so we will find healthy ways to get those big emotions out. In a later chapter, we will dig deeper into how to do so in such a way that honors God and honors ourselves and encourages processing our emotions in healthy, productive ways.
- I looked for God in unexpected places. Trauma brain means foggy brain, so be intentional to recognize God in the unexpected. Some ways in which I experienced God were in the everyday, simple things. God was with me when I heard the wind whisper through the trees, when I smelled honeysuckle, when I admired a daisy, when the store clerk gave me an extra discount, and in the random kindness of a stranger. All these little, simple things are ways God spoke peace and love to my heart. Learn to recognize God!
- I created an amazing playlist. I had music ready to go when I needed to feel calm, and music ready to go when I needed to hype myself up before doing something scary. Turn to the

arts, whether that be music, art, writing, dance, photography…whatever it may be, try your best to incorporate the arts into your life. They are so good for the brain in trauma.

- Minimize the outside noise. Take breaks from social media. Start saying "no" to any additional events that don't bring you joy and peace. In other words, create space.

To summarize, when you feel your worst, consider doing the following: 1) practice spiritual disciplines 2) find safe community 3) practice gratefulness 4) feel all the feels 5) find God in the unexpected 6) turn to the arts 7) create space.

I'd like to share a story of how creative God with me one day. It happened around six weeks after disclosure. It was Mother's Day weekend, and my family gifted me a weekend away. . . ALONE! I excitedly packed my bags and headed to the Ozark Mountains. I stayed in a quaint little cottage in the backyard of an old Victorian home. I loved it. There was a bench in the English garden, and I would sip my coffee and read and journal for hours at a time. God and I were reconnecting because there were no kids, no distractions, no triggers, no therapy sessions and no daily reminders of my husband's betrayal. It was bliss!

One of my greatest loves is being in nature. I love to be outdoors, but my most favorite hobby of all time is hiking. There is a quote by John Muir that states, "And into the forest I go to lose my mind and find my soul." I don't just know God is in the forest, I see God, I feel God, I smell God, I find God...the forest is my greatest church experience. God knows this about me and I truly think anticipates my visit just as much as I do! On this little weekend getaway, I was very close to the Mark Twain National Forest in southern Missouri. My heart could barely wait to hop in the car and find the trailhead. I had my windows down and my music cranked. I pulled over only when I saw a field of daisies that caught my eye and my heart. For brief moments, I was able to feel joy again. Lo and behold, I still had some life in me!

As I parked the car, I told God that I'd love to see something super awesome on my hike. (I request this all the time...a bear, a bobcat, a moose, you name it, I've asked for it!) My prayer went a little something like this, "Good morning God! I'm so excited for us to spend uninterrupted time together on the trail today! I'd love it if you showed me some really cool wildlife! Like...I dunno...a brown bear or some deer? You know how I love to experience you through your creatures!"

I was just a few hundred feet onto the trail when the tears began to fall as I processed my pain. I allowed my five senses to come alive and simply allowed myself to just "be." The sun was peeking through the leaves of the thick forest and my feet had to hop over puddles from a recent spring rain. The wind through the trees beckoned me to listen to the music. God music is the best music of all. As I jumped a puddle, I noticed on the ground a perfect, beautiful butterfly with black wings and blue markings. As I walked past, it fluttered and I stood there and watched it for a moment, and then continued on. A few moments later it caught my eye again, and I realized it was choosing to join me on my walk in the woods. When I stopped, it stopped. When I moved, it moved, yet there it was, always present and I thought to myself, "Well hello there. Are you my new friend?" It delighted my heart so much and I thought it was so cute. When we came upon a brook, I decided to sit and rest, with the intent of being still. I was resting for a purpose. Not for my physical needs, but for my soul. The sound of the water trickling over the rocks ministered to my heart like no worship band I'd ever heard. After a few minutes, I thought I would take a picture. In my best selfie form, I snapped a picture and remember trying to capture the butterfly as it was still fluttering about my head.

After about half an hour or so, I grabbed my backpack and continued the uphill climb, all the while admiring my butterfly friend, but mostly trekking in silence with the comfort of knowing I wasn't alone.

It was on this uphill climb that the thought occurred to me, "I won't see a bear or a moose or elk or deer today." It hit me so hard I stopped in my tracks and really took in my new friend. I saw the power of God manifested through the silent fluttering wings of an insect. I was seeing the Holy Spirit "descended like a dove" ...only it was in the form of a quiet, gentle, comforting butterfly. God whispered to me that day, but in the quietness, the message was loud and clear. I knew even if the entire world was against me, God was for me. God was fighting my struggles with me. But I knew, too, that this battle would look very different from past battles, where I came out w/ sword and shield ready to kick some trial-butt. No, not in this journey. This recovery hike would be slow. Sometimes I would have to be still and most times, my extroverted self was to be quiet and take my thoughts inward. Going against my typical "type A" personality, I wouldn't be moving entire mountains in one bold move, but would be moving tiny stones, one at a time. But by the end of it, I would look behind me and see those stones added up to huge mountains. I knew it would be grueling, long, painful, discouraging, slow, and very sad. But of all the animals, God chose one that changes...a metamorphosis from ordinary to extraordinary. But in "extraordinary," the butterfly isn't fanfare and trumpets. A butterfly doesn't have incredible strength like an ant or have a stinger like a bee. It doesn't have any superpowers. But they fly. They soar. And they are beautiful. They don't have to do anything to be admired. They just are.

But there is more to a butterfly than meets the eye.

Butterfly wings are hydrophobic, meaning they repel water. The microtopography on the wings allows water molecules to easily roll off the surface. This has an additional benefit. When water is repelled it works as a cleaning mechanism. Dirt that is collected on the wings and can inhibit flying is removed along with the water; this helps keep the butterfly's wings clean so they can flutter.

Consider recovery work as microtopography of our wings. Recovery work is the cleaning mechanism that collects dirt and removes it so we can soar. With God's revelations, we are going to feel and see ourselves as beautiful again. And with God's guidance, we are going to rise up and climb this mountain, one step at a time.

To summarize the goals of why we RISE, I have created a short acronym.

R: Recovery. I cannot control my spouse, but I can control my own safety, healing and recovery.

I: Investment. I am worth investing in my own healing and recovery, regardless of my spouse's choices.

S: Sincerity. I choose to live a life of sincerity, honesty and vulnerability with myself, God and others who are safe.

E: Empowered. I can live a victorious life through the power of the Holy Spirit.

I want to end this chapter by speaking truth over you. May these words feel like mountain spring water, cleansing and refreshing to your dry spirit.

El Roi, the God Who Sees, acknowledges your pain. God sees your need and will be your Jehovah Jireh, The God Who

Provides. God is providing for you now, in this moment, although it may not look the way you imagined.

I pray these words of truth give you just what you need to rise up, face your mountain and begin the climb towards healing.

One last thing to mention before moving on. At the end of each chapter, I've included a Q&A section with my husband, Jim.

Jim jumped right into recovery and began making amends, and the Q&A section is to help women better understand what a man in recovery looks like and sounds like. We believe actions more than words. It can be confusing when a man says he's in recovery, but his actions say otherwise. While I realize you are only reading Jim's *words*, I can verify that his day-to-day life *actions* backed these words up.

"Though you have made me see troubles many and bitter, you will restore my life again; from the depths of the earth you will again bring me up. You will increase my honor and comfort me once more"

Psalm 71:20-21 (NIV).

Heartwork Challenge:

1. Read Psalm 71. In the space provided or in a notebook, write a letter to God, journaling any thoughts pertaining to this passage and chapter. Where are you on your healing journey as of right now? Tell God. How are you feeling right now about your future? Your past? Your present? Tell God! Don't hold back. Take every feeling and let it out on your pages.

2. After writing your letter to God, take a minute to pray and ask God to help you write a letter back to yourself. Write as if God is speaking to you from His perspective. Be sure to ask the Holy Spirit to guide your pen. (Example: Dear Misty, I love how you are opening your heart to me. You can trust me, I am a safe place for you to land ...") Be willing to read your response to your recovery group if you are currently in one. (Chapter 6 will offer insight to finding a recovery group.)

3. Are you ready to enter the recovery process? Why or why not?

4. Carve out at least 20 minutes this week to get alone with God in nature.

Q & A WITH JIM

CHAPTER 1: BETRAYAL

1. When Misty first came to you with her idea of writing a book, what were your initial thoughts and/or feelings?

There was definitely fear. Fear of people knowing and fearing what they would think of me. Yet I also felt like it needed to

be done. In a way, I've known that this recovery process was an opportunity to open up doors for us to help other men and women find freedom. We just want Jesus to take this book and however He chooses, use it for good.

When I surrendered my life seven years ago, I knew my "dignity" was no longer about respecting my reputation. I was willing to be used however God wanted to use me.

2. When you read the entire book for the first time, did those initial thoughts or feelings change? If so, in what way?

I still had fear. But I had peace. I knew that it had to be done. I was okay with that. But I still was afraid. I am a very private person, so having such intimate details about us for the world to read scared me. Being known and exposed feels extremely vulnerable, which continually keeps me in a place of humility.

3. I've heard some men say that they, too, experienced trauma after disclosure or discovery due to seeing the pain they caused their wife. Was that your experience?

Not trauma, but a deep feeling of pain, sadness, guilt and shame. I felt those things because I was able to put myself in Misty's shoes and was able to think about how I would feel if the roles were reversed.

4. Can you describe in your own words what emotions you experienced before, during, and after disclosure?

Before I told Misty, I was full of fear. I was afraid that she would leave me, I had a fear of rejection, a fear of what my kids would

think, and what others would think. But my number one fear was that Misty would leave me.

In the moment, I was sick to my stomach. I felt like I was going to throw up. I was completely devastated. I had extreme regret.

After, I felt extreme sadness because I could see how much I hurt Misty. I was still afraid, because I knew she might still leave me. But there was also a sense of freedom because I wasn't hiding from her or God anymore. Freedom from my addiction was worth losing everything for.

5. Describe "freedom." What do you mean by that?

The hiding of my addiction was always a prison. There was always a fear of being found out and a constant burden to cover my tracks. As soon as I surrendered my will to God, I didn't have to carry that burden any more. There was also an immediate freedom from my sexual addiction, and I knew I never wanted to go back and feel the burden of those chains again. The relief and the freedom were like breathing new life. (Not all men have this same "immediate" freedom, but I'm simply sharing my experience.)

When I surrendered my life (the day before telling Misty everything), it felt like chains fell from my body. I even describe it as if a demon left my body and I "saw" for the first time. A weight was completely lifted. It was a total and complete release; I gave my life over to God, so I wasn't just free from my addiction, but I was starting to be set free from all my shame. My eyes were completely open for the first time. I saw who I was, I saw how my choices affected my family, and I could see so clearly. It was a significant and mind-blowing experience.

6. Did you ever have any regrets telling Misty the entire truth?

Not at the time. I wanted her to know the truth, but she began drilling me with detailed questions and wanted to know *everything*. At some point, we both contemplated that I may have shared too many details, which caused Misty more trauma. I didn't want to hide anything from her, so I was willing to tell her any detail she wanted. At the time, I didn't realize that I was traumatizing her more, nor did she. I would recommend involving a professional to help others navigate how much and how little to share. So, in a nutshell, I don't regret telling her the truth, but I do have some hesitation in the amount and the timing of specific details that I shared. The amount of details shared will be unique to each situation, which is why we advise including a counselor or trauma therapist as soon as possible.

7. What are the major differences between a man who was discovered vs. a man who disclosed? Is it possible for a man who was discovered to have a true heart change?

While I am not entirely certain, my guess is that initially, yes, there is a difference. A man who discloses has made a conscious decision to stop. He is willing to face the consequences to gain freedom. A man who is caught has forfeited that opportunity. In that moment, if someone is found out, he is faced with a choice. So, it becomes all about the heart.

Either way, I believe a man can come to a place of repentance and humility. How we end up there can differ. The man who discloses just has a jump start to the healing process. But in the end, the Holy Spirit can do His perfect work in whoever is willing.

Chapter 2: Glossary of Terminology

Education is very important in your recovery process. No doubt you have a lot of questions swirling around in your head. Take a deep breath. You are in good company here. It is good to ask questions and seek answers.

It is time to put some language to your experience. You will find two alphabetized lists of terms here. The first list is drawn from Betrayal Trauma Recovery, btr.org - a resource I use often, but was especially beneficial the first year after disclosure. They have excellent resources, including a podcast, daily and online group sessions, and individual sessions. The terms in the first list were taken directly from their website, www.btr.org, with permission. Please note that this glossary, both words and their definitions, is occasionally updated on their website.

In your own journey, you will soon come to understand that many of us experiencing betrayal trauma change over time. As we gain clarity and understanding of the trauma, the abuse, and the addiction, not only do our hearts grow, our minds and bodies align and our language evolves, too. Because of this evolution, I recommend following Betrayal Trauma Recovery on a regular basis. They do an excellent job of keeping up to date on the latest research in betrayal trauma, abuse, and sex addiction. Also, in some of the definitions you will find links to articles related to a term or concept in the definition. Use these for further information or elaboration.

In addition to their glossary, I have included some words and definitions I found to be important on my own journey, which are presented in the second list. A few terms may appear in both lists.

Education regarding your situation will give you the tools

necessary to navigate your way through tough, murky waters. Name your experience for what it is. Whether it was "abuse," "tricked," "lied to," "trauma," etc., name it. It is very important not to minimize your experiences. When you put language to it, your body will agree with your thoughts, and healing can become more cohesive as your body, soul and mind align.

As you read through the lists, I encourage you to highlight words that seem to jump off the page at you or cause you to pause. Chances are, if you had that response, it could be something you need to explore more.

Are you ready? Remember, it is encouraged to highlight, circle, and/or make notes of any words or definitions that stand out to you.

Definitions from BTR.org (Blythe, 2021)

Abuse

A way of thinking that reduces others to merely objects or servants and leads to the misuse or cruel treatment of a person. The aim of the abusive behaviors is control. Abuse is not just physical assault: emotional, psychological, spiritual, sexual and financial abuse are just as devastating with severe consequences on women and children. Women in non-physical abusive relationships often minimize their situations by saying, "He doesn't hit me, so it isn't abuse." This is a result of trauma.

Abusive people don't lose control. They are trying to assert control through lies, manipulation, anger, sexual coercion, partner rape, physical intimidation or violence.

Pornography use is emotional and sexual abuse **(https://www.btr.org/is-pornography-use-abusive-to-your-spouse/),** *even if the pornography user identifies himself as an "addict."*

Abuse Cycle

Abusers skillfully keep their victims in a cycle **(https://www.btr.org/the-abuse-cycle-actually-a-vortex/)** *that makes escape seem impossible and the abuse difficult to detect. This cycle includes the following phases:*

Grooming– *attentive, kind, helpful, apologetic, promises to seek help, admits there is a problem in the relationship*

Tension– *any behavior from the victim that the abuser sees as offensive (including the partner asking for the abuser to seek treatment for the abuse he admitted to during the grooming stage) creates resentment which builds up*

Abuse– *physical, sexual, verbal, emotional, psychological, financial, spiritual*

Denial– *gaslighting, minimizing, victim-blaming, bold-faced lying, turning friends and family against victim*

Not all abusive episodes go through this cycle. For example, lies to deceive are ongoing, and a form of controlling a wife.

Accountability

Taking responsibility for actions by acknowledging the abuse, working diligently to change behavior with a qualified abuse specialist, and doing the incredibly hard work that Lundy Bancroft describes as "living amends." An abuser's partner and/or children are never responsible for any aspect of the abuser's decisions or behaviors. She cannot cause, cure, or control it. Long-term accountability (current research indicates 3-5 years) paired with an appropriate abuse intervention program can be a sign of recovery for the abuser. However, short-term bursts of accountability are part of the abuse cycle, used to groom the partner.

Acting Out

Abusers who identify themselves as "sex addicts" act out when they commit infidelity against their partner whether with another living person, themselves (through masturbation), virtually, or through fantasy.

Addict Brain or Addict Fog

In the CSAT community, Addict Brain/Fog refers to a period of emotional withdrawal by the abuser, directed toward his partner and/or children. However, this practice of withholding truth, affection, attention, and focus from his partner and/or children is extremely destructive emotional and psychological abuse.

Betrayal Trauma

Betrayal Trauma **(https://www.btr.org/swimmer-analogy-trauma/**) *is the devastating result of a partner being traumatized by her spouse or partner's infidelity (including pornography use). Sufferers of Betrayal Trauma experience emotional, psychological, physical, and spiritual symptoms that can disrupt daily life. Healing from Betrayal Trauma is possible only if the abuse is stopped (whether by ending the relationship or setting strong boundaries in place so she cannot be abused), and the sufferer is surrounded by a strong support system.*

Blame-shifting

Transferring fault to another person in order to avoid accountability. Blaming another person for the abuse or compulsive sexual behaviors. For example, saying, "If you wouldn't do ____, then I wouldn't look at pornography/hire prostitutes/yell at you/fill-in-the-blank."

Boundaries

- *Boundaries* **(https://www.btr.org/what-is-safety-and-why-do-i-need-boundaries/)** *are the pathway to safety. Boundaries are not a way to control another person. Boundaries are the most powerful form of self-care and the most proactive action that a woman recovering from trauma can take.*
- *Boundaries are essential to recovery from betrayal trauma. Boundaries provide a plan for women to know what to do in an unsafe situation. Boundaries can help provide clarity.*
- *Boundaries can be carefully predetermined, or they can come up naturally as a predictable consequence.*
- *Boundaries are not things to be said. They are actions to keep a woman safe. They do not need to be stated in order to take action.*

Some real-life boundaries to help illustrate this definition:

- *I will only live in a home with people that I trust.*
- *When my husband has been attending an abuse intervention program for two years and has not been abusive for at least as long, I will begin speaking to him again.*
- *I will not read any emails from people who I know to be abusive. My kids and I do not spend time with people who feel sorry for my abuser and try to tell us that I shouldn't be separated from him.*

CSAT

A Certified Sex Addiction Therapist. While CSATs seemed to be the only group available to help women of partners who acted out in disturbing sexual ways for many years, research is now showing that CSATs are not trained nearly adequately enough in trauma and abuse which is devastatingly painful to the partners of abusive men.

We at BTR strongly suggest a Betrayal Trauma Recovery Coach (btr.org) for women who have been or are being abused and Center for Peace (cenfp.org) for abusive men.

Check-in

A practice of speaking with an abuser on a regular basis whether in person, over the phone, or in writing, where he has the opportunity to inform his partner of any sexual misconduct.

Some find check-ins helpful in determining whether or not they want to continue in the marriage. However, many abusers use this practice to manipulate their partners, often lying and minimizing their sexually perverse behaviors.

Codependency

A label sometimes put on victims of abuse to encourage taking some level of responsibility for the situation. This model is false and negates the reality of betrayal trauma and Complex PTSD.

D-Day

Discovery or Disclosure Day. Also known as DD. See "Discovery" and "Disclosure" for details.

Disclosure

Any time an abuser shares any detail about something that he has done that is sexually perverse, illegal, or morally wrong, it is considered a disclosure.

Discovery

When a partner's previously undisclosed sexually perverse behavior is discovered. This is most often a traumatic, shocking, and/or sometimes dangerous event for the woman. It can be discovered without any warning, or it may be suspected and D-Day (Discovery Day) confirms it.

D-day is traumatic. The woman's sense of reality is shattered, and she often finds herself experiencing distorted feelings of guilt or blame, confusion, intense fear, nightmares, despair, insomnia and so on. See Trauma for more details.

Drama Triangle

The Drama Triangle is a sociological model that is often presented to couples in troubled relationships, intended to place blame on both parties. However, in the abusive marriage, there is no Drama Triangle; there is simply an abuser and his victim.

The abuser will use all three roles in the Drama Triangle (victim, rescuer, and persecutor) to control and harm his partner, and when she reacts to his abuse she will often be labeled by him and/or poorly trained CSATS/other "professionals" as any of those three roles (victim, rescuer, or persecutor) because she is simply in horrific trauma and is trying to cope with it.

Using the Drama Triangle to try to diagnose an abusive marriage is like trying to diagnose cancer using a cheese grater. It simply makes no sense.

Emotional Affair

When your spouse or partner spends his or her emotional energy, time and attention on someone other than you, gaslighting you to protect his behavior.

Emotional Safety

A state in which a person can be open and vulnerable with another person. Several factors play into feeling emotionally safe.

Emotional safety happens when you feel loved, adequate, and safe to share your feelings, and your partner is showing healthy recovery behaviors. If you share your feelings and thoughts, he does not get angry, throw a fit, judge, criticize, mock, or ridicule you.

Empathy

A powerful tool to connect with others, respecting an individual's situation and sitting with them in their pain, rather than trying to fix or lecture.

When we feel empathy for another, we acknowledge and/or validate their pain as we place ourselves in their situation. Empathy is the ability to recognize and respond to another's pain, taking responsibility for your part in causing that pain (only if appropriate).

Empathy can also be a torturous tool in the arsenal of an abusive man, used to tell his partner that she is not empathetic if she does not condone his behavior or if she is hurt by the things he did in "the past" (even if the past wasn't very long ago at all).

Faulty Core Beliefs

Deeply-held beliefs that are not true.

For example, we may have come to believe early in our life that we need to earn love, or that we are unlovable, or that we somehow caused this trauma and pain ourselves.

BTR coaches are trained to help you rediscover your self-worth.

Fight, Flight, or Freeze

An acute stress response that happens when our physical, mental, or emotional safety is threatened—or when we perceive that our safety is threatened. Physically, we might experience rapid heart beating, rapid breathing, trembling, becoming paralyzed with fear, etc. Our body is literally reacting to a threat and goes into a type of survival mode.

Gaslighting

*A tool used by abusers to harm their victims. They psychologically manipulate in order to distort reality (***https://www.btr.org/14-gaslighting/***), causing a feeling of craziness, also referred to as crazy-making.*

Grief

A feeling of profound sadness and loss. After discovery, the woman experiences stages of grief, such as the fact that the reality she thought she had is false, and that her life has been shattered to the core. To fully heal, a betrayed traumatized woman must allow herself to grieve. Through her grief, the woman can find ways to grow.

Gut/Intuition

Abusers seek to silence the inner voice of their victims, also called the gut, or intuition, the inner voice that warns when something is not quite right. Listen to that voice: it will tell you when you are in physical, emotional, or sexual danger. Research has shown that the intuition of women in abusive relationships is almost always correct.

Honoring Emotions

Occurs by recognizing that what we feel in the moment is real, and in being willing to learn from the emotion, rather than pushing it down to avoid the pain. We can honor others' emotions by respecting the fact that, at the end of the day, it's our responsibility to own our emotions and how we choose to handle them.

Lust

An intense desire to satisfy physical appetite. A form of infidelity, if directed towards a person outside of an exclusive relationship such as marriage. Sexual abuse occurs in marriage and committed relationships when the abuser treats his partner like an object to satisfy his addiction.

Manufactured Emotional Tether

As part of the abuse cycle, the abuser comforts his partner after a period of excruciating emotional/psychological/sexual/physical abuse and the ensuing comforting and promises made (often including intense sexual "intimacy") culminates in a traumatic bond. This manufactured tether is strengthened

every time the cycle re-occurs. While an abuser may claim he feels "close" to his partner, he is mistaking "closeness" with the traumatic bond; one cannot be "close" or "intimate" with someone they are abusing. Because his partner is meeting his needs, he feels dependent upon her.

Similarly, the manufactured tether creates a sense of dependence or necessity for the partner, causing her to believe that she needs her abuser and cannot live or continue to function without him in her life.

Generally, the manufactured tether cannot be broken without a period of separation.

Minimizing

Abusers who act out in sexually perverse ways minimize their addiction behaviors by:

1. *Justifying their porn use because "guys do this all the time" or "it*

was just porn, not an actual affair."

2. *Rationalizing: "It just popped up on my screen."*
3. *Blame-shifting, saying they "turned to porn/affair because [wife/partner] won't have sex with them."*

Multi-Dimensional Partner Trauma Model

The framework used by certified betrayal trauma specialists, namely therapists and coaches, to help victims through the betrayal trauma healing process. This model has three distinct stages that are not necessarily linear: 1) Safety & Stabilization, 2) Grieving & Processing, 3) Reconnecting.

No Contact

A boundary wherein there is no contact between the abuser and the victim. It can include blocking phone calls, texts and emails, and only allowing communication through a third party.

This is a good boundary to consider when there is repeated and consistent abuse.

Objectify

Any activity that degrades other human beings to the status of an object. This includes pornography, strip clubs, prostitution, sex with self, affairs, fantasizing, identifying people by body parts and appearance, rather than personality traits and strengths.

Pornography

Any material, written or visual, used to arouse sexual feelings in a person. It is also used to satisfy sexual desires and is a tool used to degrade humans into sexual objects. Further, pornographic material is often created using underage girls and human beings who have been sold into sex slavery.

To support the pornography industry is to support child sex slavery. At BTR we firmly stand behind the truth that all human beings who view pornography are choosing to support an industry that fuels modern day child slavery. We find this despicable.

Rationalizing

Attempting to justify or explain a behavior to make it appear logical. For example, "I didn't do anything wrong; it just popped up on my screen." Or "I wouldn't yell at you if you didn't get so crazy." Any attempt to justify his behaviors based on circumstance or on the behaviors/feelings of the abuser's partner and/or children is rationalizing and is abusive.

Recovery

Women in recovery have chosen to seek safety from an abusive relationship. They know that they are not the problem. They see clearly the effect of the abuse on themselves. They are no longer in trauma (though they will still feel the effect of the abuse periodically and can deal with the triggers in a healthy way). They are physically and emotionally healthy and wake up most days feeling that life is mostly good and they are happy to be alive.

Men in recovery have not been abusive for at least 3-5 years (which includes being completely faithful to their partners and/or families if they are still married), have been in an appropriate abuse intervention program for the appropriate length of time, have dedicated their lives to living amends, and contribute in a healthy way to a peaceful society.

If their partners pursued divorce, then the man in recovery pays child support and alimony, is supportive in whatever ways his ex-partner has requested, is supportive of her boundaries, and when/if she decides to engage in a new marriage, he continues these supportive behaviors without relapsing into abusive behaviors toward his ex-partner and/or children.

Self-care

Tools to help in the healing process. In betrayal trauma, self-care refers to more than just getting a pedicure and crying on the shoulder of a trusted friend. Self-care is a choice a woman makes to learn to love herself.

A woman using self-care understands that no one can take better care of herself than she can. It is one of the most loving things she can do for herself.

Examples may include but are not limited to:

- *Giving herself permission to sleep when tired*
- *Using paper plates*
- *Joining the Betrayal Trauma Recovery Group* **(https://www.btr.org/service/btrg/)**
- *Journaling*
- *Physically taking care of herself*
- *Spending time in nature*
- *Practicing living in the moment (mindfulness and/or meditation)*
- *Expressing gratitude*

Shame

Feeling of not belonging or unworthiness. Intensely painful emotion that causes us to want to withdraw from contact with others. There is a difference between guilt and shame. Guilt = I did something bad. Shame = I AM bad. Contrary to popular belief, shame does not cause addiction or abuse. All people feel shame, but not everyone chooses to be unfaithful or to abuse someone as a result.

Sober/Sobriety

A term used by abusers who identify themselves as "sex addicts" or "pornography addicts" to indicate a period of time in which they are not engaging in sexually perverse behaviors.

Sobriety coupled with accountability and an appropriate abuse intervention program **(https://cenfp.org)** *may be a sign of recovery. However, an abuser who claims to be "sober" yet still engages in any abusive behaviors toward his partner and family is not in any kind of recovery and may be using his sobriety as a weapon to control and harm his family.*

Trauma

Abuse creates deep wounds. Trauma is the resulting emotional state created by the wounds. Betrayal trauma has a multi-dimensional impact with emotional, physical, spiritual, and financial effects.

When a woman discovers the reality of her situation, that her husband is abusive, her reality is shattered. She often realizes she has been lied to and manipulated by a person who went to great lengths to protect his compulsive sexual behavior.

When a woman is in trauma, she often experiences a wide range of thoughts and emotions. It is crucial to find help and support as soon as possible. APSATS coaches, here at BTR, are professionally-trained individuals who have been through the trauma themselves and are able to help navigate the new reality.

<u>Trigger</u>

A trigger is an experience which causes a person to recall a traumatic memory. It will throw the person experiencing it back into the emotions of the traumatic event itself.

When a woman has been betrayed, symptoms such as confusion, sadness, grief, anger, despair, and resentment may manifest. Sometimes the trigger can be noticed (being yelled at by someone) and sometimes it sneaks up and sabotages (walking down an aisle at the grocery store).

While no one enjoys the feeling of being triggered, it is important to be aware that your body and "felt sense" are telling you something important when you are triggered; listen to your intuition. While the physical and emotional reactions to triggers may be painful (and can be managed through support groups, coaching, meditation, mindfulness, and other practices), triggers are a way of your body and mind letting you know that your boundaries have been crossed in the past, and may be crossed again.

Blythe, A. (2021, January 21). 50 Things You Need to Know about Betrayal Trauma. Betrayal Trauma Recovery. **https://www.btr.org/betrayal-trauma-glossary/**

Additional Terminology/Insight

Accountability

When the sex addict/abuser/unfaithful spouse surrounds himself with accountability, it offers us some safety that he is doing what it takes to not relapse. When a man chooses good accountability, it can be a sign of genuine recovery. Unfortunately, some addicts are very good at faking recovery and learn the "right" things to say to fool those around them into thinking that they are in recovery. This book will help highlight the difference between genuine recovery and counterfeit recovery.

Addiction

The dependence on power/control/entitlement, objectification and acting out (unwanted sexual behaviors, including emotional affairs and/or attention from others) in order to get a "fix" (dopamine release to the brain). For the addiction to thrive, the addict must rely on lying, gaslighting, and manipulation. The spouse is not at fault for the abuse or acting out behaviors, nor can she fix it. If the addiction continues without professional help or intervention, it almost always escalates over time.

Addiction Cycle

Phases that an individual goes through during addiction including:

1. Preoccupation– **Fantasizing and thinking about the next time they can act out.**
2. Ritualization– **Creating an environment where they can act out; this could include creating a situation so they can**

rationalize their behavior, such as getting into an argument with their spouse. They can rationalize by telling themselves that she is mean and abusive and doesn't respect him.

3. Acting Out– See "Acting Out."
4. Shame and Despair– Feeling guilty about what they've done and saying they won't do it again, but continuing to wallow in shame/pain, which leads back to preoccupation.

These phases include forms of emotional withdrawal and emotional abuse.

Addict-Mode Behaviors

Unhealthy and abusive ways to deflect from the addiction, usually masking underlying issues. Examples of addict-mode behaviors include but are not limited to:

1. Lies
2. Manipulation
3. Gaslighting
4. Emotional, psychological, and/or physical abuse
5. Erratic behaviors
6. Withdrawing
7. Condemnation/self-righteous attitude towards others
8. Deflection

The sex addict uses these behaviors to protect his secret life of addiction.

Addictive Thinking

The inability to reason with oneself results in an addict unable to make wise, constructive choices or see the truth of his actions. See also "Addict Brain or Addict Fog" from glossary above.

Check-Ins

An organized, scheduled conversation that follows a basic outline where a person shares emotions, sobriety, and behaviors for that day. The husband with a history of sex addiction should participate in consistent check-ins with other men in his recovery group. It is not in the best interest of the spouse to keep tabs on her husband's sobriety.

Coercion

Tactics an abuser uses to persuade victims, physically or psychologically, to change their behavior and comply with the abuser's demands. More often than not, coercion includes non-physical ways to pressure the victim and exert control. This can be done overtly, such as threatening to have an affair if she doesn't comply with sexual demands, or covertly, such as sulking or giving the silent treatment.

Connection/Intimacy

A feeling of physical and/or emotional closeness, togetherness, understanding, respect, mutuality and trust between two individuals.

Core Beliefs

Basic beliefs about ourselves, other people, and the world we live in. They are things we hold to be absolute truths deep down, underneath all our "surface" thoughts. A core belief is something you accept as true without question.

Detachment

The process of letting go of someone else's behavior and/or attention, affirmation and affection. When the woman detaches with love, she allows the sex addict to be fully responsible for his behavior. She no longer tries to rescue, fix, or control the addict. This can be extremely difficult as the consequences of an addict's actions are very real, and the manufactured emotional tether has been well established.

Having boundaries can help the woman to detach with love, knowing that the addiction is something she did not cause and cannot fix. Detaching allows healing from the betrayal trauma and aids in her finding herself.

Disclosure

The term for the spouse revealing his betrayal and/or sex addiction. Disclosure occurs when a spouse discloses the truth of his betrayal and/or sex addiction.

"Trickle" disclosures are when an addict discloses acting out behaviors here and there, just a little bit at a time. They usually minimize their behavior, and it may seem like they are being honest, but it's usually just the tip of the iceberg. This is also a form of psychological abuse. Women describe "trickle" disclosures feeling like death by a thousand cuts.

Dissociation

A disconnection and lack of continuity between thoughts, memories, surroundings, actions, and identity. It is a "survival" coping mechanism when trauma has been or is being experienced. Once dissociation occurs, it often stays with a person and can become a life pattern if not addressed. In betrayal trauma, dissociation happens when a person doesn't feel safe. Chapter 13 will provide more details on this topic.

Domestic Abuse

Occurs when one spouse exhibits *cycles* and *patterns* of coercive, controlling and punishing behaviors.

- There are 14 forms of domestic abuse: child abuse, cultural abuse, emotional abuse, financial abuse, intellectual abuse, pets and property abuse, physical abuse, psychological abuse, sexual abuse, social abuse, spiritual abuse, verbal abuse, technology abuse, and power abuse. Appendix C offers more details of each form of abuse, to help you better identify whether you have been affected by one or more of them.
- Domestic abuse exists on a spectrum.
- Is identified by *entitlement* and coercive *control.*
- Can be covet or overt, but is more often subtle and therefore, confusing to the victim.
- Is not a marriage problem, but a person problem.
- Abusers are not "out of control" but rather exerting control.

- His desires become demands.
- Includes false repentance and false promises, ("I'm sorry. I promise to never do that again.") and love-bombing (showering victim with gifts or words of affection, creating doubt and confusion in the victim's mind).
- Often escalates when boundaries are set.
- Often escalates when there is a separation.
- Abusers are master deceivers and can even trick recovery group leaders, counselors, and pastors. The best barometer for professionals/clergy of whether an abuser is truly repentant and willing to change is to ask the spouse who is being abused if oppressive patterns are subsiding, which typically occurs over time and with professional assistance.
- 85% of victims of domestic abuse are women (Rennison, 2003).

Emotional Abuse

Abuse that results in the betrayed spouse doubting her self-worth and intuition. Types of emotional abuse include, but are not limited to, lying, blame-shifting, manipulation, gaslighting, name calling, avoiding, and stonewalling. Abuse is about control, so the abuser is using different strategies and techniques to deflect off of their addiction and unwanted behaviors.

Emotional Intimacy

The sharing of one's soul with another, accompanied by vulnerability, mutual respect, understanding, honesty, affirmation, mutuality, reciprocity, freedom, trust, and kindness.

Establishing Safety

Safety (as it relates to betrayal trauma): The feeling of being safe both emotionally and physically; freedom from the fear of the occurrence or risk of injury, danger, or loss, physically or emotionally. Establishing safety is an individual process for everyone. To do so, one must identify what makes him or her feel safe and then take steps to create or protect those elements. The process usually requires the establishment of boundaries to ensure and protect that safety. Chapter 8 will address this in more detail. See "Boundaries."

Family of Origin

The significant caretakers and siblings that a person grows up with, or the first social group a person belongs to, which is often a person's biological family or an adoptive family.

Sexual Fantasy/Fantasizing

An imagined space where a sex addict can escape to avoid reality. It can take the form of using sexual images—remembered or imagined—to create "porn" in their mind or an alternative reality. Addicts can be so caught up in fantasy that they become unable to distinguish reality from fantasy in their everyday activities.

Faulty Core Beliefs by Sex Addict

A sex addict may believe that they are worthless, hopeless, and/or helpless and beyond the capacity to change. "I cannot help it." There could also be the belief that they are entitled or justified in their addiction or abusive behaviors. Examples of faulty core beliefs many sex addicts have are, "I need sex to survive" or "sex equals love".

Fight, Flight Freeze or Fawn by Sex Addict

An addict may experience fight, flight, freeze or fawn during a normal conversation when they perceive they are somehow threatened (though in fact they are not), causing them to act out and/or exhibit unwanted and/or abusive behaviors.

Flooding

Flooding refers to the rush of emotions that occurs after a person is triggered. It is a strong emotional surge that can take minutes, hours or even days to subside. See "Trigger."

Gaslighting

A tool used by sex addicts and abusers to protect their addiction. It is a form of projecting or blame shifting. The goal is to alter the opposing person's sense of reality. "I never did that! You need to get your memory checked out!" is an example of gaslighting. It can be both blatant and subtle and takes effort to begin recognizing it, especially if the spouse has experienced it for many years.

Intuition

When discovery happens, it can be hard to trust or believe anything. Even the woman's faith can be challenged during this period. Many women instinctively know when something is wrong, but when D-Day happens they brush their intuition (or "gut feelings") aside.

Other women have spent years being gaslighted by their sex-addicted husband and have, essentially, been told that their "gut" is wrong.

Part of healing is learning to trust this intuition again. For example, many women do not feel comfortable setting boundaries; it feels wrong at first. Over time, as boundaries are set, the benefits are realized, and they learn to trust their intuition again.

Infidelity

Behavior or circumstance where the addict is unfaithful to their spouse. This includes porn use, fantasizing, emotional affairs, online chat rooms, masturbation, social media, etc. This is a synonym for "sexual betrayal."

Minimizing by Spouse

Spouses of sex addicts often minimize their husband's sexual betrayal and/or addiction by defending them, denial, or even blaming themselves. They do this not because of a defect in their own selves, but usually due to years of psychological abuse, gaslighting and blame-shifting done by the sex addict. Sadly, they also have been conditioned to minimize his behaviors from leaders within the church and/or others in society or dysfunctional family systems.

Narcissistic Traits

Most addicts exhibit narcissistic traits but do not necessarily have narcissistic personality disorder. Behaviors often include (but are not limited to) entitlement, power, self-contentedness, need for attention, lack of empathy, grandiose ideas/self-perception, self-righteousness, and control.

Objectification in the Marriage Relationship

The sole purpose of objectifying another human being is self-gratification. This obviously occurs in sex addictions such as pornography use, but it can also occur in a marriage relationship.

Pornography

Porn addiction is becoming the fastest-growing addiction worldwide and is only one of several forms of sex addiction.

- Porn addiction is an unhealthy and abusive coping mechanism, often a means to escape from feelings such as helplessness, hopelessness, and worthlessness.
- The danger of porn is how it affects the user's brain over long-term use. The brain requires harder and harder "hits;" this can even lead to much more serious and illegal behaviors such as human trafficking, rape, marital rape, voyeurism, and child porn.
- Because of the behaviors that often, if not always, accompany a porn addiction, experts in the field of sexual addiction consider porn to be a form of domestic abuse.
- Pornography use is often very hidden, creating a cascade of lies and manipulation, coercion, gaslighting, condemnation, blaming, and resentment.

- A person addicted to porn is often unaware that they are a porn *addict*.
- Porn is most often accompanied with masturbation.
- Porn is very male-dominant and feeds the human sex trafficking industry and violence against women.
- More information on pornography's harmful effects will be discussed throughout the book.

Relapse

Occurs when an addict steps away from recovery and returns to abusive and/or secretive sexual behaviors. Lies and emotional abuse often return as well.

Rock Bottom

A term referring to when the addict has hit a devastating low, realizing that his addiction is beyond his control and has caused tremendous damage, to the point that he reaches out for help. This is the point when he also realizes that the pain of the addiction is greater than the pain of the recovery.

It also refers to when a woman cannot handle the behaviors of her husband anymore. She steps away and seeks help for herself rather than for her husband or marriage.

Safety Plan

A safety plan is a set of actions that can help lower your risk of being seriously harmed by your partner. It includes information specific to you and your life that will increase your safety at school, home, and other places that you go on a daily basis. It is *HIGHLY ENCOURAGED* to fill out a safety plan and follow all recommendations if you discover you are in an abusive relationship. You can find specific instructions on how to do so at the end of APPENDIX D or you can call 1-800-799-SAFE for more info.

Safe Search

A manipulative, intentional, and dishonest search that a sex addict makes to cover his/her tracks and can seem like an "accident" that he/she was exposed to images where humans can be objectified. This could be internet searches, social media, or surfing TV channels.

Sexual Addiction

Sexual addiction is "the active use of a sexual behavior in a compulsive, life-destroying pattern. The behavior can include, but is not limited to, masturbation, use of internet porn, fetishes and/or unwanted sexual behavior with self or others" (Weiss, 2020).

Indicators of sexual addiction include:

- Repeated unsuccessful efforts to stop
- Escalation over time
- Spending increasing amounts of time engaged in sexual behaviors, thinking about them and the next opportunity to act out. Emotional affairs included.
- Reducing time spent engaged in hobbies, household chores, family time, etc.
- Lying or lying by omission

- Turning to sexual behaviors as an escape from stress, boredom, emotional pain/shame, etc.
- Is accompanied by many destructive behaviors and attitudes, often over long periods of time.

Slip

For sex addicts, a slip might involve clicking on an inappropriate website, viewing something sexually explicit, then stopping himself before allowing that behavior to draw him back into the vortex of chronic and compulsive sexual acting out. However, the addict in recovery will not minimize or compare current behavior to past behavior(s). He fully owns and accepts his choice, recognizes the trauma it causes towards his spouse, and begins the process of re-creating safety.

Slips are not related only to sexually acting out. They can also be lying, manipulating, gaslighting, blame-shifting, or any destructive attitudes and/or behaviors that were associated with the addiction.

Slimed

An expression for when a sexual addict in active recovery is unintentionally exposed to pornographic images. Example could be: an image pops up on an ad, a co-worker shows him a picture on his phone, etc.

Sobriety

The state of being sober. Occurs when a sex addict chooses to stop engaging in destructive patterns. Often, he will share the

number of days he has been sober. Sobriety does not equal recovery, as it deals only with the acting out. Recovery is the all-encompassing process that includes sobriety as well as addressing all of the addictive behaviors that accompanied the addiction.

"Stay in Your Lane"

A phrase to encourage a person to stop trying to control others' behaviors and choices, but rather accept that one can be responsible only for one's own choices, responses, and healing.

Therapeutic Disclosure

A written-out timeline of a person's sexual history. In a therapeutic disclosure, the couple meets with a therapist in a safe environment while being guided through the disclosure process. A therapeutic polygraph is also recommended to help make sure all the information is disclosed. Many APSATS would say a therapeutic disclosure is a non-negotiable in recovery.

Although it is emotionally painful, a written, therapeutic disclosure can be the difference between a savage tear and a surgical cut. Both hurt, but one is easier to heal and leaves less of a scar.

Therapeutic disclosures help women understand the reality of the situation. Little bits of information of betrayal here and there can take a woman back to ground zero, reliving the trauma. Because of the addict's strong desire to stay hidden (and/or believing the lie that he is to "protect" the woman from the truth), a sex addict will likely not share the full extent of his behavior during an informal disclosure. Therapeutically addressing the full sexual history is key to the process of progress, both individually and in the relationship.

Women need the full truth in order to understand the facts so they can determine their future. It will help a woman know how to set boundaries and how to keep her and her children safe. The term "therapeutic" means this is done with a professional involved. Not involving a trauma-informed third party can cause more harm to the spouse who has been betrayed, causing even *more* trauma.

Therapeutic Polygraph

A therapeutic polygraph is an excellent tool to ensure all information has been disclosed. It is important to find someone qualified and who is familiar with this kind of test. When done well, this can provide a helpful foundation on which to build trust. This is typically considered both non-negotiable and/or "optional" and is based on a case-by-case recommendation.

Traumaversary

The anniversary of a traumatic event or season in a person's life. It will often manifest in physical, mental and emotional upheaval. "The Body Keeps the Score," a book written by Dr. Bessel van der Kolk, explains the body's way of remembering significant events, sometimes at a subconscious level.

Vulnerable

Being willing to take risks and share emotions, even when things feel uncertain. The more vulnerable a woman is willing to be, the more courage she will have to embrace her healing/recovery.

It is not wise to be vulnerable with unsafe people who will likely use the information to abuse.

White-Knuckling

A phrase used to describe an addict's tenuous hold on sobriety. It also describes the sex addict who is sober but not in true recovery. He isn't watching porn or having an affair, but he is battling the urge to relapse, and it can consume all his energy to not act out. This approach usually does not work long term and is a temporary fix.

Wife Rape

Non-consensual sex in which the perpetrator is the victim's spouse. It is a form of partner rape, of domestic violence, and of sexual abuse. Coercion is often a main player in this dynamic. It doesn't necessarily look like a forced sexual encounter. Often the sex addict will use coercive tactics such as pouting, withholding love, making threats, etc., if she doesn't comply. Coercion to have sex is not mutuality.

12 Steps

Programs centered on 12 Steps of recovery that help an addict to heal and/or a spouse to heal. While there are 12-Step programs specifically for drug and alcohol addiction, a pornography/sex addict will find more effective healing through a sex addiction-specific 12-Step program, focused on pornography and sex addiction. Twelve Steps are offered for both the addict and the betrayed spouse. (Women suffering from betrayal trauma should be aware that some 12-steps geared towards betrayal trauma often place blame on *her* for the addiction.)

Finally, I want to sit on the word "abuse" for a moment longer. (Appendix C has the fourteen forms of abuse written out for your own study.) While an abusive incident can be a one-time event, such as getting punched in the face, what I am referring to in this book is the *system* of abuse. Domestic abuse is when there is a system of *patterns*. Please keep in mind that no one is perfect. We all get grouchy and irritable and say things we don't mean. In healthy relationships, there are apologies and forgiveness and making amends. In abuse, however, the abuser is exhibiting patterns in his/her behaviors as a means to exert control. Abuse is about entitlement and control. It can be overt, such as physical abuse, or covert, such as gaslighting and manipulation.

Giving language to our experience(s) is extremely beneficial and important to our healing process. It tends to diffuse the emotional charge which accompanies betrayal, helps us find a firm grip on what we are dealing with, and gives us a vision of our future. Keep climbing. You've made a lot of progress in this chapter alone, so don't give up!

Heartwork Challenge:

That was a lot of reading that I'm sure calls for some processing. If you are meeting with a group, be sure to do your work below and read your answers out loud to your group.

1. What term surprised you the most and why?

2. **How did that term make you feel?**

3. **Is there a term that you would like to learn more about? If so, which one and why?**

4. **Which word(s) resonated with your situation? List them below.**

Q & A with Jim
Chapter 2: Glossary of Terminology

1. When did you realize that you were addicted to porn?

After I told Misty about my porn "problem" and affair, I went and talked to my pastor. He had a history of sex addiction as well and was open about it. He explained some things to me and offered education. I can't remember the exact moment, but it didn't take long for me to realize I had an addiction with the proper mentoring and resources.

2. What feelings did you experience in admitting that you had more than just a bad habit, but were in fact, a sex addict?

I had a feeling of, "Wow, I'm just like a drug addict or alcoholic." It was a weird feeling. I always looked at addicts as having issues, but I was just as bad. Reading about how my brain needed a "hit" was interesting and also made sense. I felt a little nervous because specialists liken it to heroin, so I was aware of the possibility of relapse. I understood that it was more than just the chemicals in the brain that needed healing, and with God's help I could beat this. Without God, it felt like there was no hope. Knowing that God is with me even now, I know He is more than able to continually replace my pain and emptiness with His forgiveness, grace, and love. I also surrounded myself with experts to help me on my recovery journey.

3. In general, did you find it helpful to be able to put a name to some of the things you and Misty were experiencing? Why?

Yes. It helped to know that I'm not the only one. I knew I wasn't the only one when I learned that an entire dictionary was in place to describe and identify what we were going through. It opened my eyes to the porn pandemic.

Chapter 3: Common Myths

There are some common misconceptions when it comes to sexual betrayal and sex addiction. These myths are shared by yourself, the general public and/or the church.

I posed the following question to women in my betrayal trauma support group: "What is a myth you believed after you discovered your husband's betrayal?" Below are some of their responses.

"I need to be sexier and wear sexy lingerie. I need to lose weight. I need perkier boobs."

"If only I had given sex more. If only I was prettier, sexier, etc."

"If only I was prettier and skinnier."

"The reason he wasn't good to me was due to something wrong with me."

"I spoke my mind too much."

"I nagged too much."

"I wouldn't compromise my values in the bedroom, so it's my fault he acted out."

"I wasn't good enough."

"Definitely not good enough. If only I was skinnier, prettier, sexier, and more..."

"Not dirty enough for him, I was a prude, not sexy or skinny enough, wouldn't do deviant and perverted things with him."

"If I was skinnier, sexier, etc. I'm not enough to satisfy his desires. I didn't know for 27 years so I had a lot to look back on and groan."

"I wasn't spontaneous enough. I wouldn't do sexual positions he wanted me to do. I refused to have threesomes."

"I was not sexy enough. I was too skinny."

"I had to do what he wanted in the bedroom so he wouldn't look at porn, even though I didn't want to do it. I now understand that his demanding was wife rape. Realizing that I was a victim of wife rape was very eye-opening and damaging, but at the time I didn't feel like I had a choice."

Even though we each have our own story, our own version of betrayal (affairs, pornography, online chat rooms, emotional affairs, etc.) you can plainly see we all had common themes in our group.

Let's go through some of the most common myths regarding sexual betrayal. Some of these will also include some strategies for countering or managing the myths.

Myth #1: I contributed to my partner's addiction and/or infidelity.

Truth: You are powerless over your partner's addiction and sexual betrayal. There is absolutely nothing you could have done or not have done to cause the addiction/infidelity/betrayal. His addiction is a person problem, not a marriage problem.

Myth #2: If I had more sex or did what he wanted in the bedroom, he wouldn't have cheated.

Truth: You are not responsible for your husband's sexual integrity. The addict's brain is wired such that it needs a "hit" regardless of how little or how much sex you have with your partner. Again, his behavior has *nothing* to do with you.

Myth #3: This wouldn't have happened if I was skinnier, prettier, sexier, curvier, etc.

Truth: The sex addict's brain is screaming for a hit of dopamine. This will have absolutely nothing to do with the way you look or don't look, act or don't act. If they have body shamed you in any way, that is the addict talking and it is abusive. The addict's brain is never satisfied. The addict's brain is not dependent upon you. It's dependent upon the huge dose of dopamine hit it gets from looking at porn, objectifying other humans, or engaging in unwanted sexual behavior. The addict brain is also acting out as a means to escape unresolved emotional, psychological and/or physical pain, and often goes back to poor attachment and attunement from one or both primary caregivers. Pornography distorts real, authentic beauty.

Myth #4: I should forgive my husband like a good Christian.

Truth: There is more than one interpretation on forgiveness and when it is "required". I've heard some interesting teachings on this topic, and I'm still unsettled on it. All I can offer at this point, is my own experience and my own interpretation of Scripture, as well as what I believe was the message of Jesus' teachings. Chapter five dives into this topic more in depth, but, in the meantime, we can highlight some main points.

For me, forgiveness was the *process* of "letting go". I let go of my need for revenge and justice and entrusted that to God. Depending on the severity, it can take days, weeks, months, and even years. It can also take multiple times to forgive the same person.

Forgiveness is about freedom, but this was done for *my* freedom, not his. I needed a considerable amount of time to dig into every area of my life and process how betrayal affected me. I learned that hasty forgiveness is not authentic forgiveness.

Betrayal plays no favorites and will touch every area of your life: your parenting, your relationships, your finances, your relationships, your self-esteem, your dreams, and more. Forgiveness may be an ongoing process as you till through the muck and mire of your grief and pain. It is okay to give yourself time. This is *your* process. Remember, forgiveness is not condoning their behavior, nor is it reconciliation. (Refer to chapter five).

Myth #5: Forgiveness equals reconciliation.

Truth: Forgiveness does *not* equal reconciliation. Forgiveness has very little to do with the marriage in and of itself, but rather has to do with the wife's ability to start to heal. She does not forgive for the sake of her husband, but for the sake of *herself*. A husband who believes this myth (that forgiveness equals reconciliation) misses out on doing the difficult but redemptive work of behavior and character growth, as well as emotional and spiritual maturity. He misses out on the beauty of coming alongside his bride as she grieves over what was and what will never be. Her entire world has crashed. Her dreams of what she thought her life was and what she thought her life would be are forever changed and challenged. This is the time for the husband to tenderly walk this grieving process out beside his wife. He is to support her recovery process and give her space and time to heal. A wife can forgive and yet not reconcile, as those are two distinct and separate acts.

Myth #6: **If I refuse to forgive, my anger will motivate my husband's desire for recovery (and conversely, if I act like I'm okay, he will think he won't need recovery).**

Truth: **You are not responsible for your spouse's recovery.** First, this myth seems to have an underlying assumption that a person is responsible *for* someone else's actions.

Secondly, since the trauma of betrayal leaves you, the wife, feeling out of control, you may feel as though you can gain back control by influencing your husband's sobriety and recovery. But you cannot change him.

The truth is, we can enforce boundaries that may "push" our husbands into the process of recovery, but that doesn't necessarily mean his *heart* is in it. We can't control his choices nor his heart, and true recovery means a true heart change. We can control only *our* actions and *our* response to their choices. We can set boundaries, express our pain (if safe to do so), and communicate to our husbands what we expect. And ultimately, we can start our own journey toward healing. However, take note that if a man has the heart of an abuser, his need for power and control will escalate as you set boundaries and you can become more unsafe. This is why I highly encourage you to include a professional therapist who is well versed in addiction/abuse as you navigate your way.

Myth #7: **I shouldn't be honest with my feelings, because it will shame my husband and may drive him back into his addiction.**

Truth: The best gift you can give your husband is honesty, so long as he is emotionally safe.

If he is in recovery, he needs to be a part of your hurt and your pain. He needs to hear your heart and what it is feeling. You will never heal and move through this if you hold onto your feelings. Get it all out. Remember, he is not the victim. The *victim* is the victim. Your job is not to protect his feelings and/or his reputation; your #1 priority after discovery or disclosure is to create *safety* (we will discuss how to do that later). He will have to learn how to cope with the consequences of his actions without turning the fault onto you. You need to clearly define what you need from him when you are triggered and flooded with emotions. If he has established safety, then you can tell him exactly what you need and his response should settle your heart, rather than add gasoline to the fire.

In our situation, it was my husband saying things like, "I'm so sorry I did this to you," "I wish I could go back in time," "I am sorry that I've caused you this much pain," "Everything you say is true, I'm so sorry," and so on. When they respond with humility, a gentle answer, and full ownership, we are seeing good fruit.

However, a man who has the heart of an abuser or narcissism will take your vulnerabilities and weaponize them against you. Be aware that there is a difference between a foolish man and an evil man. A man in recovery recognizes and takes ownership that he has been the sole cause of your pain. If he begins to weaponize your vulnerabilities against you, you are not in a safe situation, and sharing your feelings is not advised.

Myth #8: I should have known about the porn and/or the affair.

Truth: In the aftermath of discovery or disclosure, the spouse who was betrayed will very often feel that she has been blind and will go back – usually obsessively – to look for clues that should have been "obvious". But the truth is that most porn addicts and cheating partners take extreme precaution to hide the trail of evidence. My husband used some of the following to hide his addiction/affair: 1. Wore sunglasses so I wouldn't see him take double looks. 2. Only looked at porn in secret and erased all history after each use. 3. Erased and deleted all text messages with the other woman. 4. Acted out while I was out of town with the kids. 5. Lied, a lot. 6. Deflected arguments back onto me (gaslighting). 7. Condemned me so I came to believe I was the problem, all a part of his scheming to keep the focus off his own issues. 8. Safe searches. He would purposefully search words or phrases in search engines that would appear like an "accident" in case he ever got caught. 9. Used my social media account to view other women. These are just a few! Cheating spouses become master liars, and partners are not even the slightest bit responsible for not uncovering the affair or addiction sooner.

Myth #9: I need to know every gory detail of the affair and addiction.

Truth: When it comes to how many details are needed in order to heal, every woman is different. While wanting to know details was a natural response to my world-gone-mad, there were a few details that actually further traumatized me. You may need to know only the main ideas. Spare yourself the trauma of demanding to know every detail. For me, that was easier said than done. I wanted to know everything. As you sort through what questions to ask, first ask yourself, "Is the answer to this question necessary for my healing and recovery process?" If you are unsure, speak with a trained professional to help you navigate through this. There is also something called a "therapeutic written disclosure" that will be discussed in detail in chapter nine.

Myth #10: Knowing details will only make things worse, so I don't need to know.

Truth: While it is painful to endure the narrative of your partner's betrayal, full disclosure is the only surefire way to move forward. But *this should be done strategically and well planned with a trained professional.* A full therapeutic disclosure (chapter nine) is crucial to re-establishing trust and ensuring that both partners can heal. This gives you a baseline and can be accompanied by a polygraph as well. It is not meant to "trap" a husband in a lie. It's a tool for him to prove his truthfulness since he has been lying so much for so long. It can also build trust back into the relationship and also demonstrates how committed the husband is towards recovery.

Myth #11: A few marriage counseling sessions should suffice.

Truth: There are three parts to recovery: HIS recovery, HER recovery, and THEIR recovery. Recovery after betrayal trauma is a marathon not a sprint. Each of you should be actively participating in your own counseling and then joining together for marriage counseling *once safety is established*. Marriage counseling is *not* advised until stability and safety are well documented and established. Chapter seven will discuss this process in detail.

Myth #12: **Sex addicts are all narcissists.**

Truth: **Sex addiction is a very self-centered addiction that focuses on self-gratification, but that doesn't necessarily mean the addict is a narcissist, but they will have narcissistic traits.. Dr. Jeanne King defines narcissism as having seven key attributes: 1. No empathy 2. No remorse 3. Entitled 4. Deceptive 5. Split personalities (nice in public, mean in private) 6. Emotionally Dependent (they need you to "feed" off of) 7. Controlling. While your spouse may have narcissistic tendencies, a true narcissist takes this to the extreme (King, 2020). In summary, all addicts have narcissistic traits, but not all addicts have narcissistic personality disorder.**

Myth #13: **Sex addiction is all about the sex.**

Truth: **Sex addiction is nothing yet everything about sex. At its root, it is often the result of unidentified and unresolved pain from poor attachment and attunement with one or more primary care givers, planting false core beliefs in the addict at a very early age. Objectifying other humans is used to escape and/or feel power/control. While we understand that sex addiction may be used to escape pain,** it is important to <u>not</u> minimize the abusive aspects of it.

Myth #14: **It's "just" pornography or it's "just" an emotional affair. At least he didn't have sex with another woman!**

Truth: **Pornography and emotional affairs are sadly, minimized by our current culture. Both are a forms of abuse, and both fall under the umbrella term of "sexual addiction." I personally believe that emotional affairs are often far more painful than physical affairs. It is impossible for someone to be emotionally intimate with** their spouse while they are acting out, including emotional affairs and/or viewing porn.

Porn/Sex via technology and emotional affairs is a form of infidelity and the covenant of marriage is broken.

Myth #15: **I'm safe at church.**

Truth: **Sadly, many churches are far behind on being trained properly on sexual addictions and intimate partner betrayal/betrayal trauma. They also are not aware of all fourteen forms of domestic abuse, so if there aren't bruises on you, churches often minimize the destructive impact of chronic infidelity. While we do see some evidence that certain denominations are making concerted efforts to be more proactive, there is still much work to be done. In some churches, there may be a program or basic plan set in place for the person seeking recovery from sexual addiction, but in general, there is a great lack of support and proper education to help the betrayed spouse, and if the sex addict confesses, churches often push reconciliation.**

Confession is not the same as repentance. I will break this down later in a later chapter.

The hard reality is, many spouses who have been betrayed find much stronger support and resources outside of the church walls. Chapter Seven will discuss this in greater detail.

Myth #16: **Boundaries are cruel.**

Truth: **Boundaries, when implemented properly and with the right motivation and end goal, are an expression of love for the other person as well as for yourself. Boundary-setting is a healthy** expression of a healthy response. Healthy boundaries are established to create protection for you, not punishment for him. Boundaries keep the offender accountable for his behaviors and attitudes and helps maintain safety from the foolish spouse. However, if you are married to an evil spouse, who has the pure intention to harm you, setting boundaries will not be received well, and will escalate the abuse. In this situation, boundary setting causes more harm and more unsafety, and you will need to be extremely discerning in how to handle this type of person. Again, there are safety plans already written out on the domestic hotline website, www.thehotline.org, and finding counsel that is trained in abuse is highly encouraged.

Myth #17: Being sober means my husband is in active recovery.

Truth: Sobriety is only one part of active recovery. Active recovery begins with humility and honesty. Over time, you should begin to see a change in behaviors. The fruits of the spirit (love, joy, peace, patience, kindness, goodness, faithfulness, gentleness and self-control) should slowly start to make an appearance as your husband sheds his old ways of thinking, coping, and responding to every- day life. He will exhibit patience towards you as you heal. He will not be perfect, and setbacks are sure to arise, but in general, you should see a very defined change. Due to the lying that accompanies this particular addiction, you must learn to listen to his actions vs his words. True recovery is a heart change, not behavioral modification. Look for the fruits of the spirit, and you will know. These changes will not happen if a man does not want to do what it takes to get well, and/or if he has a true narcissistic personality disorder. These traits may also take longer to shed if the husband is neurodivergent. A counselor can be extremely helpful to help you see your situation clearly.

Myth #18: Porn addicts are creepy-looking men who spend too much time on their computers.

Truth: With the increase of pornography, there is an increase in sex addiction. Porn users are all around us and are people we know, people of all ages, and people we admire and love.

Pornography is not just an epidemic problem; it is a pandemic problem. The world is hooked on porn. Do not be fooled into thinking that sex addiction is just a man's problem. Statistics are now telling us that the numbers of women viewing pornography are on the rise too. Porn shows no favoritism.

Myth #19: A sex addiction reveals there is a marriage problem.

Truth: A sex addiction is not a marriage problem; it is a people problem. There is no marriage-building exercise that can "fix" the addiction. The addiction is 100% on the shoulders of the person who is in the addiction. A marriage cannot grow so long as the addiction is present. This is one reason why attending marriage retreats and/or marriage counseling sessions is not recommended. *Focusing on the marriage, instead of the individual, will cause more harm and stall recovery efforts.*

Throughout the book, we will be tackling many of these myths and diving deeper, so you have better understanding.

Finally, let me share some staggering statistics. This reveals how pornography is truly the "new drug" of choice by so many, and the aftermath is breaking apart families and tearing down and abusing women across the world. My heart breaks for those who have been betrayed but also for the women who are often groomed into the porn industry. Women matter to God. And women who know they matter to God can change entire communities for the better.

Recent research studies, primarily by the Barna Group, reveal that initial exposure to porn begins in childhood and progresses. Let's look at some data to see the scope and effects of porn in society and the church.

1. Over 40 million Americans are regular visitors to porn sites (Hull, 2020).
2. 47% of families in the United States reported that pornography is a problem in their home (Carr, 2019).
3. The first exposure to pornography among men is 12 years old, on average (Covenant Eyes, 2020).
4. 56% of American divorces involve one party having an "obsessive interest" in pornographic websites (Covenant Eyes, 2020).
5. 70% of Christian youth pastors report that they have had at least one teen come to them for help in dealing with pornography in the past 12 months (Kinnaman, 2016).
6. 68% of church-going men and over 50% of pastors view porn on a regular basis. Of young Christian adults 18-24 years old, 76% actively search for porn (Carr, 2019).
7. 59% of pastors said that married men seek their help for porn use (Carr, 2019).

8. 33% of women aged 25 and under search for porn at least once per month (Kinnaman, 2016).
9. Only 13% of self-identified Christian women say they never watch porn – 87% of Christian women have watched porn (Carr, 2019).
10. 55% of married men and 25% of married women say they watch porn at least once a month (Carr, 2019).
11. Only 7% of pastors say their church has a program to help people struggling with pornography (Covenant Eyes, 2020).

While these numbers are staggering, I would encourage you to look at them objectively. The point of studying statistics is not to promote hopelessness, but to fight against the thought that you are on this journey by yourself. You are not alone and, as you can see, the world is in dire need of brave men and women who will rise up and climb the mountain of recovery, healing, and freedom.

Heartwork Challenge:

1. Which of these myths did you think prior to discovery? (number the ones you believed)

2. Which of these myths did you believe after discovery? Explain.

3. How do you feel about that myth now? Did this chapter change your attitudes towards yourself or towards your spouse? Explain.

4. **Rewrite the words below: It is not my fault. I am powerless to change my husband.**

5. **Did any feelings come up as you wrote those words down? If so, what? Write your thoughts below, or draw a picture to illustrate your feelings.**

Q & A with Jim

Chapter 3: Common Myths

1. Many women's self-esteem takes a huge hit after learning of their husband's betrayal. What can a husband say or do to help his wife work through those insecurities?

I think that is a good question for each wife to answer and tell her husband what she needs from him. For example, Misty told me she didn't like it when I told her she was, "hot." It made her feel objectified. She was so hurt, that even when I did tell Misty she was beautiful, my words held no weight. In her pain, she would typically shrug her shoulders or mutter, "Whatever." But even though my compliments seemed to not matter, I felt it was still important to say words like, "You are beautiful." I couldn't make Misty believe those words. She had to do her own inner work of healing from the harm I caused her, but she needed to hear those reassuring words from me. I only had eyes for her.

It is important for women to understand that, to the sex addict, it does not matter how physically attractive his wife is or isn't. He will still act out, even if she seems physically "perfect." Consider men who are married to super models, and yet, they remain addicted. (Kanye West, Tiger Woods, etc.) The selfishness and the need to numb the unaddressed pain and trauma and/or early childhood lack of attachment and attunement is why men often view porn or act out sexually. Again, it is not about you, the woman. It is about the addict and his relationship with himself, with God, and his relationship with his past.

2. If a woman were to have sex with her husband every day, or partake in whatever he wished inside the bedroom, would that keep her husband from acting out sexually?

No. It is a heart issue, not a sex issue. There is nothing a woman can do to "fix" or "satisfy" this. It is not hers to try to fix or

control, even if she could. This is something the addict has to address head-on, and he must remember humility in the process. She is not his rehab.

3. Many husbands blame their wives for their acting out. Did you do that and if so, why?

Yes, sadly, I did, and so do many other men. We do that to take the blame off of ourselves. It takes responsibility off of us. Addicts are constantly trying to avoid feelings of shame. To accept responsibility for our actions causes us shame. Shame causes us to feel so incredibly bad about ourselves, and that is exactly what we are trying our best to avoid. We will do whatever it takes to avoid feeling shame. Unfortunately, we often abusively dump our shame onto our wives and kids. But we can learn how to stop doing this and instead face our shame.

Legalism and patriarchy also fed a spirit of entitlement. Part of my healing was studying God's heart towards women and doing a deep dive in Genesis 1-3. There is a great study by Bruce C.E. Fleming that helped me unpack the original language and context.

4. Are there any myths about sexual addicts that were not included in this chapter?

One myth that comes to mind right away is: "It is something that cannot be overcome." That is false. A man can absolutely find healing and freedom from sexual addiction, as well as the abusive behaviors that accompanied the addiction.

But that leads to the next myth: "You can overcome sexual addiction by yourself/alone." As a man of faith, it took help from the Holy Spirit to brave the hard work necessary, but I cannot stress enough that the sex addict needs professional therapy. It is also essential to have a group of men to support us through our recovery. These men become a band of brothers who practice vulnerability, pray for one another, ask the hard questions and hold each other accountable.

Another myth that comes to mind is, "It isn't hurting anyone else if they don't know." Sex addiction is taking away our ability to connect with others, to be emotionally intimate, and to live lives of transparency. Our wives have good instincts, and even if they are cognitively unaware of our addiction, their bodies and souls somehow know. It also harms the women directly involved in the images we are looking at and/or humans we objectify. Women in bondage to the porn industry are being used and abused for our own self-gratification, and their lives are being destroyed. This is terribly sad. If there are other women involved, such as an affair partner, the path of destruction dominos into her family, the lives of her children, and her relationships in general. The rationalization that "it isn't hurting anybody" is a lie we tell ourselves.

Chapter 4 : Emotions

In this chapter, we will explore a practical solution to those huge rush of emotions. Feelings are neither good nor bad, they just are. However, feelings can be amazing helpers as we become a student of ourselves.

What I'm going to be teaching you in this chapter is a multi-step mechanism of identifying, naming, and learning from our emotions and then identifying and addressing something known as "Core Belief Systems." This process, which will be outlined specifically throughout the chapter, was a practical tool of my recovery process when I found myself in between therapy sessions. An added bonus is that it can become a life-long tool that grows with you. The first time I learned about it, I was clumsy and awkward. Over time, however, it became easier with practice. The information in this chapter can be beneficial for anyone with a history of childhood trauma, divorce, abuse, neglect, humiliation, perfectionism, addictions, and more.

This is the chapter where you SLOW DOWN and become mindful. The focus is on you, your past, your reactions, your emotions, and your goals. Be intentional. You will do some writing and journaling and learn to become a student of yourself.

Remember, our goal is to discover healing and create new patterns. I know I say this a lot, but it's worth repeating. That means, whether our husbands find recovery or not, we still can. We can be good parents, have healthy relationships with ourselves and others, and find internal calm in the external chaos.

Before we begin, I want you to take a minute or two to stop reading and do two things. First, breathe slowly and deeply for five breaths. Secondly, meditate/pray. As you take deep, healing breaths, ask God to open your eyes to understanding and to help you get through this chapter with a deeper understanding of yourself and His heart of advocacy towards you. Betrayal sometimes causes us to doubt ourselves and doubt in God's love and goodness. All of that is ok, but not a place we want to necessarily stay. Before we begin, may we be intention to keep our hearts open and receptive.

There are several steps necessary in ensuring that your emotions are teaching you, but not leading you:

- Allow yourself to feel emotions.
- Become aware of your emotions, then lean into them.
- Name/identify your emotions.
- Learn from your emotions. Ask yourself, "What does this emotion say about me?"

Allow Yourself to Feel Emotions

I mentioned earlier, feelings are neither right nor wrong. They just are. When we look to Scripture, we read accounts where Jesus had feelings, too. He experienced anger, anxiety, fatigue, grief, and betrayal. This is important to grasp. Sadly, many Christians believe having these uncomfortable feelings, such as anger and sadness, is wrong. But if you do not allow yourself to feel, you will not be able to heal from your hurt. Give yourself permission to feel.

Become Aware of Your Emotions

Awareness is a powerful tool we must have in our back pocket throughout the recovery process. Some people call awareness "mindfulness". It is the active process of slowing down and becoming naturally curious. If we want to heal, we must be very intentional about becoming mindful of our thoughts, feelings, and actions. Actions (or reactions) start with a thought. A thought becomes a feeling, and a feeling becomes an action/reaction. Our goal in this chapter is to logistically learn how to get beneath the emotions to the thought or belief that lives below it. It is here we can identify harmful core beliefs that no longer serve us. Identifying is always accompanied with mindfulness. That's what I'm hoping to help you with in this chapter.

We must also become mindful of how our emotions manifest in our bodies. The Bible has many examples of how emotions affect us physically. One can read through the book of Psalms, Proverbs, or study Jesus in the garden before His arrest, to easily find verses that support this scientific fact. The medical community is aware of how stress can affect the heart, the gut, and one's overall health.

It sounds simple, but for most of us, this is an extremely difficult task and many require extra resources to help us learn how to identify. A person can be aware that they are "off," and yet be unable to properly identify what their feelings may be. Many women reading this book may have suffered from years of abuse, and for the sake of survival, have numbed out. Mindfulness is the tool to bring you back to yourself. This "art" of identifying your emotions will become a beneficial discipline in your life, so instead of ignoring your feelings, press into them.

Name and Identify Emotions

The picture to follow is called a "feelings wheel." Feeling wheels are tools to help properly identify the emotions we are feeling. After seven years of counseling, I still have to refer to my laminated "feeling wheel" to find the right descriptive words. Before you spend any significant amount of time studying the picture, I would like to make some clarifications on feeling wheels in general.

First of all, there are many versions of the "Feeling Wheel." Some are called "Emotions Wheel," some have eight inner-circle emotions, and some are color coded. Some variations set up the inner circle as pairs of opposite feelings. They can range from simple to complex. I invite you to do some exploring on your own and choose one that resonates with you. There's no right or wrong. For teaching purposes only, I have chosen one that is based on "Nonviolent Communication" by Marshall Rosenberg, Ph.D.

When it comes to betrayal, we can be all over the wheel within the same 10 minutes! There was one situation in particular I remember telling a mentor that my feeling wheel was like my own version of "Wheel of Fortune." I told her I could "spin" the feeling wheel and wherever it landed would properly describe how I had felt at any given time in the course of that day. Some days are like that. But properly naming our emotions forces us to slow down and dig deeper. As we breathe deep and meditate/pray, we turn inwards and can start to look past what is on the surface. We become "Inspector Gadget of our soul" as we discover more about ourselves.

Note that the outer circle generally points deeper into the inner circle. Outer emotions are superficial. Inner emotions are underlying, deeper emotions.

Feelings Wheel

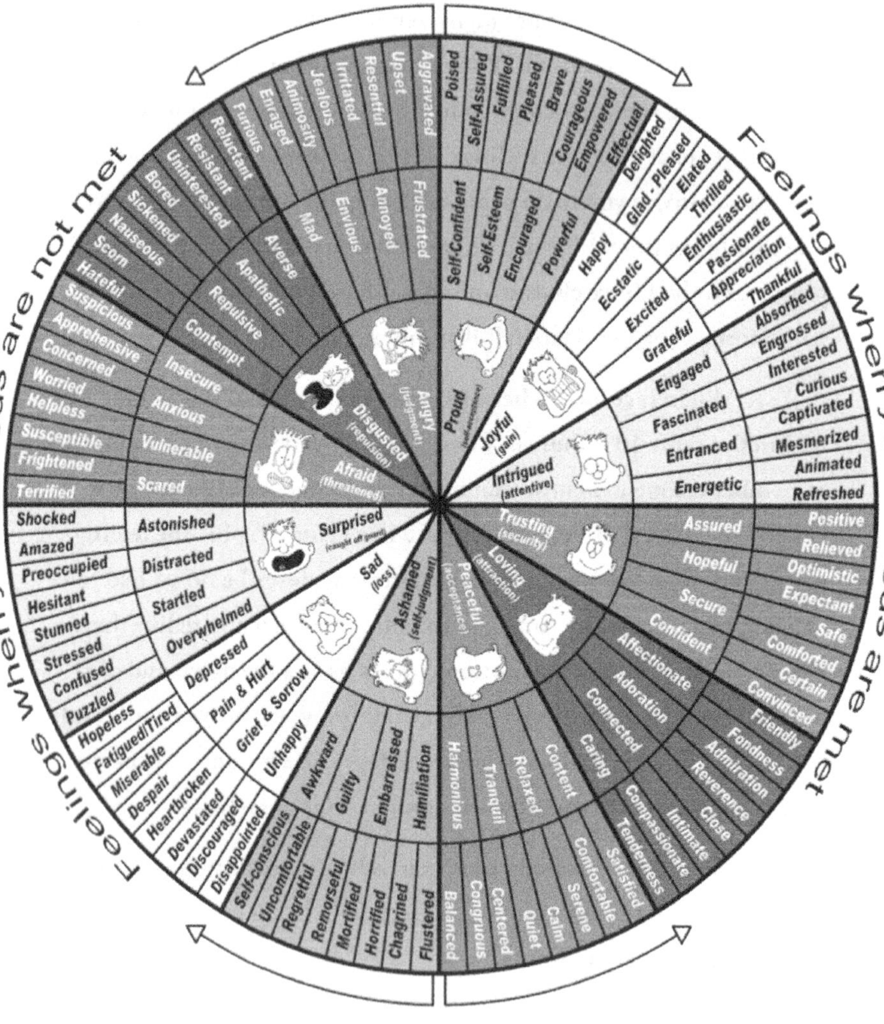

Feelings when your needs are met

Proud (self-assurance): Self-Confident, Self-Esteem, Encouraged, Powerful; Poised, Self-Assured, Fulfilled, Pleased, Brave, Courageous, Empowered, Effectual

Joyful (gain): Happy, Ecstatic, Excited, Grateful; Delighted, Glad - Pleased, Elated, Thrilled, Enthusiastic, Passionate, Appreciation, Thankful

Intrigued (attentive): Engaged, Fascinated, Entranced, Energetic; Absorbed, Engrossed, Interested, Curious, Captivated, Mesmerized, Animated, Refreshed

Trusting (security): Assured, Hopeful, Secure, Confident; Positive, Relieved, Optimistic, Expectant, Safe, Comforted, Certain, Convinced

Loving (attraction): Affectionate, Adoration, Connected, Caring; Friendly, Fondness, Admiration, Reverence, Close, Intimate, Compassionate, Tenderness

Peaceful (acceptance): Harmonious, Tranquil, Relaxed, Content; Satisfied, Comfortable, Serene, Calm, Quiet, Centered, Congruous, Balanced

Feelings when your needs are not met

Ashamed (self-judgment): Awkward, Guilty, Embarrassed, Humiliation; Flustered, Chagrined, Horrified, Mortified, Remorseful, Regretful, Uncomfortable, Self-conscious

Sad (loss): Depressed, Pain & Hurt, Grief & Sorrow, Unhappy; Disappointed, Discouraged, Devastated, Heartbroken, Despair, Miserable, Fatigued/Tired, Hopeless

Surprised (caught off guard): Astonished, Distracted, Startled, Overwhelmed; Shocked, Amazed, Preoccupied, Hesitant, Stunned, Stressed, Confused, Puzzled

Afraid (threatened): Insecure, Anxious, Vulnerable, Scared; Suspicious, Apprehensive, Concerned, Worried, Helpless, Susceptible, Frightened, Terrified

Disgusted (repulsion): Averse, Apathetic, Repulsive, Contempt; Reluctant, Resistant, Uninterested, Bored, Sickened, Nauseous, Scorn, Hateful

Angry (judgment): Frustrated, Annoyed, Envious, Mad; Aggravated, Upset, Resentful, Irritated, Jealous, Animosity, Enraged, Furious

Based on Nonviolent Communication by Marshall Rosenberg, Ph.D. May be duplicated for personal use and for teaching Nonviolent Communication. Graphics and organization of feelings and needs wheels by Bret Stein. artisantf@hotmail.com Revised 1/1/11

Now that you have learned to name your emotion, what do you do with it? How and what can you learn from it? Remember, emotions are our teacher, not our leader.

The following section will take us to the next level in healing. We will unravel what our emotions are wanting us to know about ourselves so we can respond to our trauma in healthy and productive ways.

Learn from Your Emotions

Emotions can point us deeper into something called "Core Belief Systems." Let's refer to our vocabulary list from Chapter 2. Core Belief Systems (CBS) are defined as "basic beliefs about ourselves, other people, and the world we live in." They are things we hold to be absolute truths deep down, underneath all our "surface" thoughts. A core belief is something you accept as true without question. Here are some other ways to describe a CBS:

- it can be conscious or subconscious
- it contains our experiences, emotions, thoughts, ideas, attitudes, memories, self-talk, perceptions, values, desires, and opinions
- it is not always based on objective truth
- each of us has multiple core beliefs, each unique to our own experiences
- a CBS is often planted in our soul in early childhood, in some cases can begin in the womb, or be passed down generationally.

There are some key words that you need to understand. Core beliefs are deep down. "Deep down" means these were more than likely seeded at a very young age, or at least prior to the age of 18 years old. The other key words in the paragraph above are "without question." Even if these beliefs are false, the mind tricks the soul into thinking the belief is true, when it is actually a lie. We don't typically examine our CBS. We allow it to steer us, unquestioned. But what if the CBS is not true? What if you are being led through life unknowingly and unaware following something that is not in your best interest? We want to observe that.

A false CBS can greatly hinder us as individuals, because it is a lie. The lies might become emotional blocks and infiltrate our relationship with ourselves and with others. The lies might affect our parenting style and how we respond to our children. There is truly so much benefit from doing this soul-work and I cannot stress enough how important this work will be. You'll be doing this work with a solid therapist, but what about when you are at home? Is there something you can do on your own to help you work through flooding of emotions? The answer is yes!

The best tool I have used to discover my CBS is called the "Life Event Revelation Chart," which is a chart we call "LERC" for short. This chart was developed by a healing ministry. Full detailed instructions on how to use this tool can be found in the book Rational Christian Thinking by Gary Sweeten and others. Regardless where you fall on faith and religion, I encourage you to be open because it really is a great tool to work with.

If you don't fully understand yourself and how you operate, you could potentially remain in unhealthy cycles. LERC can be a tool to help you recognize and identify the lies, and then replace those lies with beautiful truths, transforming your heart and mind. For me, it helped me begin to see myself as God saw me: beautiful, good, a warrior, intelligent, kind, and capable.

The easiest and most practical way to explain this chart is to literally involve you in filling it out as you are reading along. Grab a pen or pencil and let's walk through this process side by side.

Before we begin, take a few minutes to study the chart on the following page. Look at each box and read what is to be written inside. Notice the arrows. This will all make sense soon. I don't expect understanding quite yet, just observation. Your new-found ability to identify and name your emotions will equip you to move into this next major part of the tough work we are doing.

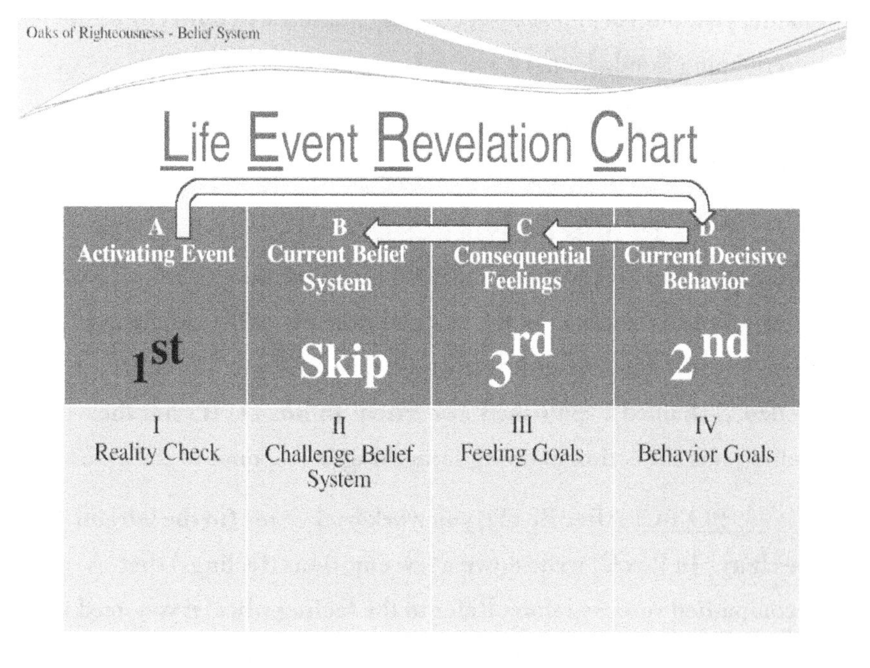

The top row is considered "Phase 1." The bottom row is "Phase 2."

Between Phases 1 and 2 you will ask yourself 6 questions.

Top Row: Phase 1

BOX A: Before we begin this exercise, I want you to think of the most recent event in which you reacted to a situation with strong emotions or "flooding" of emotions that didn't necessarily match the circumstance. For example, if your grandma dies, a natural human response is grief. If your husband was caught looking at porn, your natural human response would be anger. Your intense response is appropriate to the event. I'm not talking about that. I'm referring to a time when you were triggered or flooded with emotions that didn't seem to match the situation at hand.

Here is an example: Your child responds to you with a disrespectful tone and rather than responding calmly and firmly, you shame, yell, punish and accuse, creating a cascade of both child and parent being flooded, angry, hurtful, and upset.

Now it's your turn. Think of an event, and write it down in BOX A. You are writing just the event.

BOX D: After filling in Box A, you then skip over to Box D and write down HOW YOU RESPONDED to Box A. This is a list of unwanted behaviors. In the original example of the child being disrespectful, I can imagine one would possibly write words such as "yelled", "shamed", "punished", or "cried" in Box D. It's not the feeling, it is the action of doing something in response to the event.

BOX C: After Box D, you work backwards (to the left) on the chart. In Box C, write down a few emotions (feelings) that accompanied your reaction. Refer to the feeling wheel if you need it. In regard to the original example, someone might write "anger, fear, disrespected, hate."

BOX B: Lastly, identify and write any belief systems associated with the feelings and behaviors. Once you write a belief, ask yourself the question "Why" and see if you can keep digging down. You are trying to get down to your Core Belief System. The CBS typically starts with the words, "I am..." Let me show you an example from the situation between the parent/child mentioned above. Here are some Core Belief Systems that might come out:

- My child doesn't respect me. ("Why? Because my desires don't matter.")

- My desires don't matter. ("Why? Because I'm not loved.")
- I am unloved. ("Why? Because I am unworthy of love.")
- I am unworthy of love. ("Why? Because something must be wrong with me.")
- Something is inherently wrong with me as a person. ("Why? Because I am not enough.")
- I am not enough. (Core Belief)
- Because I am not enough, I will be abandoned. (Core Belief)

See how that works? It is a sequence of thoughts that takes us deeper. It takes some practice and you may not always be able to get to the root CBS, but with practice and time you begin to discover so much about yourself. You may see patterns and common themes. Below are some common negative Core Belief Systems.

I am not good enough.
I am incapable.
I am stupid.
I am inferior.
I am nothing.
I'm worthless/I am unworthy.
I am unimportant.
I am a bad person.
I am ugly.
I am unlovable.
I don't matter.
I am not valued.
I am alone/I am abandoned.
I am a failure.
I am rejected.

BEFORE MOVING TO PHASE 2, ASK YOURSELF THESE QUESTIONS: **(It's okay if you can't answer them all, but give it your best shot!)**

1. **Can you remember a time early in your life when you remember having those same thoughts or feelings? (Oftentimes, the CBS can be traced back to early childhood years.)**
2. **Is this thought nurturing your physical, emotional, and spiritual life?**
3. **Is this thought helping you achieve your goals?**
4. **Is this thought keeping you out of inappropriate conflict with others?**
5. **Is this thought keeping you out of inappropriate conflict with yourself?**
6. **Did this thought ever benefit you in some way?**
7. **Is this thought still beneficial and serving you in some way?**

<u>Bottom Row: Phase 2</u>

<u>BOX I</u>: **Reality Check**

Go back to the original "Box A" where you described the event. Is there any part of your perception that could have been false? Did you make any assumptions or misconstrue any part of your event? If so, rewrite the event objectively and correctly.

<u>BOX IV</u>: **Behavior Goals**

Again, jump all the way to the right. If this event were to happen again, how would you <u>like</u> to respond? Write it down. This is your behavior GOAL. Let's go back to the original example. The initial reaction to the disrespectful child was "yelling, shaming and

crying." The goal response, however, might be "stay calm, validate his/her feelings, discuss and practice a better way to speak to me."

BOX III: Feeling Goals

Working to the left, consider how you would feel if you responded in a healthy, productive way. How would you feel? Refer to the feeling wheel if needed. Example: content, productive, peaceful, encouraged.

BOX II: Challenge Belief System

Replace your false CBS with truth. The truths can be words of affirmation about yourself and/or, if you are a person of faith, truths you have learned from God's Word. For instance, if you had the CBS that "I am abandoned," you can replace it with, "God will never leave me or forsake me. Deut. 31:6." The false CBS, "I am unloved" can be replaced with, "I am loved by my family." This process takes practice, so if you find yourself struggling, ask a friend, counselor, or mentor for help in replacing those old thoughts with new thoughts.

It's really powerful when you start to identify your CBS. It means you are starting to make some headway in your recovery journey. The process outlined above has several descriptive names: re-framing, re-training, and renewing are a few words that may be used to describe LERC. I, personally, like all three of those verbs. Let me share why.

The prefix "re" stems from Latin origin and means "again and again." That means that each of these verbs carries a sense of ongoing action. Re-framing means that again and again, we have to look at, think about, and express our beliefs differently. This has to become an exercise and can be accomplished best, in my opinion, through keeping a journal, meditation/prayer. I want to stress that this is not a one-time occurrence.

Ephesians 4:22-24 states that part of becoming more like Jesus, we are to put off the old and put on the new. I was able to identify my old thought, and then replace it with new thoughts, almost always about myself and my self-hatred. This tool helped me to starting loving Misty.

It is powerful to do this exercise and it helps free us, not just temporarily, but sometimes permanently! Naming our feelings helps these feelings lose their tight grip on us. The "taming" of our emotions comes into play as well, because you will find your mindful self better equipped to *respond* to conflict rather than *react* to conflict. When I slow down, take some deep breaths, feel where the emotion is in my body, I am able to respond calmly.

Identifying the core belief will often take us back to our Family of Origin and/or childhood experiences. Learning how to dig out a CBS may require a professional. Sometimes we have childhood trauma, such as divorce, abuse, or neglect, that actually causes our brains to wire improperly. The good news is that our brains can and do heal. With the proper tools, we can often un-wire the damage and then rewire our brains. God can use all kinds of tools, people, and resources to accomplish this. I encourage you to stay open and willing to prioritize your emotional and mental health, even if that means utilizing resources that are outside your typical tools.

Our team of counselors was a key factor in our ability to heal and restore. Some of the biggest reasons people avoid counseling seems to be lack of money, inconvenience/time, and/or fear of the pain it may bring. This was the case for us in our early days after disclosure. Allow me to put it in perspective. If a loved one were in a terrible car accident and suffered a crushed lung, would you allow the

EMT's to transport your loved one to the hospital to get life-saving care? Of course! You wouldn't say, "I'm sorry, let me call my bank and make sure I have enough money in our account." No, you would see the dire situation, recognize that it was life or death, and you would simply trust that it would work out. Now, consider your current emotional state. After betrayal, you are, emotionally speaking, in a state of crisis. Your spouse has left you emotionally bloodied and ruined. Remember in Chapter 1 when we discussed trauma and its effect on our physical bodies? Trauma can cause physical symptoms such as hormonal imbalance, weight gain, weight loss, stomach problems, anxiety/depression, extreme fatigue, pain, PTSD, sleep disorders, sexual dysfunction, chronic illnesses, and more. If left untreated, deep emotional disturbances from trauma can cause even more serious diseases and autoimmune disorders. The impact of trauma is *real*. Ignoring our emotional fragility is risky.

Seeking professional help may require sacrifice. It may mean working extra, not spending as much at Starbucks, creating space in your schedule, or making financial sacrifices, but do consider counseling and prioritize it if possible. You will never regret it. We will address what kind of therapist to look for in a later chapter.

If you are in an unsafe situation where paying for professional help could put you at greater risk, there are many free or greatly discounted online resources, too.

If you are anything like me, you will have many sleepless nights. Use the night hours to wrestle with God, sharing your heart, begging for reprieve, asking for help. . . lay it all out before Him. Jesus is anticipating this kind of relationship with you. Be totally honest with Him at all times. Let your heart and soul bleed before Him. Can I admit something to you? I cussed at God. A lot! He heard every word in the book. Have you ever heard someone say they had to work on forgiveness towards God? Welp, I did! Suppressing our true feelings does not work well in our favor. I recognized my anger and hate and sadness, wrestled with God about it, and eventually worked through it, productively. There is no condemnation through Jesus. You are allowed to be and feel without judgment.

A Bible book I loved to read was Nehemiah. In a short summary, Jerusalem had a temple, but the walls surrounding the city of Jerusalem were ruined. There was no protection for Jerusalem from further attack. Nehemiah traveled to Jerusalem and used his leadership skills to rally a citywide construction crew. Within a few weeks, the walls around Jerusalem were built and standing tall. The sturdy wall caused the surrounding enemies to lose their desire to attack, so they backed off. Before Nehemiah showed up, Jerusalem was in bad shape. She was exposed. Vulnerable. Unprotected. Destroyed. Abused. She used to feel beautiful, secure, and enjoyed financial prosperity, but that was no longer her reality. Jerusalem needed re-building.

I was my own version of destroyed Jerusalem. My husband's betrayal nearly destroyed me, and it would have had I chosen to allow it to become a part of my identity. I am not betrayed. I am a human who experienced betrayal. Language matters.

What I want to highlight is that many of us had the misconception that our foundation was strong. Betrayal has a way of revealing things, and part of that is teaching us that our foundation may have been full of rubble and rot and our soul may need a totally new building program. Betrayal is evil. Yet betrayal is what I personally needed to take place to see my situation for what it really was. D day, (Day of Disclosure), became my Day of Awakening.

Everyone comes into a marriage with baggage. Some of us have more than others due to father/mother wounds, neglect, divorce, bullying, sexual abuse, or more. I entered my marriage with baggage filled with neatly folded memories all tucked away, padlocked in and never to be thought of again. Enter betrayal. Not only does betrayal have a unique way of opening up every suitcase, but every memory spills out onto the dirt road of our lives. Disorganized, dirty, and chaotic, I frantically and desperately tried to pick up each article of clothing to stuff back into my suitcases. I felt an internal prompting to stop trying to stuff everything back in. Rather, I was to pick up each clothing item of memory, and hold it in my hands. Smell it. Feel it. Remember it. Grieve it.

I resisted at first. It hurt to visualize the 7-year-old version of myself, standing alone, feeling unloved and abandoned. It felt sad to relive the pain of my father making fun of my developing body in middle school. But when I submitted to it, I finally began the arduous task of rebuilding.

As a person of faith but not religion, I would envision Jesus partnering with me. We unpacked this together, piece by piece, memory by memory. If an article was stained or dirty, we would hand wash it together before neatly folding it and tucking it back into the suitcase. If a memory was too hard to face, we would save it for later. My spirituality played a role in giving me the stamina to go through this.

Logistically, a counselor who specialized in trauma guided me through the process, and little by little, I started to rebuild my foundation. Core Beliefs are very powerful. They can keep us stuck in unhealthy cycles, untapped to our full potential as women. To address core beliefs, one has to start from the ground, up. You'll never experience true healing until you learn how to filter present day circumstances with a clean filter. This is why counseling is such an amazing tool. It will guide us to clean our dirty filters, and sometimes, we might heal more quickly, too, because counselors keep us on track.

You may feel like "exposed Jerusalem" now but remember we can rebuild! Restoration and repair is on the horizon! But also keep in mind, Nehemiah didn't rebuild the wall all by himself. He used all kinds of people, from young to old, to help. Seek out these resources. It takes a tenacious and brave woman to work on her recovery. Jump in with both feet and get going. Resolve in your mind that your walls are worth rebuilding. You are a beautiful city with a glorious light ready to shine to the world around you. You can square your shoulders, once heavy with weight, and stand tall and strong and say, "Hey! Look at what I did!" Your walls will be solid, firm, and strong. Because your foundation will now be laid properly, you won't be shaken when life gets hard. People will be drawn to your streets and you will be able to offer hope and comfort to other women who are hurting. It is so important to keep that vision ahead of you! See it. Literally, right now, close your eyes and see the new version of yourself. The future you. The *whole* you. The *real* you. The *healthier version* of you. Do you see her? This is where you are headed. Remind yourself often of her.

There is a song that I listened to over and over again during the "rubble" phase of my recovery. We briefly talked about the importance of music, but it truly is a great tool to aid you in your recovery process. I made a playlist that was specific to the needs of my heart. Songs that reminded me of hope and recovery. I needed songs that helped me practice gratefulness. To this day, the song below is still a favorite: "Rebuilder" by Carrollton. Read the lyrics, or better yet, find the song online and take a listen while you read.

Through the rubble and the wreckage,
I'd forgotten who I was
You reached out for my hand
And found me in the dust
My soul had given up
But You wouldn't leave me undone
Rebuilder
My walls were crumbling
Restorer
You brought the light into the room
And filled my lungs
So I could learn to breathe again
My shelter
My warmth in the coldest night
My Helper
You held me up till I could stand
On the promise that You are
Rebuilding me

John 8:32 says, "You shall know the truth, and the truth shall set you free" (NIV).

Heartwork Challenge:

1. If you didn't do the LERC chart, do so now. You can do it alone or with a friend or recovery group. Be sure to share it with someone you trust.

2. **Proverbs 20:5 says, "The purposes of a person's heart are deep waters, but one who has insight draws them out (NIV)". Read that a second time. What do you think that verse is saying?**

3. **How can it apply to you in your current situation? Take a minute to really meditate on that verse. When you have a thought, a word or a picture, write it in the space below.**

Q & A WITH JIM
CHAPTER 4: EMOTIONS

1. How is naming emotions important for you in recovery?

It helps me identify root beliefs and experiences that have contributed to the addiction. It also helps me better communicate with Misty and identify false perceptions. It has helped me parent with more compassion and be a more loving husband, because I consider how the other person must be feeling. It has also helped me become a safe man.

2. What Misty refers to as "LERC," you refer to as "The Vortex." Can you explain what that means, and how it is helpful in your recovery?

The vortex is a term my men's support group used to dig deeper into our behaviors. It starts with surface, broad feelings and ideas and digs deeper and narrows it down to a core belief system. The core beliefs have created filters that I interpret life through, some of which are "dirty." Identifying these false beliefs helps me to see why I react the way I do, and then begin to transform my reactions into responses that are healthier.

3. Is it hard for you to name your feelings? Why or why not?

Yes, it is extremely hard. To some degree, I was conditioned to suppress my feelings in the hyper religious environment I was raised in. My feelings were not important and were even punished at times. (For example, if I was angry, my legalistic upbringing taught me that anger is sin, so I was not allowed to feel angry.) I also had the perception that certain feelings can be a sign of weakness. Misty and I both grew up in a very legalistic environment, and feelings were not valued. We are learning that feelings can give us answers as to why we react the way we react. We don't want to live our lives based on how we feel, but our feelings offer insight. I am also neurodivergent, and it can be challenging for me to identify feelings. I do much better with logic.

4. Have you noticed patterns of similar feelings and/or Core Beliefs among other sex addicts?

Yes. Many addicts struggle with a fear of failure and fear of rejection. In general, most of us have strong feelings of hopelessness, worthlessness, and helplessness. Most of us didn't have the tools in place to cope, and that resulted in us making harmful, life-destructive choices. Most of us can attest to having poor attachment and attunement from one or both primary care givers.

5. How does the addict transform those feelings of hopelessness, worthlessness, and helplessness?

I can speak only of my own experience and there were multiple steps I had to pass through in order to transform my thoughts. First, I had to truthfully see myself for who I really was, and it was pretty messed up. 2. In humility and brokenness, I told God how sorry I was for trying to live my life without Him in it. I

asked Him to be a part of my life and to heal me. Then I began the work of making amends with others. 3. Accepting the grace Jesus gave me is where the transformation really began. I literally felt the weight of my addiction lift from me, and I no longer carried the task of trying it alone, because I knew everything must come into the light. I must be fully known. There was comfort in knowing I could seek help and resources now. 4. Knowing how Jesus saw me, as good, I could then begin to shed the shame and self-hatred and start seeing myself as Jesus sees me. Through His eyes, I am fully known and fully loved.

There are some great resources that go into more detail of how to shed shame. Approach recovery holistically and nurture the body, mind, and soul.

Chapter 5: Grief and Forgiveness

In 1969, Elisabeth Kubler-Ross identified five stages of grief: denial, anger, bargaining, depression, and acceptance. Since then, psychologist and author David Kessler added another stage: finding meaning. This is just one of many models that are designed to help us understand grief. Having read several different acronyms or stages on the topic, I found that the model mentioned is what most resonated with me. Regardless of which model you relate to, the most important thing to remember during grief is this: be kind to yourself. This is a season to turn inward and shower yourself with grace. Let's discuss why.

The more I've studied betrayal trauma, the more I see parallels between the grief of sexual betrayal and the grief one experiences after the sudden loss of a loved one. In betrayal, you grieve the death of your dreams, the death of your memories, and the death of your future. All that you thought was, wasn't. What you think is, isn't, and what you thought would be, won't. Betrayal affects the past, present and future.

Although painful, one must enter grief as part of the healing journey. The stages are not linear. In fact, they can overlap, repeat, and one can fluctuate between stages minute by minute.

In this chapter, you will take the time to intentionally consider how betrayal has affected you and what losses have occurred because of it. This is an important step to your healing because not only are you specifically naming your losses, but you are acknowledging the effect these losses have had in your life. This process will eventually move you into a state of acceptance. Acceptance can then gently move your heart into a position of letting go. Letting go is what can catapult you out of the dark forest of grief and rejection. Without it, your capacity to experience freedom and be the best version of you may be hindered. You may wonder what you need to let go of. This will vary from person to person.

On this healing journey, one cannot arrive at the peak of healing without first trudging through the treacherous forest of grief. There is no going around it, and there is no rushing it.

Before we begin the climb, I'd like to take a short detour and explore what happens in the brain when D-day occurs, and how this pertains to the process of grieving.

Hormone Problems? Betrayal Trauma Could Be Why

Difficult and overwhelming experiences cause the brain to go into the "flight, fight, freeze, or fawn mode," or, more scientifically, an "acute stress response." An acute stress response gives us the energy required to make fast decisions in the face of life-threatening events such as natural disaster, crime, or physical attacks. But a stress response also occurs with a life altering event, such as losing a loved one or being betrayed. Whether life altering or life threatening, your brain goes into the same primal response, because it cannot distinguish between the two. To help us react quickly in the face of perceived danger, the brain triggers changes in the adrenal and nervous systems.

The adrenal glands respond to the stress response by sending out a huge dose of cortisol. This is a good thing for short-term periods, but releasing cortisol, which is a hormone, over a long period of time begins a cascade of hormonal issues that can wreak havoc on the body. Some of the issues that could begin to pop up are sleep disturbances, weight gain or weight loss, migraine headaches, thyroid issues, and more. Understanding that you will more than likely be in a constant state of stress over a long period of time, it is a good idea to have your hormone levels checked on a regular basis to ensure you stay as healthy as possible. Talk to your doctor about getting a full hormone panel one to two times per year.

The adrenal glands are not the only part of the body that takes a huge hit from betrayal trauma. The nervous system does, too. A traumatic experience causes your neurons to fire more rapidly through certain areas of your brain. This is meant to help you act in a clearer and faster fashion, giving you a sense of hyper-vigilance or super alertness in the face of danger. In relation to betrayal, many women feel the strong need to over-control, be hyper-vigilant in their husband's recovery, or take on the role of private investigator for weeks or even months after discovery. This is a normal response due to trauma, and serves us when needed, but a response we may want to move away from when it no longer serves us.

The physiological happenings inside your brain are important to be aware of as you begin the grief process because it helps you remember to be kind to yourself. Our brains are designed to work this way. We aren't sinning simply because we are having trauma responses trying to help us seek safety. Staying long-term in a trauma response will begin to harm our bodies. Over time, as safety is established, healing these trauma responses will be necessary for them to lessen. Time will not necessarily heal the damage trauma has caused. Safety in all aspects of our lives is what heals the damage trauma has caused.

The stress response will be in full force during grief. The many ranges of emotions are normal and healthy. Let's look at the stages of grief and how each phase can affect you as you simultaneously deal with trauma.

Shock

As mentioned earlier, the stages of grief are not linear. The stages can be cyclical or out of order, and one can experience more than one phase at the same time. It is unpredictable and sporadic. However, my own personal experience, as well as most women in betrayal trauma I know, say the initial phase upon discovery is shock. Typically, shock can last a few days to a few weeks. Your body and thoughts do not align during this phase, so you may require extra support from a safe community. (We will discuss safe people later). Among the women who have been betrayed, the most common effects of shock are forgetfulness and absent- mindedness. While grief takes on many forms, we tend to have commonalities between us. Below, I have listed a few specific ways you may notice shock affecting you, so give yourself permission to ask for help if needed. Remember, be kind to yourself.

- Making silly mistakes. When in shock, a person may be more liable to make silly mistakes, such as driving the wrong way down one-way streets or forgetting to turn off the burner. You may find yourself making mistakes at work, especially when it comes to details.
- Forgetting to take care of your own basic needs. This includes eating and drinking, doing laundry, showering, personal hygiene, and attempting to sleep. This could also be depression, and if it becomes debilitating, talk to someone who can help.
- Forgetting important responsibilities. This includes taking care of dependents such as children, elderly people, and pets. Ask for assistance if you find yourself unable to take care of your dependents appropriately.

- Forgetfulness in general. You may forget basic information that helps you make sense of what has happened. It may be necessary for others to repeat information several times.
- Susceptibility to other complications, such as depression, family breakdowns or chronic illness.
- Unable to remember information. Your nervous system is dysregulated during grief, and a dysregulated nervous system cannot retain information. Even reading this book and having reading comprehension could be extremely difficult and exhausting. This is normal, due to the grief and trauma you are experiencing.

Shock does not necessarily require a specialist but be aware that your brain is under an extreme amount of stress. But with time and acceptance, the initial disruptions of shock usually subside. (If they don't, talk with a professional.) Experiencing shock is both normal and expected after betrayal trauma.

I highly suggest that you have multiple practitioners lined up to address specific ways to properly support your body. Here are some suggestions:

- Primary Care Physician (PCP): meet with your doctor and fill them in on your stress and discuss options and ideas of how to best support your body during high stress. Discuss any lab work that may need to be done.
- OB/GYN: have your hormones checked regularly, and even possibly more often than normal during this stressful time. Due to the nature of your spouse's sex addiction, it is advised to get checked for sexually transmitted infections. That appointment in and of itself was extremely traumatic for me, but don't let the fear of the results keep you from learning the truth of your situation. Also, be sure to regularly check your breast health. I highly recommend thermography, as it can detect pre-cancerous cells years in advance and is safe

and effective. Thermography offers you the gift of time. You can stay ahead of things through the use alternative methods and nutrition to maintain good breast health.

- Naturopathic Doctor: find a good holistic doctor who understands the emotions and the impact those emotions have on the body.
- Holistic Digestive Health Specialist: Rest and digest is the phrase you will hear often when talking about stress and its correspondence to gut health. Finding a gut-brain practitioner could be a naturopathic doctor or someone with certifications who understands the ability to support the body's stress response naturally, such as biofeedback. Supporting your body through proper nutrition will also be extremely important during recovery.
- Mental Health Support Practitioners: trauma-informed counselors, abuse and addiction informed clergy, massage therapists, equine therapy, forest bathing, etc. There are many different avenues for you to support your mental health. A good psychiatrist may be in order to keep an eye out for debilitating depression and anxiety.

Denial

Another area of the brain that is heavily affected by trauma is the amygdala. The amygdala is a small, almond-sized area of your brain and is both the alarm center and the emotional center of your reactions. It interprets with feelings over logic, and to protect you, the brain responds with emotional shock. Shock causes some to feel numb or nothing at all. A friend of mine called it "emotional anesthesia." This response initially protects the body from becoming too overwhelmed all at once. But over time, the danger is that we become too appreciative of this numbing effect, which can potentially move some into a more permanent state of denial to cope. While denial is a normal part of grieving, we most certainly do not want to stay there. Like a gentle river, grief should always be in motion.

We live on fourteen acres in a rural area of Missouri. During the spring, one of my favorite outdoor activities is to go hunting for morel mushrooms. For me, the hunt is just as fun as eating the fried mushrooms, but eventually our days of hunting come to a screeching halt. Around mid-April, the forest gets thick with a native plant that I am highly allergic to: poison ivy. Poison ivy is an invasive plant and over time, it can completely take over entire areas of our woods. One time, I was so focused on looking at the forest floor that I didn't realize I had wandered into an entire area of poison ivy sprigs. The vines were rising out of the ground with gnarly fingers and hairy fibers that seemed to say, "I dare you to go ahead and try!" I could have denied that I was standing amid poison ivy, but that does not make it go away. Denying does not fix the problem. It also does not address or mitigate the problem. It compounds it. Denial is never our friend. And much like poison ivy, betrayal is invasive. It affects many different areas of our lives. It creeps into parts of us that are perhaps unexpected. While we are focused on the initial assault, it is sneaking past our attention, and attacking on multiple fronts. In this chapter, I am encouraging you to do something that may seem counter-productive: purposefully and intentionally enter the dark forest of grief. Let me explain.

Allowing yourself the freedom to fully enter grief is equivalent to tying your hiking boots in double knots. It is entering a state of mind in which you know there will be hard work and you'll need firm footing. Yet, at the same time, your heart will also need moments to rest, slow down, and loosen your laces for a while. Grief is a funny thing. It works on its own timetable. You cannot help but move through the phases once you enter, but you also cannot rush it. There may be times when you may feel "stuck" in a phase, like denial or anger or sadness. This can happen, so finding a good therapist is important. Seeing a professional may help you process and continue that fluid motion of gently moving in and out of the phases. Taking the time to journal may be adequate to keep that forward motion going, too.

Let's begin the ascent into the forest of grief. First, we need to look at some of the areas of loss that may have occurred as a result of your husband's betrayal and/or addiction.

- your relationships/friendships.
- your mental health.
- your physical health.
- your emotional health.
- your family of origin.
- your spouse's family of origin.
- your parenting.
- your finances.
- your church/church family.
- your ability to love and be loved.
- your ability to trust.
- your dreams/goals.
- your marriage.
- your past memories.
- your birthday/anniversary/holidays.
- your cognitive abilities/your memory/concentration.
- your capacity to manage life in general.
- your family vacations, both past and future.

- your sex life.
- your self-esteem.
- your spirituality.
- your eating habits
- your energy levels
- your sleep
- your daily routines
- your social life and interactions
- television and movies that you once enjoyed

This is *not* a complete list. Wow! Isn't that mind blowing? Does this list surprise you? Does it validate you? There is a legitimate reason why you feel foggy-brained! Your brain has experienced trauma from betrayal, and you have had many losses. It has affected almost every area of your life. For what it's worth, I'm so sorry for your losses.

I'll never forget a humorous moment during a recovery group meeting. Fifteen women came together every Tuesday night to learn, discover and grow. One night, we were discussing the many ways our lives had been affected by betrayal. The leader was in the front of the room and our recovery books were all open to a page where we had to specifically name our losses. We got to the section of cognitive function/memory/concentration, and my friend, who was sitting next to me, nudged my arm with her elbow and pointed to her book. I silently read her scribbled answer but tried desperately to stifle my laughter at her words, "I can't remember shit!" When I was unable to contain my laughter, the leader looked curiously at me and said, "What's so funny, ladies?" When I read her answer out loud to the group, the room erupted into applause and laughter and cheering and validation. We were a room full of warrior women who couldn't remember shit! I suppose I could add to the list our ability to discuss betrayal without saying one cuss word!

In a nutshell, the point is this: betrayal brings loss. And a lot of it. Loss is accompanied by grief. Grief will cause you to fluctuate in and out of very strong, human reactions due to the trauma. Do not deny your body permission to feel the uncomfortable rushes of anger, sadness, confusion, and more. Press into it. The better you become at allowing your mind, body, and soul to align, the more efficient you will become at hiking through the dark and cold days of grief. Better days are coming, friend. Soon, rays of sunlight will begin poking through the trees and warm your skin and your soul. You are forever changed, but joy will and does return.

You are not alone in your forest. If you are a person of faith, invite Jesus on this difficult hike with you. Your goal is not deliverance *from* grief, but deliverance *in* grief. The passage below is one I read every single morning for three months. I worked on memorizing it, but my foggy brain couldn't use memory function, so instead, I opened my Bible app and read it. It is a special chapter to me because I love how it offers hope. By looking at the tense of the verbs, you can see that David is writing both in the present and past tense. In verse ten, David prayed in the present tense, "Help me out of this!" and in verse eleven he says in the past tense, "You did it." Just those two sentences alone are enough for my heart to feel hope.

Psalm 30 (The Message)

1 I give you all the credit, God—
you got me out of that mess,
you didn't let my foes gloat.

2-3 God, my God, I yelled for help
and you put me together.

God, you pulled me out of the grave,
gave me another chance at life
when I was down-and-out.

4-5 All you saints! Sing your hearts out to God!
Thank him to his face!
He gets angry once in a while, but across
a lifetime there is only love.
The nights of crying your eyes out
give way to days of laughter.

6-7 When things were going great
I crowed, "I've got it made.
I'm God's favorite.
He made me king of the mountain."
Then you looked the other way
and I fell to pieces.

8-10 I called out to you, God;
I laid my case before you:
"Can you sell me for a profit when I'm dead?
auction me off at a cemetery yard sale?
When I'm 'dust to dust' my songs
and stories of you won't sell.
So listen! and be kind!
Help me out of this!"

11-12 You did it: you changed wild lament
into whirling dance;
You ripped off my black mourning band
and decked me with wildflowers.
I'm about to burst with song;
I can't keep quiet about you.
God, my God,
I can't thank you enough.

Forgiveness

While writing the outline for this chapter of grief and forgiveness, I really struggled. Each topic alone has entire books written about them, so it is no wonder why this internal struggle was taking place. I would highly encourage you to do your own digging and take personal responsibility on ensuring that you are not rushing either process and that you feel freedom to explore each topic and decide for yourself what Jesus taught and what He would tell you to do in your situation. A podcast that helped me was the Bible Project, Sermon on the Mount series, episode 23. Tim Mackie does a deep dive into what forgiveness is/isn't and I found it truly helpful.

I first want to clarify that I believe "forgiveness" and "letting go" cannot be separated out, although some will say otherwise (I will explain this below). Secondly, I recognize that there are two schools of thought on forgiveness and whether it is required when there is not a genuine heart of repentance. Third, I recognize that many women have been spiritually abused by being told they "should" forgive their husbands seventy times seven, or they "shouldn't" keep a record of wrongs, often keeping them in abusive relationships. Fourth, many Christian circles push or rush forgiveness to take place, resulting in a lack of genuine forgiveness.

Let's take our time together to sort some of this out, with the caveat that my theology/ideology may not align with your theology/ideology, and we can agree to disagree. What I desire most, is for you to pursue what brings you peace.

Forgiveness and Letting Go

Let's put a definition to relational forgiveness. I couldn't find an "official" definition that resonated with me, so I came up with my own. For me, forgiveness is "the ongoing process of an intentional and voluntary decision of letting go my need for control toward an individual, group, or institution who has harmed me, allowing me to overcome feelings of resentment and/or vengeance which sets me free to be the best version of myself." Letting go is "the act of releasing my need for control of the other person and their outcome." In other words, "letting go" is the act, "forgiveness" is the process of that act.

These two concepts go hand-in-hand, and that is why I personally believe I am called to forgive, even if the offender is underserving and unrepentant (Matthew 18:21-35). But there are some things forgiveness is *not*. Let's list some of those things below. Forgiveness is *not*:

- Trust
- Reconciliation
- For the benefit of the other person
- Forgetting
- Tolerating sin
- Always a one-time event
- Ignoring behavior
- Letting someone off the hook

Forgiveness also does not take the place for certain consequences. Let's list some of those things below.

Forgiveness does not mean:

- You condone or excuse the other person's behavior

- You no longer feel the pain of their offense(s)
- You release the other person from natural consequences, including judicial court rulings.
- You continue allowing abuse and/or unwanted sexual behavior
- You stay in the relationship or reconcile
- Legal pardon or that you cease from pursuing legal justice
- You continue to allow him/her to harm you.

Now that we have basic, fundamental knowledge, let's look at forgiveness a little deeper.

.

Forgiveness is Your Choice and Your Timing

Sadly, there is often pressure for betrayed spouses to swiftly offer forgiveness with the intent of restoration of the marriage. That pressure can come from others of influence in our lives, such as clergy, our spouses, our friends/family, or even our own selves. For starters, the grieving process is not the time to focus on the forgiveness process. Again, allow yourself *time* and *space* to unravel and name all the ways you've been betrayed. The ironic thing is this: when you allow yourself to grieve, you are indirectly working on forgiveness and letting go. They go hand in hand. The two are intricately intertwined. When you work through grieving over each of the areas mentioned above, you get both closure and openness. The closure of grief opens your heart towards letting go. What a strange but empowering process.

With the basic understanding of how grief is the gateway that ushers us towards letting go, let's take out our emotional compass and set our feet on the path to forgiveness.

Our path may be considered a bit unorthodox, for lack of a better word. You see, I used to have the false notion that forgiveness was for the benefit of the other person. I had a horizontal focus, as I put more energy into thinking about how it would make the other person feel. I believed the person who benefited most from forgiveness was the person on the receiving end. I was wrong. Our emotional compass is taking us on a path less traveled. It is often not recognized by the church, by others, by us and/or by our husbands.

Because of this, you may find your spouse isn't completely on board with not rushing this process. It will take some education on his part to fully understand what you, the spouse he betrayed, are going through. If your spouse is saying or implying by his actions, "Get over it already!", you need to set a boundary, because this is unsafe. If he gets frustrated or defensive, you need to set a boundary, because this is unsafe. Words such as "Get over it already" are reactions not responses. Reactions come from emotional immaturity and instability. (Responses come from personal ownership and stability). Reactions might mean sobriety, but not necessarily recovery. Sobriety addresses only the acting out. Recovery addresses all the unwanted behaviors that went *with* the acting out. (Reminder: acting out refers to the addict's primary method of dopamine release, such as masturbation.)

While you cannot be in control of your husband's sobriety or recovery, you can be in control of your response to him. And when it comes to grief and forgiveness, you get to be in the driver's seat. Your journey is for you. Forgiveness is not for your spouse. It is for *your* freedom, not his. A husband in true recovery will respect that his wife needs space and time to grieve, and her process of forgiveness is her choice.

My most favorite explanation on how to forgive God's way is taken from the book, The Cure by Lynch, McNicol, and Thrall. If you love to read and you're a spiritually minded individual, this is a must-have! Chapter five was life-changing for me regarding how to forgive God's way. I referred to it repeatedly when working through my forgiveness process. I'm going to highlight the main points below and add a few of my own thoughts and experiences.

The Order of Forgiveness from The Cure

1. You admit something happened. While this step may seem obvious, it is surprising how much we deny that someone has abused and betrayed us. Admit that we have been wronged. Do not minimize it.

2. You get in touch with the consequences of the act done against you. This is "counting the losses" like the ones mentioned above. It is intentionally going through and realizing all the ways betrayal has affected one's life. Not doing so doesn't make the losses go away, but rather buries them alive where they will take root and begin to define you. The process of counting the losses is a sacred, although sometimes scary, process.

3. You tell God what happened to you. This is my favorite part, pouring out my heart before God. Telling God *all of it*. Journaling, praying, crying, not just *to* God, but *with* God. You invite God into this process with you. As you let go, you place complete trust in God's justice on your behalf.

4. You tell the offender you've forgiven him *only when he repents,* for his sake. This is where I believe, sadly, many in the church community get it wrong. They think your forgiveness is for the other person's benefit. But forgiveness is for *your* benefit. Yes, we can internally offer forgiveness to our husbands regardless if they repent or not. But if we tell our husbands that we forgive them before they have the opportunity to repent, we rob our husbands of their own life-freeing repentance. Repentance and brokenness are crucial to your spouse's recovery. Give him that opportunity. He should be able to clearly identify all the ways his choices have injured you. It is okay to say, "Thank you for your apology, but I need more time before I can forgive you."

I've stated before and will say so again, forgiveness is not necessarily a one-time act. It could be an ongoing process for many days, months, or even years. Getting an apology from our spouses will build trust, but it is not a prerequisite for us to be able to forgive. This realization should greatly encourage your heart. Trust and forgiveness are two separate entities. You can forgive your spouse, and thus find freedom and healing, with or without his apology.

One of my favorite explanations of forgiveness was given in a short Instagram post by a page I follow called *jimmy_on_relationships*. In the post, he says, "Why can't we just forgive and move on? Because forgiveness doesn't lead to closeness or safety or connection. Now forgiveness can lead to peace…that means we forgive them to let go of the debt that they owe us. That's why we say people owe you an apology. It's because they took something from you. There's a debt, there's a wound, they hurt you, and we can intentionally let go of that resentment and cancel the debt that they owe us because we know they can't really pay us back anyways. But at the same time, forgiveness alone doesn't lead to trust being rebuilt, does it? And a relationship lives or dies based on trust. We can forgive and move on, but if that person is still in your life and you're asking, "Why can't I just forgive them and everything feel ok?", that's just not the way it works. Your body is too smart for that. It knows they are not a safe person. It knows they aren't trustworthy. Why would your body want to give more of itself to someone who is only taking advantage of you or hurting you? If someone isn't interested in listening to your pain and validating your experience as real and being curious and taking accountability and repairing any hurt that they have caused, you can forgive them all you want but you'll never feel close to that person, will you? Now that's not to say that closeness after a betrayal isn't possible. It absolutely is! But only if both people are working towards repair and reconciliation and that takes not only forgiveness from one, but also a willingness to take accountability and validate wounds from the past with consistent change in behavior. Forgiveness is wonderful but intimacy and trust and connection will always require more than just forgiveness."

My final thoughts on forgiveness are directed right at you. I want to take just a moment to present the whole point of recovery work: restoration. I'm not talking about restoration of your marriage. I mean restoration of *your soul.* That is where our focus is. I truly believe this process of letting go and/or forgiveness will help restore *you*.

You have much to grieve, dear one. It's okay. I did too. Take your time with this. Don't rush it. Don't push it away. Press into it. And when you are ready, consider if you should begin the process of forgiveness, and/or if there is anything worth letting go.

You are loved. Don't forget that. You are very brave, and I am so proud of you.

Heartwork Challenge:

Be prepared to put in extra time with this week's "Heartwork Challenge." Naming all the losses takes a lot of thought, effort, and intention. You do not want to rush this. If you need to spread this out over a few weeks, that is perfectly acceptable.

1. After each bullet point below, reflect and write out how betrayal has affected that particular area of your life. If you want to work through forgiveness, pick one of the bullet points and work through the forgiveness steps as outlined in this chapter. If you are reading this book with a group, consider sharing something you learned from the challenge.

- your relationships/friendships
- your mental health
- your physical health
- your emotional health
- yourself
- your family of origin
- your spouse's family of origin
- your parenting
- your finances
- your ability to love and be loved

- your ability to trust
- your dreams/goals
- your marriage
- your memories
- your cognitive abilities/your memory/concentration
- your capacity to manage life in general
- your family vacations, both past and future
- your sex life
- your self esteem
- your spirituality
- your eating habits
- your energy levels
- your sleep
- your daily routines
- your social interactions (how do you feel when you and your spouse are at social events such baseball games, church, concerts, etc.)
- your birthday/anniversary/holidays

Q & A with Jim

Chapter 5: Grief and Forgiveness

1. Misty shares how disclosure pushed her in to full blown grief. Did you expect grief to be a part of her healing process?

Yes, but to see it made it more real and raw.

2. How did you support Misty during her grieving process and what affect did her grief have on you?

It varied. Sometimes I didn't know what to do, so I responded by withdrawing, which did not help the situation. Sometimes I was physically near her, and let her vent to me and was supportive. I would say things like, "I'm so sorry I hurt you" and would do my best to validate her feelings. Sometimes I did it right, and sometimes I did it wrong. But I definitely didn't try to "fix" her. I humbly admitted that I caused her pain.

Admitting that it was my fault resulted in overwhelming feelings of shame and guilt. My men's support group helped me work through the shame I felt because of the pain I caused her. Seeing her in pain would cause me to feel so much shame, so it often forced me to work through some of my own garbage in order to be present and supportive for her. The key was giving my shame over to Jesus and reminding myself of who I am in Christ. I felt like trash, but Jesus saw me as beneficial, adored, and whole. I had to remind myself of that often. That without my addiction, I was growing into a good, safe man.

3. Have you had to grieve anything in regard to recovery? If so, what?

I've heard of some men having to grieve the fake friendship with porn or the affair partner. I personally never experienced any grief in giving up my relationship with porn or the affair partner. I did, however, grieve over the pain I caused my wife.

I've also had to grieve over the loss of my privacy and hiddenness. I'm very introverted, and recovery forces you to be completely open and honest, and that is very hard for both the

introvert and the addict. So, in one sense, I felt so relieved to not have that lie to constantly cover up, but in another sense, the honesty and openness has made me feel embarrassed and vulnerable.

4. Did you ever wish Misty would "hurry up" and forgive you? Why or why not?

Yes. It was hard. Her pain would cycle, and she would constantly have to go back to the beginning which was a constant reminder of what I had done. Part of my impatience was my own selfishness, because it felt shameful to be reminded. Seeing her hurting so badly surfaced feelings of helplessness. This is one reason why behavior modification techniques for sex addicts in and of themselves don't work. The man in recovery has to continually go back to who he is in Jesus, because he cannot and will not get his emotional needs met through his wife. This cycle can be a very long process, which is often why men give up. I prayed often for God to give me patience. Forgiveness can't be hurried. The wife can't rush grief, and she can't rush forgiveness. It is her choice. When my feelings of shame surfaced, it was my responsibility to see my therapist and address it.

5. Have you had trouble forgiving yourself throughout this process?

Yes, at first. There was so much shame and guilt. But the constant reminder of who I am though Christ and how Christ sees me, allowed me to forgive myself fairly quickly. It also helped to know that even though it was my choice 100%, to do what I did, there were also legit reasons why I chose that path. Pressing into the early years of my life was important for me to understand the reasons why I became an addict, and none of it had anything to do with Misty.

Chapter 6: Finding Your Safe People

In the last chapter, we learned how grief and forgiveness go hand in hand. In this chapter we are going to focus on helping you find your tribe. Your safe community. You might think that it's best to face this by yourself, alone, and trauma tricks the brain into thinking isolation is in your best interest. You can try and do this alone but doing it with a safe community of others can be so life-giving. There is power in community. But you need specific support for your specific trauma.

Let's discuss some practical, foundational principles to finding your "recovery tribe."

Everyone Needs a Ralph

Our family has always been partial to Golden Retrievers. Their love for the great outdoors and loyalty to their "pack" make for the perfect family companion. For ten years now, we have been blessed with the sweetest 100lb Golden Retriever named Ralph. Ralph is "extra" special in so many ways. For starters, we learned early on that he has food allergies, so his Gluten-Free lifestyle fits in perfectly with ours. He never chews his bones, but rather kicks into his natural instincts and walks around our property looking for the perfect spot to bury them, in case he'll need food later. Ralph absolutely hates the mornings. He prefers to sleep in late and gradually comes to life. In fact, if you try to convince him to get going more quickly, he will look at you with his big brown eyes that say, "Do I have to? Please don't make me!"

Part of my self-care regimen is going on hikes or paddling in my canoe. Ralph is my self-care sidekick. When I row, Ralph loves to swim and follow the canoe, and when I hike, he likes to forge ahead and lead the way into our grand adventure together. He has the knack of knowing when to follow and when to lead.

But the one thing I love most about my Ralphie-Boy is his loyalty. He loves me when I'm cranky, when I'm crying, when I'm angry, when I'm content, and when I'm excited. He loves me no matter what.

If only all humans could have that same attribute.

Early in my recovery process, I realized very quickly that finding a human version of Ralph was easier said than done. Nonetheless, I also recognized it was a key component to my healing process and one I needed to prioritize. But with my trust so incredibly shattered, and my heart guarded, it was exceedingly difficult to even think about living out my pain with another person.

In those early, raw months, I felt so overwhelmed with pain. Jim was also in recovery, but still learning how to respond rather than react. He was learning how to shed unwanted behaviors that went along with his addiction, and therefore I deemed him "unsafe" for my heart to rest. He was working on his sobriety, emotional maturity, and spiritual maturity.

Some experts in the field of sexual addiction state that whatever age a person is first exposed to pornography, their emotional maturity freezes at that age, regardless of how many birthdays follow. This would put my husband at an emotional age of about 13 years old, which is not exactly a "safe place" for me to expose my heart and soul. He had some growing up to do, and I had to create some safety.

So, then what? I began asking God to give me discernment. I sought out resources to guide me. I found a solid counselor, who eventually sent me on to a trauma specialist, and both were a great jump start to the healing process and I definitely benefited from their guidance. From there, I was recommended to see an APSAT, and she led me to an amazing recovery group specific to spouses of sexual betrayal. As you can see, it took a while to find the right people. The task was challenging, but eventually worked out. Now, seven years later, there are many more resources online for women in betrayal trauma. Hopefully, the task of finding a safe community will be easier for you than it was for me.

There are many books on the topic of creating your tribe, one of my favorites being Safe People by Cloud and Townsend. Here are some characteristics that define a "safe person:"

- allows freedom to share without condemnation/judgment.
- doesn't feel threatened by differing opinions.
- doesn't have a "right way" or "wrong way" mentality.
- encourages me to develop my own values rather than what they or others believe my values should be.
- exhibits trustworthiness and doesn't share my personal life with others without my permission or talk about me behind my back. Likewise, they don't share others' personal lives with me without their permission.
- loves me & accepts me, just as I am.
- offers conflict-resolution in a loving and beneficial manner.
- lives a life of transparency and authenticity and can admit their own struggles openly.
- doesn't over-spiritualize issues.

- validates first, then gently directs me to principles that align with the teachings of Jesus.
- doesn't feel responsible for me.
- doesn't try to "fix" me, but rather listens and loves.
- gives advice only when asked for it.
- is confrontable, meaning I know I can go to them in love, speak the truth, and not fear that it will change our relationship.
- loves without an opinion or agenda.

God created us for human connection. He created community. He knows and sees and understands that we are not meant to get through this hard life alone, and we can see that demonstrated time and time again through the Old and New Testament. Isolation is not in our best interest. I'm not referring to solitude, which is a discipline of self-care and rejuvenation. Solitude is healing, isolation is not. But it is very important that as you seek community, you find safety.

Since your husband is not deemed safe, where do you find your safe people? Your family? Your friends? Your church? Your co-workers?

Initially, the safest person might be a professional counselor. (Chapter seven will discuss a counseling.) Then, as they help you find your footing, you can begin the process of seeking a group to rally around you and help you heal. The goal is to find people whom you can share life with. They are individuals who value living life with transparency and authenticity.

You may find that your closest friends are unable to meet the requirements of safety in regard to betrayal. Some of your dearest friends have beautiful souls and hearts, but for whatever reason, they may be emotionally unable or unavailable to take on your hurts. Learn to be okay with this. You can find the right people during the right season. He may highlight unexpected friendships or bring you brand new ones to fill this role.

The most encouraging place for me to find my safe people was through my support group for spouses of sexual betrayal. These women were all ages, and our husbands were all over the spectrum in the recovery process. Some of the husbands were still in active addictions, and some had been in active recovery for years. Some of the husbands were considered "dry sobers" meaning, they hadn't looked at porn, but were still displaying addict-mode behaviors such as gaslighting, defensiveness, blame-shifting and resentment. But because our group was focused on our healing, not our husband's recovery, our hearts were bonded on the quest to heal. Let's take a minute and discuss what kind of group you can deem "safe" for your heart.

Finding a Group

I would encourage you to find a group that utilizes a trauma-based approach to your recovery. This kind of group will find resources that understand and acknowledge what your brain, body and soul are currently going through, and will also offer insight and tools using a holistic view. It will consider all aspects of your recovery process, and most importantly, this kind of group will highlight the importance of establishing *safety first*, trust second.

Let's define "safety first." "Safety first" means that the number one priority for you is to ensure that you are safe physically, psychologically, spiritually and emotionally.

You may not be aware if you are "safe" or "unsafe" in your current circumstances. The biggest indicator on your status is the presence of one emotion: fear. As you begin to dissect all the areas of betrayal trauma, you may discover that your safety is compromised. Some of us can establish emotional safety by simply implementing boundaries. If the spouse is truly in recovery, he will be respectful to honor the boundaries. If you feel more unsafe after setting boundaries, you could possibly be in a more dangerous situation.

If you don't feel safe, get in to see a counselor as soon as possible and find a good lawyer to protect yourself as you create a plan of action to establish safety. There is also a national domestic abuse hotline that you can call at any time to find an advocate to help you establish safety. Call 800.799.SAFE (7233) for more info.

This kind of situation is far outside a support group, so surround yourself with knowledgeable people who can properly assist you. They can also help you determine if you are in an abusive relationship if you feel confused or uncertain of what is happening in your personal situation.

Support Groups

A support group will recognize that you cannot build trust without first establishing safety. This book will guide you how to do so. Safety should be well documented and established before building trust and before you work on emotional intimacy with your husband.

You will also know you're in the right kind of group when the sole focus is off the husband and is on your healing. This doesn't mean they ignore your spouse's abuse and betrayal, but rather that the recovery work and discussions are focused on your healing process while, at the same time, equipping you with the proper tools on how to deal with the addiction, abuse, and betrayal and emphasizing your safety.

I personally believe it is also important to be in a group that doesn't idolize the institution of marriage. While not everyone may agree with this, the reality is that some women are in very dire situations with men who have no desire to be well. We believe that God, in His goodness, has provided divorce as a way out of abusive situations, including apathy and neglect. If you want to read a book on divorce, I recommend The Life Saving Divorce by Gretchen Baskerville.

In a nutshell, a healthy group is full of life and vitality. Members are committed to their healing and prioritize being present at meetings. They have a vision and most importantly, they meet women right where they are in gentleness and love. It views every member as bringing value and worth to the group, because no experience is wasted when we are working towards authenticity and healing.

Although most of the women in my group are grieving, they display incredible strength, beauty, and a hunger to become more like Christ. I know I can call any of them at any time and get prayer, support, feedback when asked, validation and love. I wish I could tell you every church and every group who claims to be a support for spouses of sexual betrayal have all the right tools, but that just isn't so, and you could find yourself more traumatized from the wrong group. A leader/facilitator should never forcefully give counsel, unless asked for it. They should never push a woman to rush into forgiveness, trust, or emotional intimacy. There should be mutual respect and a basic understanding that each woman is on her own personal journey and this will look many different ways. A group facilitator encourages autonomy. Because of this, there is loads upon loads of grace towards one another. There should be openness and acceptance, even if there is disagreement. At one of my meetings, I heard our group facilitator say the words, "Love without an agenda." A healthy group knows how to love others without inserting their own agenda or exerting control.

Before you attend a group, it is perfectly acceptable and appropriate to ask the leader/facilitator some questions. You can do this in person or by phone, whatever is most convenient. If you have multiple groups in your area, you can contact each of the leaders prior to attending so you can weed out groups that may not be the right fit. Keep in mind, some of this may not make sense quite yet, but we will address these details later. This might be another good page to use a sticky note tab as a quick reference when needed.

Here are ten recommended questions to ask the leader/facilitator:

1. Tell me how this group was born.
2. How do you feel about full disclosure? Polygraph? (Full disclosure and polygraphs are encouraged but not required. The decision varies from couple to couple, human to human.)
3. What is the structure of your group meetings?
4. What resources or books are you currently using? What have you used in the past? Future?
5. Is there any philosophy or author that you base your teachings on? (Mark Laaser, Anne Blythe, Sarah McDugal, Natalie Hoffman, Leslie Vernick, etc.). This will help you determine underlying philosophy and possibly, even theology.

6. Is the group open to women whose husbands are not in recovery? (It is my opinion that the group should be focused on helping women who have experienced betrayal trauma, not dependent upon what their spouse is/isn't doing.)
7. Is this group faith based? (This will vary depending on what you personally value. For me, this wasn't important so long as my choice of choosing faith was respected.)
8. Will I have opportunities to hear other members' stories and/or share my own? (Hearing from other women in the group is powerful, healing, and encourages authentic living.)
9. Does the group acknowledge betrayal trauma? (This is *very important* to get proper support.)
10. Will I learn about how to create safety and build trust? (Safety should be of *highest* priority.)
11. Does the group follow a co-dependency or co-addiction model? (I find this to be problematic because it places blame on the victims.)

It takes a lot of vulnerability and courage to step into a room or online zoom session of women you don't know. I remember feeling so anxious. But finding the right group is crucial to your healing process. Joining the wrong kind of group could be detrimental to your healing process. Don't take this decision lightly. You've been through enough trauma. It would be a shame to go through more trauma due to the wrong kind of group. You can ask your therapist for resources on finding groups that are offered in your area. If there are no known groups, there are plenty of online groups for you to explore. A good place to start would be www.btr.org or www.wildernesstowild.com. I currently have a free online support group, and you can find it by visiting our website at www.risetoheal.com. If you have any trouble finding your safe people and recovery group, don't give up. There are many online resources and group chats where you can immerse yourself in loving, healthy, supportive groups.

What About Family?

You may be wondering whether or not to even tell your extended family of your husband's betrayal. It is not my place to insert my opinion because, in all honesty, it depends. There are so many variables involved. Because of the unique set of circumstances with each betrayal story, I feel this is something that should be discussed thoroughly with your spouse (if he is in recovery) as well as with a counselor. Be intentional to use discernment and wisdom and include a professional to help you map out the plan of action.

Family is often not formally educated on sexual betrayal, and therefore will not understand the abusive aspects of pornography and sexual addiction. Sexual betrayal is extremely complex. It requires a lot of education to know and understand how to respond, how to relate, and how to support.

If you are in active recovery, your family may not understand why you are doing what you are doing. They typically do not have the full picture and may feel confused by how you choose to go about your healing process. But remember, you do not have to defend yourself. Stay the course. Boundaries may need to be established so you can keep your focus. You are not obligated to explain your course of action. This can be very difficult. There is nothing you want more at this time than to be heard, seen, loved and accepted. Letting go of their expectations towards you may be a process. In time, and with practice, you will learn to accept that not involving family may the wisest choice.

Sexual betrayal is often misunderstood, so your family may have a propensity to minimize your spouse's choices, not as a way to make you feel better, but as a way to make *themselves* feel better. This can be for any number of reasons, but regardless of what those reasons may be, it can be extremely hurtful to you.

Don't get me wrong. Families are beautiful things, and we love our families very much. As your first exposure to any form of social contact, your family is who taught you how to live, how to interact with others, and how to make your way in the world. They are also the first group of people you learn to trust or not trust. As such, your family of origin is largely responsible for your thought patterns and behavior, especially when it comes to relationships with others as well as your relationship with God. If there was any kind of breakdown in relationships during your early years, this could have created unhealthy family dynamics and therefore, greatly affected your thought patterns. For example, if the father was emotionally unavailable and/or physically absent, a person could grow up having feelings of abandonment, rejection, or a deep fear of being alone.

You may have experienced abuse and/or dysfunction by your family of origin. Many dysfunctional family systems experience something called enmeshment or entanglement. (This will be detailed below.) You may experience some pushback from enmeshed family members as you begin to recognize dysfunctional patterns and set healthy boundaries. *You can begin to untangle yourself from enmeshment even if your loved ones aren't on board.* This is called self-differentiation.

Some women choose to confront the abuse/dysfunction head-on with their family members, either face-to-face or through a letter. Some women choose to confront the abuse/dysfunction head-on through counseling or through a letter that is read to someone *outside* the family as a form of "therapy" and healing. Whatever the case may be, the point of confronting family of origin is *not* so you get reconciliation or repentance from those who've hurt you. The main reason is for you to finally create autonomy. Autonomy, or self-differentiation, is the ability to act out of your own values and interests. Practicing autonomy is learning how to speak up for that little girl inside you who never found her voice or who tried speaking up but wasn't heard. It is for you to discover your self-respect and self-worth. It is proclaiming your behavioral, emotional, and cognitive self-government.

Your family of origin had a considerable impact on your social, emotional, and spiritual development. As many studies attest, your family of origin helped to shape your worldview, determined how you related to and interacted with others and with God, and even had a big effect on your mental (and possibly physical) health. These influences will impact much more than your past; the way you were raised affects every aspect of your future, too! That's why it's often helpful and strongly encouraged to consider your family of origin if you're working through trauma, mental health concerns, or similar issues.

While it might seem pointless, shameful, scary or embarrassing to address concerns about your family of origin, it's not uncommon to carry childhood hurts and traumas into adulthood. This is largely because children are wholly dependent on others, and this dependence can render them helpless in the face of abuse, divorce, neglect (physically and/or emotionally), and generational issues like dependence disorders, enabling, addiction, mental health disorders, denial and general unhealthy family dynamics. When children feel helpless, abandoned, unloved, or unimportant they can develop beliefs that may be harmful later in life. It can even impact who they choose to marry! Again, these feelings that occurred when you were a child became a part of your Core Belief System mentioned earlier in this book.

Consider a car's oil filter. People ought to regularly change the filter because they know that a clean filter is essential to an optimally performing engine. If one doesn't change the oil filter, it can become clogged and cause severe damage to the engine. Your internal "filter" is the same. We all come into marriage with a "dirty filter," and if we don't address the muck from our past, our current day circumstances are going to be processed through a malfunctioning and "dirty" filter. That results in our reacting to things in non-healthy ways and patterns that will not promote wholeness.

Sometimes, family dysfunction can be hard to recognize. Tawnya Kordenbrock, a licensed professional clinical counselor, has written a wonderful article called "Ten Signs of a Dysfunctional Family." With her permission, I am including the article to follow. Since we all have a degree of dysfunction in our relationships, you will likely recognize at least one of the elements described.

Ten Signs of Family Dysfunction, by Tawnya Kordenbrock

1. Perfectionism

If you currently feel like nothing you do is good enough, there's a high probability you got this view from your family of origin. Sometimes it's conveyed with words such as, "Smith's always succeed. If you're going to be in this family, you can't fail."

Other words could be, "You should've done it this way ______." Or "Why did you do it that way?"

It's also conveyed with frowns, glares, and smirks. Continuous correction also creates perfectionism.

All of these lower a child's self-image and increase feelings of guilt. H. Norman Wright calls them "torture words."

2. Rigidity

Rigidity refers to inflexibility in family rules.

For instance, "We always go to church on Sunday mornings." You may have even had to sit on the pew with a fever and nausea just to fulfill the rule.

Another example could've been: "Be silent when dad walks in the door from work." Or "Children should never be heard at the dinner table."

This is different from guidelines that promote respect. Instead, they are hard and fast rules.

3. Silence

Silence is dysfunctional when it's used to punish. It brings deep and lasting damage to others by disregarding their worth. In fact, it's abusive.

A milder form is insisting others guess what is wrong with you. The dysfunction here is not valuing the relationship or the other person enough to actually state your hurt or desires.

Such actions can also be described as cutting you off, giving the "silent treatment," or acting as though you are dead to them.

Not only is hurt inflicted, but you are deprived of learning how to work through conflict. You also learn to not have your own opinion or to disagree, since the pain of the resulting response is so great. It can also be used as a passive-aggressive way to manipulate a situation.

4. Repression

Repression involves dampening or denying feelings in order to express only "acceptable" emotions.

In these families, hurt and anger are unacceptable and therefore must be stuffed.

Unfortunately, stuffed emotions come out in other ways, such as cutting, addictions, physical ailments, people pleasing, and compulsive behaviors.

Even more, stuffing feelings isn't discriminant — joy and happiness can also get repressed.

5. Triangulation

Just as a triangle involves three sides, triangulation involves three people. It occurs when one person uses another as a go-between for the person with whom he or she is upset.

A classic example is a dad who tells his daughter, "Go see if mom is still mad at me. Tell her I love her and see if you can get her to see my point of view."

Or, if mom and dad are divorced or separated, the child is a messenger, giving updates on the other parent. Or the child could become an appeaser for both sides.

This style of interaction, first of all, short-circuits direct communication. More importantly, it puts responsibility on the child for the relationships of others. As an adult, he or she could become a fixer of others' problems and struggle to recognize their own emotional needs.

More sadly, the child carries a weight he or she isn't meant to carry and is being used.

6. Double Messages

This could be as severe as receiving an "I love you," or an "I'm so sorry," from an abusive parent to a statement of "I trust you," while going behind the scenes to check up on you.

Double messages say one thing while simultaneously showing the opposite.

They injure by bringing confusion to the real meaning of words.

They also injure by bringing confusion to your intuition. For instance, when mom tells you "Dad doesn't have a drinking problem, he just needs to relax after a hard day of work," this negates the evidence you've seen that point to dysfunction. It teaches you to ignore your inner sensors that alert you to danger.

7. Lack of Fun

Fun is important for the health of a family. It provides fertile soil for growth.

Fun is an indicator that the family enjoys being around each other and feels safe.

When fun is absent, safety and respect for individuals is also absent. If your family never had fun, there was probably also abuse, rigid rules, and/or repression of emotions.

At the same time, don't mistake hurtful humor as genuine fun.

If your family never had fun together, ask yourself why.

If you were always alone or away from home when you had fun, it was likely because some type of shameful behavior existed in your home.

8. Martyrdom

If you pride yourself in how much pain and abuse you can stand up against, then you learned this dysfunctional behavior as a child.

Parents teach this when they alleviate their stress with too much alcohol, when they escape relational pain by overworking, or punish themselves by overeating.

As a child, you may have learned it by being told to "suck it up" when you were hurting. Or, you were told to be quiet about your pain because someone else's feelings mattered more.

This can happen when a parent is too emotionally distressed to handle everyday conflict or if a parent (or other family member) is chronically ill and the role of everyone else is to support the struggling person.

9. Entanglement

Here's one that's especially tough to see when you're in it. The behavior is justified by labeling it as love.

Entanglement is being overly wrapped up in each other's lives. In such an environment, it's hard to tell where you begin or end because your life is dependent on the behaviors of everyone else in the family.

This is also known as enmeshment. You can know if you're enmeshed if you spend a large amount of time trying to figure out the problems of other family members. Or, if you see yourself as responsible for their emotions.

In a healthy family, healthy boundaries exist where everyone is responsible for solving their own problems. This doesn't mean dad wouldn't ask for help. However, it does mean that he doesn't consider mom the reason for his problems. It also means mom doesn't see herself as the solution or the source of a solution.

In an enmeshed family, when one person is down, the whole family is down. When one person is up, the whole family is also up. H. Norman Wright describes it as being on a giant swing together.

10. Abuse

This includes physical, emotional, and sexual abuse. It also includes neglect and witnessing someone else being abused or fighting.

Neglect encompasses not only a lack of basic needs but also a lack of proper discipline or attention. If no one was in charge, due to substances or emotional distress, then as a child you were left on your own.

Also, your parents may not have physically or verbally abused you, but exposure to their fights was equally damaging.

Any type of abuse greatly strips the family "soil" of nutrients. It leaves family members starved for emotional safety and care.

It leads to all types of struggles when you are grown. Most of these struggles will be rooted in shame and self-hatred or low self-image.

The Effects of Living in a Dysfunctional Family

You likely noticed at least one of the above relational styles as belonging to your family. What were the effects of this family dysfunction on you?

One effect is that it taught you unhealthy rules about emotions and how to handle them. This in turn affects the level of intimacy you will have as an adult.

Living in a dysfunctional family also forces you to play a role instead of being seen and valued as an individual.

Kordenbrock, T. (2020, December 20). 10 Signs of a Dysfuncional Family
https://www.arenewedlife.com/10-signs-of-a-dysfunctional-family/

If any of the above resonates with you, know that you're not alone. There are many people with a history of a dysfunctional family of origin. Most are unaware of how it is affecting them until a crisis is present. Often, it takes a life-shattering event to gash open our souls and allow us to do the necessary work to piece ourselves back together again.

Although the process of addressing family of origin is tedious work, I cannot stress enough how much you can bloom in the process. You will start to view the world around you with 20/20 vision. You will begin to replace the dirty filter with newness of life! Remember the butterfly? This is when you see the impact of the microtopography of the wings. Living Water transforms you into a new creature and cleans your wings so you can begin to soar! The metamorphosis takes time, patience, grace, and work.

Trust

Another reason to clean the filter is so you can learn how to trust again. (Trust is a whole other topic we will talk about more extensively later on, but it is worth mentioning now as yet another reason to address your family of origin.) When my husband's betrayal happened, my family of origin filter was very dirty. Because of unresolved hurt, a poisonous, vile septic waste bubbled up from deep within. I felt like Yellowstone National Park, the human version of a super geyser! Calm on the surface, but tumultuous events

happening deep underneath. Hate, mistrust, cynicism, and anger: it all came pouring out and wouldn't stop. It took two years of intentional, faithful counseling to finally move through the pain and begin to focus on the pain in my own marriage. For some, recovery looks like three steps forward, two steps back. But even in the parts that feel like moving backwards, you are still making progress.

Recovery is a marathon, not a sprint.

It is important for you to wrap your mind around the mountain you are facing. According to Betrayal Trauma Recovery, healing from betrayal takes, on average, three to five years. That is an average, mind you, and takes into account a woman who is doing "all the things" to pursue wholeness. If you remove the counseling, the recovery books, and support groups, you can expect those numbers to increase, as your healing will take longer, and it is entirely possible that your healing will be all together hindered.

Hearing that your recovery can take an average of three to five years may sound daunting. You may think your marriage or spouse isn't worth the work, and you would be correct. That sounds harsh, but I cannot stress enough how important it is to shed the goal of "saving your marriage." Let me tell you an eye-opening sentence that may leave my church goers in a frenzied state, gasping at my audacity to dare blaspheme the sacred institution of marriage. Here goes nothing: recovery isn't about saving your marriage or your spouse. We are on a journey to save you. This is about you. You are worth the work, so keep your eyes on the prize, which is a much healthier version of you! If both you and your spouse are in active recovery, you will see the positive impact that independent healing will have on your marriage. So, in an indirect way, your marriage *will* be deeply impacted, but it is *not* the main focus. This idea is counter to what many churches and church leaders will push. Churches tend to push couples into marriage therapy before safety has been established and sobriety has been set. If your husband is in active recovery, couples therapy will most definitely be a part of your journey, but much later. In the beginning, when you find yourself at the trail head, it is wise for you to take one path and your husband to take another. The destination for both paths will be the same, to become safe, healthy, whole individuals who will be able to make clear decisions on their future together. Your paths may eventually merge back together, and it may not. For a season, each of you needs some space and time to work on just yourselves. There is power in the words, "Time will tell."

Ask yourself this question: "What is my goal in recovery?" If you desire a life full of joy, peace, love, unity, good health, deep relationships with others, emotional intimacy with safe people, and an open and honest connection with God, you will prioritize your safety first, and your own recovery. Trying desperately to save the marriage will not get you to this goal.

We own a pet hedgehog named Spike. When you first reach in his cage to hold him, he sticks his quills out and hisses. It's like he is saying, "BACK OFF!" The good news about Spike the Hedgehog is that he doesn't stay prickly forever. Once he warms up to the idea of being outside his glass cage, he relaxes, explores, and enjoys his time outside his glass box. I think he even likes it when I scoop him into my hands. He rolls up into a little ball, his cute little nose wiggling at me, and relaxes in the safety of my hands. We can all learn from Spike. He thinks life outside his cage means danger, but it actually means more opportunities. This is your time to break free from old, preconceived ideas of what recovery should look like. God is scooping you out of your comfort zone and inviting you to see the world differently, from a different perspective. It may seem strange, odd, or wrong, but relax your spiritual and emotional quills. As you let go of the resistance you may feel towards recovery and learn to be open, you will find a path of discovery, exploration and opportunities that will rock your world.

Heartwork Challenge:

1. Who do you feel is a "safe" place for you to land? Write their name(s) below.

2. What do you think it means when I said, "Safety First, Trust Second"?

3. Why do you think that "safety first, trust second" is important for you to understand in regard to churches and groups?

4. Have you told your extended family of your spouse's betrayal? Why or why not?

5. **When you read that recovery on average takes 3-5 years, how did it make you feel? Explain.**

6. **Have you felt invalidated by someone after sharing your spouse's betrayal? Without naming names, write out your experience.**

Q & A with Jim
Chapter 6: Finding Your Safe People

1. Why do you think it is important for sex addicts to find a recovery group?

Misty is not in charge of my recovery or sobriety. While she has "full access" to knowing whatever she needs to know in order to feel safe, we both agreed that it wasn't in her best interest for me to unload my daily struggles on her. I needed men to connect with. Being able to share specific struggles with a group of "safe" men allowed me to not be hidden and kept pain, temptations, and struggles from building up inside. We (sex addicts) need a village to help encourage us through the challenges specific to sex addiction, abuse, and relationships in general. Having a group of men to consult with helps keep me from being hidden. Hiding, keeping things in the dark, is a core reason why addicts may continue in their addiction. It is so important to bring things into the light.

2. How did you feel about Misty finding a recovery group? Have you noticed positive or negative changes in her since she settled in a recovery group focused on sexual betrayal?

I saw her hurting so badly and there were things I knew I couldn't help her with, but other women could. I was glad she found a group that met her needs. I have undoubtedly noticed huge, positive changes in Misty since she joined a recovery group.

3. Why do you think it is important for a sex addict to receive counseling without his wife?

Because addicts have to work out their own crap before they can work out their marriage. Going to individual counseling has helped me dig deeper into the issues that contributed to my addiction, helped me identify abusive behaviors and allowed me to grow into the man I desired to be. I had a "dirty filter" that needed to

be replaced. Cleaning our filters not only helps us deal with the addiction but will benefit the marriage as well. It has also made me a better dad. Sometimes I have to revisit my filter and clean it again. It will be a lifelong process. Another reason is it takes a trained professional to explain and help me explore the importance of attachment and attunement in my early years. That has been very important to my recovery.

4. How has your recovery group helped you personally?

It has helped me learn my identity in Christ and not as an addict. That has changed my life. It is so important to really grasp that, because I couldn't get affirmation from my wife during recovery. She was in too much pain as she processed my betrayal. The group also helps me by showing continued support, prayers, and responding to "SOS" texts.

It feels like a sense of purpose when I am able to offer support to other men on their journey too.

The men in my group have also been a safe place for me to be real and vulnerable. It is encouraging to know I'm not alone in the struggles.

5. How have recovery and counseling helped you in marriage?

I have a true intimacy deficiency, as do many addicts. Both recovery and counseling have definitely taught me how to be emotionally intimate. I'm still learning, but I have definitely improved, and it has gotten easier.

It has helped me identify when I am vulnerable to act out and/or when there are warning signs that I need to dig into. Many reactions are the surface behaviors and I need to see what's lying underneath. I can now identify my triggers and be more proactive.

I am still working on communicating better. Forty years of doing things a certain way is hard to reverse and it doesn't happen overnight, but slowly I am improving. The key is to approach conflict in humility. Inevitably I will experience pain in conflicts,

but my recovery group mentor is constantly reminding me to take that pain to Jesus, and to continue the hard work of becoming an emotionally intelligent man.

6. What things should a man look for in a sexual addiction recovery group?

Ideally, one should see the following:

- **Obviously, one that is for sex addiction. (SA)**
- **One that uses structured curriculum such as a 12-step.**
- **A group that encourages professional sex addiction and abuse informed counselling.**
- **A group that encourages full disclosures and polygraphs.**
- **A group that focuses on heart transformation not just behavior modification.**
- **A group that recognizes the abuse and the importance of respecting your wife's boundaries.**
- **A group that encourages you to listen to your wife and really hear what she has to say. (She is the best barometer of our recovery because she knows us better than anyone else.)**
- **A group that helps you dig into root causes.**
- **A group that helps you identify your triggers that make you more vulnerable to act out.**
- **A group that helps you understand basic human needs: attunement, responsiveness, engagement, ability to regulate arousal, how to be strong enough to handle negative emotions, a willingness to repair. (Adam Young, www.adamyoungcounseling.com)**
- **A group that teaches you what your wife needs and how to recognize abusive behaviors that accompanied the addiction.**
- **A group that teaches what contribute to acting out and how to combat those lies and make constructive choices instead of destructive choices.**
- **A group that is open, transparent, and vulnerable with one another.**

- A group that explores all aspects of grace, boundaries, admitting our wrongs, and speaking the truth in love.
- A group that encourages discipleship and life-long recovery.
- A group that recognizes the dangers of masturbation/fantasizing.
- A group that isn't afraid to ask the hard questions.
- A group that clearly identifies objectification.
- A group that helps the men reframe sex and marriage as God intended- one of equality, mutuality and respect.

Chapter 7: The Church and Counseling

Porn is the Trojan horse to our homes. It is straight from the gates of hell. Fight the New Drug is a non-religious and non-legislative organization that is raising awareness of pornography's harmful effects using science, facts, and personal accounts. Their website outlines how porn hijacks the brain, damages relationships, and affects the world. The site also reveals current statistics and the latest research that clearly shows how pornography is often the precursor to all kinds of more serious crimes, such as rape, child molestation and human trafficking. If you are seeking information on the harmful effects of pornography, that particular website is an excellent place to start.

So, if a non-religious organization has clearly defined and researched the harmful effects of sexual addiction, where does that leave the church and clergy? What about counselors and therapists? Can you trust that all counselors are properly trained in sex addiction? Do all clergy and counselors fully understand the complexities associated with sex addiction?

In this chapter, I will discuss whom you can turn to in this time of crisis and get the proper support needed to aid in your recovery process. There are some key things to look for when seeking professional counsel.

The Church

When it comes to proper understanding of sexual betrayal, emotional/physical affairs, pornography, sex addiction, and the abuse that sex addicts inflict upon their spouses, the church, in general, is sadly falling far behind. There is a great lack of education,

prevention, and recovery programs for sexual addictions and for spouses of sexual betrayal among Christian communities.

There are also deeply rooted patriarchal views and messages about sexuality within the church that are extremely destructive and harmful. I highly suggest the book, *The Great Sex Rescue: The Lies You've Been Taught and How to Recover What God Intended* by Gregoire, Lindenback, and Sawatsky. It details the dangerous messaging in some of the most popular evangelical books on marriage and sex addiction, such as *Every Man's Battle* and *Love & Respect*.

Sex addiction doesn't play favorites. Its evil clutches reach into all cultures, have no socioeconomic boundaries, and don't care about race, age or gender. It has become a worldwide pandemic, and most heart breaking, it has infiltrated our churches. I am not referring only to the congregation, but to the church leaders as well. The statistics of how many are addicted to porn is mind-blowing, and the numbers increase on a daily basis (Covenant, 2020). When we find ourselves in crisis, one of the first places Christians run to is the church. We look to the church for safety, hope, and answers. Can we trust our clergy to know and understand the complexities of sex addiction and betrayal trauma? The hopeful answer is: maybe. A more accurate answer is, more often than not, no.

The use of pornographic material among Christians continues to rise, reaching near epidemic proportions in the church. In 2016, a team of researchers from The Barna Group, a visionary research and resource company based out of California, launched a nationwide study about pornography called "The Porn Phenomenon." It was a massive research project examining teenagers, young adults, and Americans in general, as well as pastors and youth pastors. More than 3,000 people were interviewed, with specific questions covering a wide range of pornography-related topics. Shocking statistics released by the Barna Group revealed that 57% of evangelical pastors struggled with porn, either currently or in the past. 55% of pastors who use porn live in constant fear of being found out. The vast majority of the faith community believe pornography is a bigger problem in the Church than it was two decades ago. But many do not know what to do about it. The church is in desperate need of open dialogue on this topic, but sadly, it is often presented with so much shame, that it drives the addict deeper into hiding with a great fear of being found out.

The numbers of porn use by those in the church are staggering. If your pastor is not actively sharing their own intention in prioritizing sexual integrity, if they are not teaching the congregation strategies of how to live in freedom from our over-sexualized culture, there may be concern. We live in a day and age where sex is everywhere. No one can escape it. Pastors ought to be leading the way in sharing specific and practical strategies for keeping our minds and hearts geared towards a healthy view of sexuality while being immersed in a world that sells cheap, hook-up sex. They need to be teaching men about patriarchy and how to stop objectifying women and instead, viewing women as whole people. Youth pastors should be equipping the young on what to do when, not if, they are exposed to pornographic images. All churches should have a well-researched plan of action in place when someone reaches out and confesses of their sexual addiction. Teens should feel safe to openly discuss the topic of sex, objectification, mutual consent, sexual content, and sexual addiction. Churches should be properly equipped and educated on how to best support the spouse suffering from betrayal trauma. Churches "should" do all these things, but sadly, they don't.

I wish I could tell you that all clergy can be trusted with your heart on this matter. The reality is many clergy have not yet become a safe place for spouses of sex addicts. In fact, I'd go as far to say that many clergy have become more of a safe place for the addict to continue acting out! In addition, many clergy attach shame to sex, so sex addicts, both men and women, remain in the church pews, hiding behind their masks. Sadly, they remain in bondage. If clergy doesn't come clean, why would their flock? We must find a way to change this dynamic. Clergy needs to learn how to hold sex addicts accountable and how to be a safe place for the spouse who has been betrayed. A place where she can find validation, safety, and healing.

Generally speaking, the church has a lack of education and training on how to properly navigate the many layers of sexual addiction and domestic abuse. There is a huge need to educate clergy on how to respond to both the addict and the spouse who has been betrayed, using an abuse informed and trauma-based model. The lack of proper training can leave the couple without the proper support, which enables the addict, leaves the spouse feeling confused and misunderstood, and oftentimes creates more harm and additional trauma.

In my support group of about 70 women, almost all of us have experienced some form of church trauma and/or spiritual abuse during our recovery. Spiritual abuse occurs when someone establishes control and domination by using Scripture, doctrine, or a leadership role as a weapon. I asked the women in my group what experiences they had in their church. Some of the most common themes were:

- telling the wife to be quick to forgive.
- telling the wife that she is over-reacting.

- a push to be emotionally intimate or trust their husband before safety had been established.
- not teaching healthy boundaries.
- assuming the husband is no longer acting out or is in sobriety without any accountability set in place.
- wives being told to have more sex with their husband.
- asking wives how they contributed to their husband's infidelity.
- pushing husband and wife into marital counseling but not individual counseling.
- not requiring a full disclosure from the husband.
- not understanding the abuse cycle, and not recognizing porn addiction as a form of domestic abuse/minimizing.
- not knowing the distinct difference between sobriety and recovery.
- telling the betrayed spouse that God hates divorce, so that is not an option.
- telling her that she is suffering for Jesus, and this is a good thing.
- telling her to submit more, and that doing so will bring him to salvation.
- saving the marriage institution becomes higher priority than saving the individuals within the institution.

Absolutely none of the counsel above would be supported by properly trained sexual addiction and sexual betrayal professionals because they have a deep understanding of the many layers involved.

To add to this common church dysfunction, many pastors, according to the Barna research I mentioned earlier, are also addicted to objectifying women. Pastors will more than likely lose their position if they admitted to their addiction to objectification. Sadly, they often believe the lie that the risk of losing it all outweighs the glory of newfound freedom in Christ.

As we learn more and more about the emotional, spiritual, and mental battle that goes on inside so many pastors' hearts, and the hearts of their wives, we realize the enormous task that needs to be done in the Church. Being a pastor who is open about sexuality and who offers real, practical strategies to stop objectifying humans would be an amazing platform to help other men and women find freedom.

There are organizations, such as Covenant Eyes and Psalms 82 Initiative, that are helping churches by equipping and educating, but there is still much more work to be done. I pray for a day when we see the church rise and lead the way to freedom from the consumption of humans for sexual gratification. I also pray for a day when we see the church properly recognize the abuse wives have suffered under their husbands' addiction and a program in place to offer her safety, healing, and support.

Over-spiritualizing

Another issue that you may experience among Christians and churches is their propensity to over-spiritualize. Over-spiritualizing is a form of intellectualizing in which a person over-extends the intended meaning of a text or presumes God's intention in a situation with the purpose of avoiding or minimizing uncomfortable feelings. Christians, for example, may take a verse or spiritual truth and try and use it as a way to leap-frog over the pain or disappointment of any given situation and jump straight to a simplistic, pat solution. While God's Word has amazing mysteries and truths, it was never meant to help us avoid reality, but rather, to live well *in* reality. It seems too often, Christians feel pressured to say something spiritual; otherwise, they are failing at their job as a Christian. But when I observe conversations more intently, what I have noticed is this: Christians who are the most uncomfortable with uncomfortable emotions are the ones who tend to over-spiritualize the most. Read that again, and let it sink in. In the process to push people *to* Jesus, they forget one very important thing: to validate the other person's feelings. When we fail to enter someone's pain, we leave that person feeling unimportant, unloved, invalidated, and sometimes judged and condemned for their feelings.

As an unhealthy coping mechanism and a means to escape pain, we, the ones who have been betrayed, can also over-spiritualize, even to our own selves. When we over-spiritualize, we are doing the *opposite* of our intentions. We are stalling our own healing, because what we are doing is actually avoiding those emotions that feel really ugly. We also often misunderstand the feelings as being wrong, when they are often legitimate trauma responses to what we have experienced. Emotions can feel ugly, but they can also direct our healing if we listen with genuine curiosity of what they are trying to tell us.

When we over-spiritualize, we are sending the message that those feelings are too much for God.

Let's look to Jesus as our example. In John 11 we read about the death of Lazarus. In verses 33-35 it states, "When Jesus saw her weeping, and the Jews who had come with her also weeping, he was deeply moved in his spirit and greatly troubled. And he said, 'Where have you laid him?' They said to him, 'Lord, come and see.' Jesus wept (ESV)." Did you catch that? He entered into their pain *before* offering hope. He didn't rush hope or force it. He didn't insinuate they shouldn't be grieving. They could just *be* and then Jesus Himself entered into that pain *with* them. Oh, how I love this! This story should be our example of how to respond to all who are in suffering, and it should give you great insight as to whom you can trust your heart with and whom you can't. Some people, as much as they try, just don't know how to enter into these ugly human emotions. And sadly, many of those people are in the church. We have lost the art of lamenting and its sacred purpose, which is to release the deep pain.

Don't misunderstand. Jesus did eventually get to the offer of hope and ended up resurrecting Lazarus from the dead, but not before He took His time sharing in the hurt and pain with people He loved. When we allow Him *in* to our pain, instead of trying to push our own selves *out* of it, we are holding out our hand to Him saying, "Jesus, help me. Jesus, be near." That's an invitation that He holds with sacredness and honor.

Over-spiritualizing squelches emotional intimacy. When someone pours their heart out, that person needs kindness, assurance, and validation. He/she doesn't need someone to control their situation or to "fix them." The moment that a person is met with how God has a plan and how they need to trust more, that person's feelings are completely invalidated, and the person is pushed away. They don't want preaching or teaching or instruction. They want a listening ear. The least we could do before jumping in and offering advice is ask the question, "May I share my experience with you?" When you find a person who will remain quiet and simply sit with you in your pain, you have found an incredible gift.

Counseling 101

When it comes to counseling for betrayal trauma, the first choice would be to find an APSATS (Association of Partners of Sex Addicts Trauma Specialists). This is highly preferred over a CSAT (Certified Sex Addiction Therapist) because more often than not, a CSAT will not recognize *betrayal trauma*. You need someone who will be well-versed in both trauma and the many forms of domestic abuse. You also need someone who fully recognizes the emotional and psychological abuse that accompanies sex addiction. APSATS will also coach you on how to recognize abusive behaviors and patterns in your marriage. It may take some time calling around, or doing online searches, to find the right person. If you'd like to find someone online, I will strongly suggest starting with Betrayal Trauma Recovery at www.btr.org. I also highly recommend life coach, Sarah McDugal, or attending sessions with Leslie Vernick, who specializes in emotionally destructive marriages. Michelle Mays offers counseling and has good material as well. Keep in mind, some counseling centers are able to meet online, and some are licensed to meet only within their state. Don't assume that having the proper credentials and letters behind the name automatically equals the right fit. It is acceptable to interview a counselor and/or coach and find out their credentials, their modalities, and their approach.

Here is a list of 12 questions you can ask a counselor to see if they are the right fit for a spouse who has experienced betrayal.

1. **What are your credentials? (You definitely want someone who acknowledges betrayal trauma and abuse.)**

2. What are your thoughts on trauma in relation to a spouse's pornography use? (Betrayal is traumatic, so stick with a counselor who recognizes the trauma inflicted.)
3. Do you have strategies to help me learn how to set clear and concise boundaries? (You will need help navigating and setting boundaries.)
4. Do you view pornography use as a form of abuse? (Chronic porn use is a form of domestic abuse.). Why or why not?
5. Do you incorporate modalities such as EMDR to help the brain process trauma? (This tells you they understand the effects of trauma on the brain.)
6. Do you believe in HIS recovery, HER recovery, then, when safety is established, THEIR recovery? (Safety first. Always. There may be rare occurrences when marriage sessions may be necessary in the midst of individual counseling in order to work out the "how-to" of establishing safety. The thing to listen for is the counselor's understanding that emotional intimacy *cannot* be built until safety has been clearly established.)
7. Are you faith-based? (This is optional but is important for some to know. I don't believe one should let it be a deal breaker, because often non-faith based therapists are more trauma/abuse informed.)
8. Do you address family of origin? (This could be very important to your healing process.)
9. Can you recognize addict-mode behaviors and educate me on how to recognize them? (You will need this skill.)
10. Do you support a therapeutic written full disclosure? (This should be standard practice with CSAT /APSATS.)
11. Are you trained in how to facilitate a therapeutic full disclosure? (There is a very strategic way to approach

therapeutic disclosure. This will be addressed in a later chapter.). If not, do you know someone who is?

12. How do you feel you could help me most on my recovery journey?

As you call around, you may come to realize that one person may not meet all your needs. To date, my husband and I have met with four different counselors. Each of them has their own set of strengths and specialties. Recovery takes a village! Sometimes you may meet with a counselor who isn't a good fit or you "outgrow". That happened to us as well. The questions above should help you minimize wasted money and time.

Recovery in General

As mentioned in a previous chapter, betrayal causes our brains to go into natural "fight or flight" instincts due to the trauma our brains have endured. To combat that trauma, I had a strong need for knowledge. If only you could see the closet full of books I ordered and articles I printed. I spent hours upon hours researching online and journaling my experience and thoughts. I spent money attending workshops and fully immersed myself in a topic I never thought I would need to know. I became consumed by my need for knowledge when my life felt out of control.

Then there is the other side of the coin. Some spouses feel it is too overwhelming and too painful to read any material on it. They refuse to learn, refuse to accept and refuse to address it. The trauma of betrayal can cause us to either over-control or stick our heads in the sand. So, what is the best way to handle it? Neither obsessive knowledge nor withdrawal sound like the best options.

Let me encourage you that there is a place in the middle. It took me some time to discover it, but once I did, my healing process really started to take off. Keep in mind, healing is an individual process. No two stories are the same, so no two approaches are exactly the same. *It is a very personal and individual experience.* We must offer respect towards our sisters in healing.

It is also important to note that when it comes to sex addiction and sexual betrayal, there are three different parts to recovery. There is his recovery, her recovery, and their recovery, should the couple choose to stay together. Again, *this is not necessarily linear*. It will be messy. In the midst of our individual recovery, we had marriage sessions on a regular basis simply to work on communication and conflict resolution, *not* emotional intimacy. Don't misinterpret what I'm trying to convey. Emotional intimacy is the end goal, but not the initial goal until certain parameters have been set. Because of our history of stonewalling, and due to the years of gaslighting and lies, I initially felt unsafe to have confronting conversations. There were times I put my concern "on a shelf" and waited for our scheduled appointment where I knew it would be a safer environment. Having proper support to truly be able to recognize the addict-mode behaviors made me feel empowered that I had help; someone was in my corner and I wasn't alone. On the flip side, sometimes I was put in the "hot seat" and challenged in my thinking. The filter through which I saw certain situations was clouded and murky due to past trauma I had not dealt with. I had a difficult time expressing my feelings. I needed help. We needed help. That is why I want to be very clear that recovery for all three units (his/her/their) is simultaneous. The mix-up occurs when therapists and/or clergy entirely skip over the "his/her" individual therapy and jump right into marriage counseling and push for emotional intimacy. This is almost certainly doomed to fail, because the husband is often still immersed in addict-mode behaviors, safety has not been established, and a therapeutic disclosure has not yet taken place. A wife simply cannot even think about emotional intimacy until safety has been clearly established through strong boundaries, she knows the full truth and sexual history of her husband, and the trust-building process has begun.

It is also important to note that sex addicts who are not truly interested in getting well may use therapy sessions *against* his wife. He will take what she said in sessions, and on the way home, weaponize her vulnerabilities. This puts her in a dangerous situation, so it is very important to avoid joint sessions until stability and safety is well documented.

His/her recoveries typically take place simultaneously. It is recommended that this be on a very regular, consistent basis. You could see the same counselor (at different times) or each find your own counselor. Once this is set in place and safety has been established, marriage recovery can begin, if and only if both partners are *all in.* While the exact structure can look different ways depending on the circumstances, marriage counseling should *not* be viewed as the only form of recovery. Remember, each of you has your own recovery to work on so when you do come together and work on your new partnership, both of you have cleaner "filters" and can see the situation more clearly. Also keep in mind, your choice to heal regardless of your husband's choices is exactly that: your choice. Over time, you can begin to work on emotional intimacy with your husband, but it is recommended that you do so only if he is "all in" and in active recovery and *safety measures have been clearly laid out.* Emotional intimacy is the happy side effect to recovery work and will happen naturally as you begin to trust again. As you gain deeper understanding of your emotions and discover your core belief systems, your new-found inner self will pour into other relationships

in a healthy, honest, open way, even with your husband. If your husband isn't in active recovery, you can still work towards this goal as you connect more honestly with others who you deem as safe. Regardless, the choice as to whether or not you enter marriage counseling is yours. His recovery is his *responsibility*. Your recovery, and the recovery of your marriage, is your choice.

How Will I Know That My Husband Is "Safe?"

There is no exact moment in time when your spouse becomes safe for you. Every situation is unique. It depends. What does your heart need in order to create safety? That is the million-dollar question. When you feel your heart has identified what it needs to be safe, and your husband is displaying active recovery and tending to what your heart needs, trust will follow. Your husband will have been in his own recovery work and is showing through his actions that he is committed to the process.

When it comes to sexual addiction, we must believe our spouse's actions, not his words. 1 John 3:18 says, "...let us not love with words or speech but with actions and in truth" (NIV). Look at your husband's fruit. Fruit reveals the heart. What are the fruits of the spirit? Love, joy, peace, patience, kindness, goodness, faithfulness, gentleness, and self-control. When you start to see the fruit, that is a welcome sign that your heart can begin to work on trust again. You can also determine if he is safe when you see him have an "all in" attitude. I've mentioned this multiple times already, but I cannot stress this enough. He needs to be showing you through his actions that he is committed. Fully committed. That means there has been stability to his sobriety. This can be evidenced through various means, such as attending a solid men's group, seeing a counselor, and respecting your boundaries.

I also believe you can know if he is safe by looking at his relationship with finances. Money speaks. Very loudly. Is your spouse a reckless spender? Is he an over-controller? Do you feel like you have to hide purchases? Does he give you full access to all areas of your finances? Is he a reckless spender? Is your spouse financially abusing you? (Appendix C lists more details on how financial abuse can look). Do not flippantly read past this paragraph, because this is a very solid barometer you can use to determine if your spouse is showing signs of emotional safety. If you want to do your own personal Bible study on how money reveals the heart, simply do an online search on "Bible verses and managing money." As you read each verse, evaluate. It can be an amazing and simple tool to help you determine if your spouse is safe or unsafe. Proverbs 22:1 states, ". . . a gracious spirit is better than money in the bank" (MSG). When it comes to your finances, does your husband exhibit a gracious spirit?

Keep in mind that initially after disclosure, his actions may be clumsy. He will not automatically be perfect, nor will he ever be. As the more emotionally and often spiritually mature spouse, you will need to ask God daily to give you eyes of discernment towards your husband in recovery. Sex addiction is accompanied by many abusive behaviors, such as gaslighting, resentment, blame-shifting, control, lies, and legalistic condemnation. If a husband is in true recovery, you will see a <u>*gradual*</u> decrease in these behaviors <u>*over time*</u>. It won't happen overnight, and expect there to be moments of regression but, in general, you should see improvement and genuine changes over time.

Were you a Seinfield fan? There is an episode where the gang meets their opposite selves. They call it "Bizarro World." Somewhere early on in our recovery, Jim and I made an agreement to enter into our own version of Bizarro World and do opposite of what we had typically done when conflict arose. I was queen of silent treatment, or flat out ignoring and stuffing my feelings. Jim would also withdraw or became rigid and resentful. We each assumed the other person should automatically know what our needs were, so in our withdrawal we remained silent, allowing resentment to take hold. Jim would become so rigid in his "my way or the highway" attitude that he was completely irrational and impossible to work with during conflict. I tend to be queen of stonewalling. Some couples may yell and raise their voices. Some married couples may utilize both techniques. Whatever the case may be, resolve now to be *opposite you*. We have to get rid of our old ways of dealing with conflict. Again, this will feel very unnatural initially, but as you do the opposite, allow yourself to find that healthy balance with input from trained professionals to guide you to a healthier way of relating to each other.

You are having to "undo" years and years of established patterns and coping mechanisms. Marriage counseling will come in very handy for specific arguments. I had to learn how to advocate for my safety. Sometimes I would ask for a time out during conflict. I would "put the conflict on a shelf" and let it wait until our next counseling session. I would clearly state my needs to my husband during the wait period, so he was aware that I was struggling and needed space. Saying things like, "I am having a hard time finding words to match my feelings, so please respect that I need some space as I sort it out, and we can address it at our next counseling session." or "I feel very anxious in regard to this conflict, so please respect that I would like to discuss this further with our counselor." Boundaries were set until I felt safe again and Jim respected my boundaries.

I almost always felt *better* after joint marriage counseling sessions. That is because my experience was with a man in true recovery. If you leave marriage sessions feeling defeated, confused, misunderstood, or in greater conflict than before you went in, something is definitely off. Either you have a terrible counselor, or you are dealing with a man who doesn't want to get well.

While some women need permission to leave a marriage, I had to give myself permission to stay. There were two valid reasons why I knew God was calling me to stay. The first was my husband's brokenness. He was completely broken over his lies. He took full responsibility for his actions. He no longer blamed me or justified his addiction and behaviors. Secondly, Jim was humble. He knew he needed help. He became active in a recovery group. In essence, he was showing a true commitment to the process and his fruit revealed this to be so. As I've mentioned before, due to years of our husband's lies, we need to listen to their actions, not their words. You know the old phrase, "Actions speak louder than words?" That will be your motto as you move forward into recovery. You will refer to this phrase in making the hard decisions of, "Should I stay, or should I go?" You will use this phrase to know if you need to set a boundary, which will be discussed in the next chapter. You will use this phrase when in the middle of conflict-resolution and determining whether or not you need to include a counselor. The presence of brokenness and humility will be absolute key to aiding you in your decisions. Some abusers will fake brokenness and humility, but over time, you will see good or bad fruit.

On another note, you cannot expect perfection from either yourself or your spouse. Our recovery process seemed to constantly be three steps forward, two steps back. This "ebb and flow" process felt like it happened on a weekly basis the first year or so. Just keep reminding yourself that even in the steps back, you are still moving forward, even if your marriage isn't. Over time, if the two of you get healthier, you'll start to notice longer periods of peace. You may notice that working through conflict becomes productive and healthier. Instead of stuffing, ignoring, yelling or withdrawing, you both begin to utilize the tools you're being taught and find they are working. It isn't easier by any means. It is work, but it is rewarding work. We don't expect perfection, but we should see progress. If you don't' see progress in the relationship, then you will be faced with some hard decisions. You might decide that the pain of the past is too great to continue in the marriage, even if he is in recovery. That's okay too. There are deep consequences to abusive behavior, and sometimes those consequences don't allow for a relationship to continue after one party broke the covenant, even if both participants do the work of getting healthier. He broke those vows when he chose to sexually act out, not you.

The above will contribute to your determining whether or not your spouse is "safe." The further they get themselves into recovery, the more you should see fruit that they are changing from the inside out.

Attending a sex addiction group and going to counseling won't necessarily determine if he is deemed "safe" or not. He may be attending just to appease you.

If your spouse is in recovery to appease you, it is doubtful that true recovery will last long term. They have to be in recovery for themselves, just as we have to be in recovery for ourselves. Recovery is very self-focused. I mean that in the most positive of ways. We are focused on our own path, our own healing and our own faults. We are focused on healing from our own family of origin and we are reflecting on how we take ownership of communicating our needs and setting boundaries.

Recovery is not taking ownership of your spouse's choices. Let me say that again: there is ***nothing*** you could have done or not done or said or not said, to stop your spouse from sexual addiction,

and there is nothing you can or cannot do or say to make him recover. Stay committed to your own recovery, focus on how to set up boundaries for your protection and to hold him accountable, but do *not* take on responsibility for his choices or behaviors. In the coming chapters, you will begin to learn the difference between holding him accountable and trying to control his recovery process. The first can be productive and beneficial. The second will not be conducive to your healing process nor his.

Heartwork Challenge:

1. **What was your initial reaction when I mentioned that your goal isn't to save your marriage? Be completely honest.**

2. **Are his actions telling you that he is in recovery? Why or why not?**

3. **Read some or all of the following verses. After the verse, write in your own words or what you think that verse means. If you are in a group, you could split these verses up and have individuals read them out loud.**
    - **Prov. 15:22**
    - **Prov. 11:14**
    - **Prov. 24:6**
    - **Prov. 19:20**
    - **Psalm 119:105**
    - **Psalm 32:8**
    - **John 16:13**

Q & A with Jim
Chapter 7: The Church and Counseling

1. From your perspective, why do you think pastors remain hidden in their porn addiction?

I'm not a pastor but I would imagine it is because they have a greater potential to lose everything, including their position of power. Men that are *not* in ministry may feel shame, but they don't always lose their jobs over coming clean.

2. Does it shock you that the Barna research group discovered 57% of pastors have a history of a porn struggle? Explain.

No, I'm not shocked at all. In fact, I wouldn't be surprised if that statistic is even higher. I say that because of the potential impact that would affect a pastor if they actually admitted to it. Our culture is bombarded with porn—it is blatantly out in the open--every single day, and pastors are human, too. Pastors often don't know who to talk to when they are struggling. They remain hidden in their struggle, and when we remain hidden, the sin has power over us and keeps us in bondage. I also believe there are misinterpretations of Scripture, especially Genesis 1-3, that keep Christian men in a spirit of entitlement. Deep diving into the original language and context of those chapters really changed our lives for the better.

3. When does porn cross the line from being a "struggle" to being an "addiction?"

That's a tough question. Addiction is anything that a person goes to in order to escape. However, most people don't realize they are even doing that, so they don't see that they have a problem. Author Mark Laaser states that it doesn't necessarily mean a person always goes back to the same thing over and over again. He implies that if you are using something to numb out, address stress or pain, or look to something to fill an emotional need, it could be an

addiction. But addictions are cyclical, regardless of how much time lapses between those cycles. (You can type the words "abuse cycle" in a search engine and view for yourself what the cycle looks like.). It also escalates over time.

4. One of the most common things wives hear from clergy after learning of the husband's porn use, is that they need to have more sex with their spouse. Is this statement abusive to the wife, and does that enable the addict?

It's abusive because it puts the responsibility and blame on the wife for something she has no control over. It doesn't matter how much sex an addict has. It's not a sex issue. It's a heart issue. Telling a wife to "have more sex" is basically feeding his addiction. It is pure selfishness, and all about his own self-gratification. For the addict, the whole purpose for sex is to feed his need for another dopamine release. Take the wife out of the picture, then how do you help the addict? For instance, what if the wife had some kind of physical impairment that left her unable to have sex? How can the church help his addiction now? Do you see the point? That response is not placing accountability on the addict, but instead, enables him and keeps him in his addiction and it is also creating great harm to the wife.

Chapter 8: Normal Responses and Boundaries

In an earlier chapter, we noted that there are common myths when it comes to sexual addiction. There are also common reactions by the spouse who was betrayed. Below you'll find a list of some of the normal reactions based upon the trauma the one who betrayed has inflicted upon his spouse.

The abuse that accompanies sexual addiction will create a plethora of flooding emotions. I am highlighting this because you may not feel like yourself, and that is completely normal. As you enter healing from the trauma, the brain retrains and rewires, and you will reclaim who you are.

You could be one, two, or a mix of multiple. Highlight the responses that you relate to.

- Hypervigilant: In a strong desire for truth after years of being lied to, betrayed partners will become detectives. They search for evidence of cheating, check phone bills, check browser histories, read emails, read texts, look at credit card bills, phone apps, and more. They might also hire hackers and/or private detectives, surreptitiously install tracking and monitoring software on digital devices, or do whatever it takes to catch them in the act. This is a trauma response, and it serves you well when it is needed.
- Sporadic and Unpredictable Mood Changes: Spouses who have been betrayed can be sad and depressed, filled with rage and anger, and then desperately affectionate, loving, and even sexual all in the same day. Their moods can swing from one extreme to the other with little to no warning. She longs for deep connection and to be loved and cherished by her

spouse. This is a trauma response. In recovery, you will learn how to regulate your nervous system.

- Beat Up Self Esteem: Betrayal causes one's self-esteem to take a huge hit. She can suddenly feel unattractive and unlovable, too fat or too ugly, even when those feelings do not mesh with reality. Comparing oneself to other women becomes the norm. This can result in obsession with appearance, or she can react by being the total opposite, in which she completely stops taking care of herself. She may hate her body, and therefore avoid any physical contact, or completely disconnect during physical intimacy. She may suffer in silence, feeling deeply insecure everywhere she goes, as she compares her body to all the women around her. It can be mentally and emotionally exhausting. This is a trauma response.
- Sexually Charged: She may seek out sex with her cheating spouse, despite his infidelity. Maybe she is trying to feel desirable again; maybe she is trying to use sex to control the cheating spouse's sobriety; maybe she thinks that if she offers enough sex at home, her spouse won't feel a need to act out; maybe it is because she has the false belief that it is her fault her husband cheated, so she offers more sex as a means to satisfy the addiction. She may also seek out sex from other men to have "revenge sex". This is a trauma response.
- PTSD: She may be so triggered, she steers away from entire situations to avoid the feeling of dread, knowing she will be triggered. There may be a deep fear of intimacy and fear of being hurt again. She may avoid going to certain areas of the city, neighborhoods, or stores if they remind her of the trauma he caused. It can literally apply to anywhere at any

time. It may show up during physical intimacy, in the grocery stores, or at church. This is a trauma response.

- Ultra-Independence: Because her trust has been violated by the person or persons who should have kept her safe, she may be driven to do things on their own. There is an attitude of, "I can do this by myself." When others offer help, she has a hard time receiving. Somewhere in her life, she came to believe that receiving meant weakness. She can sometimes be labeled as a "strong woman", but the deception is that she is relying on her own strength and independence as a means to keep people away. There is often a lack of true authenticity and vulnerability. She rarely, if ever, allows people to see her faults. She may have a deep mistrust and possibly even hate towards all men. There is a spirit of ultra-independence, often a sign of being significantly hurt by people who were supposed to keep her safe. This is a trauma response.
- Micromanaging: Because her relationship is out of her control, and she no longer trusts anything her spouse (or anyone else) says or does, she might try to micromanage all aspects of life—family finances, childcare, chores, free time, etc. This may be necessary for her safety, but it could also be a trauma response. She will need to determine if her actions are serving her best interest and well-being.
- The Fighter: Because of deep wells of pain and anger, she sometimes reacts like a feral cat backed into a corner, such as snarling and lashing out in any number of ways. She might call the spouse who betrayed names, devalue the good things the he does, tell the kids and neighbors what about the infidelity/addiction, and more. Lashing out is the defense

mechanism in response to the abuse she has suffered. This is a trauma response.

- The Inquisitor: Sometimes, she wants to know every little detail of the addiction—what happened, with whom, where it occurred, how many times, and all sorts of very specific, and sometimes explicit, information that may not be necessary for healing, and sometimes incurs more trauma. This is a trauma response. She will need to slow down and ask herself if knowing that information will serve her and help her gain clarity on her future.
- Depression/Anxiety: She may become severely depressed. Due to the trauma that has occurred in the brain, she may become highly unmotivated. She may become extremely fatigued and often cannot get out of bed. She may have thoughts of suicide or self-harm. She may have panic attacks, sometimes severe panic attacks. This is a trauma response.
- Shutdown: Due to the trauma, she might avoid talking about it at all costs. It is also common to alternate between Inquisitor (obsessive questioning) and Shutdown (avoidance). One minute she wants to know everything, the next minute she may want to bury her head in the sand. She may also use the tactic of shutting down as a means to exhibit a false sense of control. Shutting down can be a coping mechanism. It can also be used as a means to try and make their spouse feel the same pain they are feeling or as a means to try and control their spouse's recovery/repentance. This is a trauma response.
- Reactive Addict: She might try to escape her emotional pain by engaging in her own types of behavioral addictions such

as shopping/spending, eating, exercising, spending hours on social media, or acting out sexually. It can be any kind of hobby or interest but taken to the extreme as a means of escape or numbing out the pain. This is a trauma response.

- The Mother Hen: She may try to "mother" her spouse and does everything to ensure her spouse gets better. She might schedule all the counseling appointments, order his recovery books, give constant reminders that his counseling appointment is approaching, and other mother-hen type behaviors. She may base her own recovery upon whether or not her spouse is in recovery. This is a trauma response.

I wanted to briefly take the time to highlight one more coping mechanism that I have seen often but can be missed by many therapists if they aren't trained in betrayal trauma. It is similar to denial or avoidance but does even a bit deeper and further. It's called betrayal blindness.

Dr. Jennifer Freyd, one of the founders of researching betrayal trauma, coined the term "betrayal blindness." I like Dr. Freyd's explanation because it feels much more aligned with what I have seen some women exhibit. Michelle Mays, author of *Betrayal Bind*, defines it as "not allowing yourself to see what is going on, to connect the dots, or to fully engage with reality, because if you did, the information would threaten your relationship with the person who is most important to you." Michelle Mays goes on to say, "Without clarity by a therapist of how betrayal blindness factors into the cycle of attachment ambivalence, and impacts couple's dynamics, therapists can go in misguided directions regarding individual and relational healing. Couple's therapists can mistake betrayal blindness for a betrayed partner's willingness to repair or forgive and go down the road of trying to heal the relationship before the betrayed partner has come fully into awareness and emotional connection with their own experience around the betrayal." (Mays, 2023). If this sounds like you, take this terminology to your therapist and do some of your own reading on how to address it. It requires a gentle and patient approach.

We just hit on the most common reactions to betrayal. Maybe you could add some more to the list! Let me assure you, these reactions are *normal*! I know you may feel crazy and unlike your normal self, but you've been hit hard with trauma, and it is a *lot* for you to navigate through. Plus, the trauma causes a physiological change in the body, and taps into a deep, primal part of our humanity. It takes time and effort to undo the physical and relational damage his actions have caused. It is so involved, there are entire books written on it. I recommend reading the book *Betrayal Bind* by Michelle Mays. She highlights attachment and relational aspects of betrayal and betrayal trauma that I found to be extremely helpful to learn.

I'd like to point out that it is possible to have these patterns showing up before you even knew about the betrayal. Your instincts are strong, and it may be that you were exhibiting some of these patterns as a protection response to the abuse you were unaware of. It is also possible that these patterns were established as a response to childhood trauma, such as neglect, family of origin dysfunction, legalism/spiritual abuse, divorce, or any form of child abuse.

While all these reactions are completely normal due to trauma, that doesn't mean they are always in your best interest. You don't want to stay in these patterns. Your goal should be to move into a posture of pro-active not re-active. Shedding trauma responses and learning how to emotionally regulate in the face of chaos takes practice and tools.

Establishing Boundaries

To be pro-active, you first need to establish some boundaries to create safety. Safety, as mentioned before, is your number one priority after betrayal.

The first step in doing so is learning how to create boundaries and why we create boundaries. I love how boundaries, when used properly, create emotional health and are created by people with emotional health. Boundaries keep us off the crazy train of cyclical behaviors and patterns.

When I was talking to my husband about boundary setting, he stated, "Boundaries are for protection, not for punishment." After years of recovery and me setting a lot of boundaries with him, this felt so encouraging that he, on the receiving end of boundaries, recognized the purpose.

Boundaries are an expression of love, out of a heart of love. It is mostly for *you*, not for your spouse, although he can most definitely benefit as well. Boundaries are in place to help you feel emotionally, and sometimes physically, safe.

Safety in a marriage is the under-structure that builds security, intimacy, trust, and the sense of oneness that a healthy attachment can foster. You know you are emotionally safe when you start to see key changes in your husband's character. Changes like having more empathy, being less defensive, showing integrity, being reliable, living in honesty, being quick to apologize, exhibiting humility, and staying committed to recovery work. These are all positive signs that your husband is becoming a safe man. He also must honor the boundaries that have been established.

I love the definition and description by Anne Blythe, owner of Betrayal Trauma Recovery, in her podcast "How to Stay Safe

When Your Husband Is Unfaithful" (Blythe, 2016). In the podcast, Anne draws on the work of Dr. Adam Moore, a licensed marriage and family therapist who specializes in treating sexual addictions. Below are the main points pulled from the podcast that I found to be very helpful.

Boundaries Provide Safety

Boundaries Do the Following:

1. **Define limits of relationships.**
2. **Are healthy responses to someone violating you.**
3. **Keep you safe while someone who has hurt you rebuilds trust.**
4. **Protect you from repeated harm.**

Boundaries Are Not:

1. **Retribution.**
2. **A way to force someone to act the way you want.**
3. **A way to avoid pain.**
4. **An excuse to emotionally disconnect. (Moore, 2014)**

Let's put some language to your boundaries. Next are some boundaries to set in place for yourself.

Examples of personal boundary statements:

1. **I cannot control my husband's response, but I can control mine. That means I can stay calm and firmly state my needs and desires.**
2. **Since I cannot control my husband's responses or behaviors, I'll let go of trying to control doing so. I am not in charge of**

his recovery. I can set up my expectations and boundaries and if they are not met, enforce consequences.

3. I will choose to take care of myself through self-compassion. This is a season where I have permission to turn inward and focus on my healing. Once safety has been set, I can begin working on trusting him again. I am not required to share my feelings and needs with him until safety and trust are in place.
4. I get to choose when and how I will begin trusting again.
5. I get to choose the timing of forgiveness.
6. I give myself permission to grieve, as long as I need.
7. Regardless of his choices, I can still work on my own path to healing.
8. When I am struggling, I will reach out for help and seek safe people with whom to share.
9. I am not responsible for my husband's addiction nor his sobriety, yet I also no longer have to comply to his addiction and abuse.
10. If/when my husband is acting out, I can still choose to love myself and prioritize my needs.

I love statement #4, where you read the phrase, "I get to choose when and how I will begin trusting again." I cannot express enough how this was such a huge part of my recovery. If you have someone in your circle encouraging you to share your feelings with your spouse when safety has not been established, come back to these statements and read them over and over. You are not "required" to open your heart to an unfaithful spouse. Ever.

This is one of those areas where uneducated individuals or untrained professionals could potentially do more harm than good. They mean well by encouraging emotional intimacy with your

spouse, but you cannot accomplish it when safety hasn't been established. Our spouses have quite a bit of maturing that needs to take place before this can happen. Which leads us right into the next section of relational boundary statements. These statements are examples of relational boundaries.

Relational boundary statements sound like this:

1. **Regardless of what you do or don't do, I will continue to work on my healing from the consequences of your choices.**
2. **I will sleep alone in our bed or in the guest room if you choose to use pornography, break the covenant of marriage in any way through unwanted sexual behaviors, or if you act out your pornographic fantasies on me. We will not sleep together in the same bed until I feel safety has been re-established. An in-house separation may be implemented, or you may be asked to move out should you choose to break the marriage covenant.**
3. **When you attend a weekly support group specific to sex addiction, it makes me feel safe and more willing to work on trusting you again. If you choose not to go, I'll be limited in my capacity to trust.**
4. **If you blame me for your behaviors, choices and perceptions, I will not try to reason with you or defend myself any longer. The conversation will be put on hold until I determine what I need to feel safe once again.**
5. **I will not have sex with you when I feel coerced, emotionally disconnected or unsafe.**
6. **I feel unsafe if you are not making a concerted effort, through counseling and/or personal recovery work, to discover the "why's" of your addiction and abuse. If you refuse to have empathy and understanding of how your**

addiction has affected me, if you continue to lie, manipulate and gaslight me, or if you continue to be lazy in your recovery process, I will move toward separation from you. In this state of addict-mode behaviors, you are not safe to be around.

There is so much wisdom, love, and healing in these boundary statements.

Sex will be discussed more in detail in a later chapter, but let's take a brief moment and look at #5. "I will not have sex with you when I feel coerced, emotionally disconnected or unsafe." I don't know about you, but I put an insane amount of pressure and guilt on myself to have consistent sex with my husband, not out of a heart of connection and love, but from a place of fear. Fear that if I didn't, he would be more tempted to act out. Fear that if I didn't, I would be labeled a "bad wife." We will explore where these feelings of guilt may have started in the chapter on sex.

There were many times that I felt emotionally unsafe or disconnected from my spouse while in recovery. Because of that, I gave myself permission to *not* engage in sex for as long as my heart needed to heal or until safety was established. There is no need to put unnecessary guilt on yourself. This is a consequence of his choices, and his role during this time is to offer whatever support you need in order to heal. (You are not withholding sex as a means to punish him or control his behaviors, but to give you the space needed to heal, with the hopes of coming back together once your heart is ready and safety has been reestablished.)

Defining your boundaries can be difficult, especially in the beginning while you are still learning how to do so. It may be helpful to write them down and discuss with your counselor, group leader, or other women who have been in your shoes. Some of the women in my group had really solidified this process and were extremely helpful for me.

Creating a Boundary

Before we begin, I want to re-iterate that sometimes there are domestic abuse situations where setting boundaries is not safe. If that is the case, seeking help from a Domestic Violence Shelter is advisable. The shelters have many resources to help someone understand the level of abuse they may be experiencing and have connections to lots of other resources, not just a place to live temporarily. For those who choose to stay in their current relationship, boundary setting will be a must in the recovery process.

When it comes to creating a boundary, how does that look?

If your boundary involves your husband's behavior and your response to that behavior, it is important to share it with him *before* the offense occurs.

Think of how you talk to your kids. "If you do ______________, then __________ will happen." I use this approach with my kids constantly. Typically, I have my child narrate the statement back to me in his/her own words so I can check for understanding. This is not a bad idea to use with your husband as well. Sometimes we can say things one way, but our words can be perceived another. Checking for understanding is always a good idea. It is unfair and unrealistic to enforce a boundary if that boundary hasn't been clearly laid out. State your expectation and don't be afraid to ask him to repeat it back to you. Doing so will ensure he clearly understands in the event that a boundary is crossed.

Boundaries will vary from person to person. You will come up with your own list of boundaries, based upon how your husband acted out prior to D-Day.

Boundaries will change/evolve over time and as his recovery becomes more solidified and you feel safer. Here are just a few examples of boundaries I set early on in recovery:

1. At bedtime, the phone was to be turned off and in a different room. No phone use during the night or while I was sleeping, and no phone allowed into the bathroom. (The phone was his main source for viewing porn.)
2. No going on business trips alone with a female co-worker. (He had to discuss this with his employer.)
3. Install internet filters (We chose Covenant Eyes.)
4. He must be active in a men's sex addiction support group. (This group meets weekly.)
5. He must have two accountability partners. (We discussed the options together.)
6. I can contact accountability partners any time.
7. He must consistently attend counseling sessions.
8. No more rated "R" movies or movies with sexual content of any kind.
9. No defensiveness, blame-shifting, or gaslighting during conflict.
10. He must be reaching out to other men on a regular basis and be connecting emotionally with others.

Below are some ideas for consequences I used when a boundary was crossed. The consequences can be set before the offense occurs, or you can leave it open and ask your spouse to pick which consequence he would like to incorporate. You can adapt and personalize them to your specific needs:

1. Add in an extra counseling session.
2. Call accountability partner (in my presence).
3. Call his group leader (in my presence).
4. A written apology, to be read at a marriage counseling session. (only if joint sessions have been deemed "safe".)
5. Sleep in a guest room until safety is re-established.
6. Attend a conference on sexual addiction recovery.
7. Complete the Amends Matrix, as outlined in the book, Worthy of Her Trust.
8. No screen time for "x" amount of time.
9. Attend an extra recovery group in our area.
10. Take a polygraph every six months the first two years, then once per year or as needed to establish safety.

Once you have your boundaries outlined, it is time to share your boundaries with your spouse. It is important that he understands your boundaries so both of you are on the same page. (We put some of these in place together, collaboratively.) He may get defensive, so if you foresee a negative reaction, consider if you want to share the boundaries alone with your spouse, or with a trusted counselor who understands the different forms of abuse.

Once your boundaries have been clearly laid out, you must take on the task of learning how to enforce them.

Enforcing Boundaries

Enforcing boundaries means consequences are not only set in place but are then followed through. Enforcing can be challenging and feel extremely unnatural. Initially, I remember feeling guilty, selfish, and clumsy. Over time, I started to feel differently about boundary setting and enforcing. It started to feel less like selfishness and more like self-compassion and empowerment. I was finding my voice. Remember, more often than not, spouses who have been betrayed have been under years of abuse. Destructive attitudes and behaviors such as condemnation, gaslighting, and shifting the blame have been the husband's go-to resolution in conflict. Sex addicts will use these strategies to justify their behaviors and keep the focus off of them. It is death by a thousand cuts, so she doesn't even realize their souls are being crushed. This soul-crushing process happens at a slow rate, often occurring over many years. Because of this, we are often unaware of what is even happening. That is why enforcing boundaries takes practice.

Blythe's podcast offers some specific tips from Dr. Moore. He suggests simple steps to help you enforce a boundary with your spouse. I have summarized the steps below.

Four steps to help enforce boundaries:

1. Slow down and breathe. Respond as the mature adult that you are. Do not react, respond.
2. Remind him of your boundary and consequence that was set and the goal is not punishment for him, but protection and safety for you.
3. Follow through with the consequence.

4. Help him understand that your boundary is in place until you feel safe again, and not for a set period of time. You are in control, not to punish but rather you are creating space to heal.

Enforcing a boundary is part of the climb that can be foggy. I've read so many varying ideas of what type of consequences should happen and how they should be enforced. I have a strong opinion that consequences should lead the husband further into recovery as much as possible. Defining and enforcing boundaries can be very difficult for wives of unfaithful men for a variety of reasons. However, our safety depends on it. It's often the defining process of our recovery and the true start of our healing. This is also an amazing opportunity for your husband to live out his love and devotion towards you. If he truly understands his role during your healing process, he will put his feelings aside and remember that he is to offer full support. In humility, he remembers the reason why boundaries are in place. By humbly abiding by your boundaries, he can begin the process of rebuilding trust and be held accountable for his actions.

To help clarify my point, let me list out some specific examples of how and when a boundary could be set. This is an important topic, so I want to make sure you have a good handle on how to use this tool properly. To further assist you, I've included some examples below.

Example #1

Boundary: Husband is to turn off his phone at night and put it in another room when going to bed. Failure to abide by this means the husband has to call his recovery group leader and complete the amends matrix, which will be discussed with both the wife and his counselor.

Crossed Boundary: Wife wakes up and finds husband on his phone while in bed. She explains, "When you look at your phone, it makes me immediately think you are relapsing, and I feel unsafe."

Enforced Boundary: Husband calls his recovery group leader in the presence of his wife. He completes the amends matrix and then discusses it in a counseling session.

Example #2

Boundary: Husband is working hard on shedding the gaslighting and/or blame-shifting during conflict. Failure to do so results in counseling sessions, by himself, on this topic. A marriage counseling session may be scheduled once he has addressed his addict-mode behaviors. (Reminder, marriage sessions occur only if you've seen signs that he doesn't weaponize joint sessions against you). The husband agrees to sleep in the guest room until safety has returned to the marriage.

Crossed Boundary: During an argument, the husband begins blaming his wife, telling her she is the reason for his behaviors. She calmly states, "When you shift the blame onto me, it reminds me of how we used to deal with conflict. These are old patterns and do not benefit either of us. I am not feeling safe in this conflict, so I'm enforcing a boundary until you can learn to discuss this with emotional maturity and respect."

Enforced Boundary: Husband moves to the guest room, attends his counseling sessions alone, and when ready, invites his wife to a session together to discuss and resolve the issue. Once this has happened, he returns to the marriage bed. If he refuses, you cannot force him. In those cases, you need to determine what you can do to feel safe. (Perhaps you move to the guest room instead of him.)

While I wish I could tell you every husband will respond to your boundaries with patience, grace, and love, we all know that is an unrealistic expectation. Especially in the beginning, where new relational dynamics are being set in place. The dysfunctional hamster wheel of cyclical patterns and behaviors you've both been on for so many years has come to a complete halt. You have jumped off the wheel and the two of you are, in many ways, starting completely over! It is an abrupt U-turn of the marriage.

According to the Psalm 82 Initiative, an organization that advocates for victims of domestic abuse, there are four pillars of the abuse cycle: coercion, control, entitlement, and compliance.

Because of this, it is important for you to be prepared for both positive and negative responses.

Sometimes setting boundaries and consequences not only establish safety, but also reveal the heart of your husband. If he is *not* in recovery, enforcing boundaries could make things worse between the two of you. People with the heart of an abuser *hate* boundaries. He may become more abusive, more isolating, or continue acting out. Setting and enforcing boundaries may be the tool needed to be used in order for you to know what decision to make in regard to your future. Setting the boundary allows you to clearly see your situation and how unsafe or safe it truly is. You can then move forward in making the best decision for yourself and your children.

Remember, God is pro-people before He is pro-institution. Consider the woman at the well. Jesus lovingly offered her His Living Water. He didn't offer to restore her marriage(s), He offered to restore her! He is for you, not against. God doesn't expect you to stay in an unsafe marriage and continue to be abused for the sake of staying married. Divorce can be a beautiful gift from God as your Jehovah-Jireh, providing you a way out of a toxic relationship to find healing and freedom.

Traumaversary Boundaries

We've been looking at how to set boundaries with your spouse to create safety in the marriage. Now we are going to look at how to set boundaries to create safety towards yourself. One of those areas is how to honor difficult dates in your trauma timeline. This is called a "traumaversary."

A "traumaversary" is the anniversary of a traumatic event or season in a person's life. It is significant because it can be really hard on a person, manifesting itself in a variety of ways. A person can experience physical, emotional, mental and spiritual upheaval and instability.

According to the Anxiety and Depression Association of America, traumaversaries can trigger someone to experience migraines, stomach aches, flashbacks, nightmares, sleep problems, difficulty concentrating, fatigue, anger, grief, and more.

I have mentioned multiple times how important it is to be vulnerable and transparent. I want to practice what I preach right now.

Today marks my seven-year traumaversary. Seven years ago today, my husband told me the truth. Seven years ago today, my life was turned upside down. Seven years ago today, I found myself physically harming my own body to lessen the pain I felt inside. Seven years ago today, I asked my husband to leave because I was scared for my own safety, and the safety of my children. Seven years ago today, I felt like my life had ended. Seven years ago today, my self-esteem was annihilated. Seven years ago today, a dark cloud and heavy fog descended on my mind. Seven years ago today, I found myself emotionally free-falling in a deep abyss. Seven years ago, today.

Traumaversaries can be both known and unknown. In fact, I have a friend who actually shares the same traumaversary as myself. A couple of days ago, I sent her a text, letting her know that I was thinking about her and praying for her. She replied by telling me that she had been in an emotional funk all week long and blamed it on hormones. She had completely forgotten that it was a traumaversary, but her body remembered. I find it mind blowing that our bodies are designed to remember, even when we are cognitively unaware. But when we are aware of a traumaversary approaching, what can we do in preparation, so we don't spiral out? Are there things we can do to lessen the emotional flooding? The answer is yes. Let's walk through some simple boundaries for yourself that you can put in place to prepare your heart and mind for traumaversaries.

1. Create a plan. Prior to the event, take time to sit and outline what you need. This process will be individualized to your unique situation. It could look many different ways. Do you want to schedule an extra counseling session? Do you want a day alone or a day with supportive family/friends? Do you want a night alone in a hotel room to process and grieve freely? Do you want to arrange a babysitter so you can have a day to yourself, or do you want to arrange a family day packed full of fun activities? Whatever it is, be intentional to

eliminate extra stressors. Clear out your schedule, if possible. Consider easing your schedule the week prior to and after the traumaversary.

2. Commemorate. In the process of creating a plan, be careful not to plan so much that you distract yourself from remembering. Part of remembering is allowing yourself space to feel. Don't use busyness as a coping mechanism to suppress your feelings. Definitely chisel out time to honor your pain. This could be an entire day to do so, or a short 20-minute walk in the woods. Maybe it is spending time writing in your journal or donating to a charity that supports battered women. Whatever it may be, choose to remember.
3. Continue to feel. Remind yourself that it is okay to feel. Grief has many faces. If you feel sad, let it out. If you feel anger, let it out. If you feel confused, let it out. Whatever it is, let it out, and give yourself permission, space and time to do so.
4. Count your blessings. Gratefulness heals. Practicing a heart of gratefulness will rewire our brains and heal us from the inside out. In my home, we use the phrase, "Find the rainbow in your cloud." We don't deny our emotional "clouds," but we seek out and look for the "rainbows" along the way. Name them, and practice a heart of gratefulness.
5. Practice Contentment. There is something to be said for simply being content. Contentment is acceptance. When we can get to a place of accepting our past, our bodies align with our emotions and we find peace. Be content with where you are in your journey. You are exactly where you belong, right in this moment. Discontented people desire to be someone else, be somewhere else, or have something else. Be the opposite of that kind of person. Being in a state of contentment is an art. A choice. A state of mind. It is choosing to take what life has thrown at you and deciding to be at peace with it.

Trigger Boundaries

Another area of creating safety towards yourself is learning how to respond to a trigger. A trigger is an experience (real or perceived) which causes a person to recall a traumatic memory. They are those super-reactive places inside you that become activated by someone or something outside of your control.

When triggered, a woman suffering from betrayal can respond many different ways. She may withdraw and isolate or shut down emotionally. She might feel depressed. She may feel angry or respond in an aggressive way. Whatever the case, the reaction is intense because she is reminded of the act of betrayal. The "flooding" of emotions can last anywhere from a few minutes to a few days, to even a few weeks.

Unlike a traumaversary, a trigger can be very unpredictable. The random "pop ups" can range from annoying to debilitating. It can happen during sex, watching TV, or a trip to the grocery store.

When dealing with triggers, it may be helpful to re-read chapter 3 on "Emotions." Below are some tips on how to address triggers.

1. Name it. Naming your feelings is being aware of your feelings. Too often we tend to ignore, suppress, or minimize our feelings. (Refer back to the feeling wheel if you need assistance.) Become a student of yourself, and when you feel like you are in an emotional "funk," press into it rather than ignore it, blame it on something else, or minimize it. Pressing in to our triggers means we fully feel the uncomfortable emotions that accompany the trigger. By

doing so, we can work through the trigger, then eventually out of it.

2. Claim it. Claiming our trigger means we accept the impact the act of betrayal had on us. We recognize the trigger, name the emotion(s), then dig to find the origin. In chapter 3, you learned how to use the LERC to trace back to false Core Belief Systems. Triggers will give you an opportunity to LERC again and again. Let me rephrase that for the sake of emphasizing: triggers are windows of opportunities. Don't ignore them or rush through them. Lean in. Press in.
3. Tame it. When we take the time to name the trigger, and claim the impact betrayal had on us, we can then find ways to tame our triggers when they arise. This is a discipline that will happen over time as you climb our mountain of recovery. Taming could also be called emotional regulation. You can "bring yourself down" through techniques you've picke dup in therapy and/or support group sessions. Deep breathing, tapping, meditation, taking a walk, listening to music, or petting your dog. There are many ways to tame and regulate.

Keep climbing. Soon, you will be above the tree line and your head and heart will "clear out" and you'll see the amazing, breath-taking views. Your effort will pay off.

Heartwork Challenge:

In today's heartwork challenges, be prepared to set aside a little more time than normal to complete your work.

1. BOUNDARY TIME! This is going to be one of the most important exercises you will do: make a list of boundaries and consequences. This will vary from person to person, and I found

it helpful to go over these with other women to get ideas. Be sure to protect at least a good half hour to work on your boundary/consequence list. Think of everything you need to feel safe. You will present this list to your spouse, either alone or with a trusted counselor.

2. Go back to the start of the chapter and read through the typical responses. Which ones did you fit under? Remember, there could be multiple! If you are doing this book in a group, share your responses.

3. Expand on your feelings and thoughts on setting boundaries. How does setting a boundary make you feel? Does it feel natural? Empowering? Scary?

4. Write out a recent time you felt triggered. Name it. Claim how it affected you. Take that same trigger and practice the LERC strategy in the space below.

5. OPTIONAL: Can you think of a Biblical account or example of boundary setting? Feel free to work with a partner on this exercise. Be sure to include Scripture references.

Q & A with Jim
Chapter 8: Typical Responses and Boundaries

1. Misty worked very hard to create safety by setting up clear boundaries. What did you think or feel about her boundaries?

The boundaries she set up made me initially think, "I'm not a child" or "I can handle it." But I quickly realized the boundaries were beneficial not only to build safety and trust but also for me, personally. One of the boundaries Misty set up was that I couldn't use my phone at bedtime. This was something I did for many years and my phone was one of the ways where I consistently acted out. Now, every night I place my phone on Misty's nightstand or it stays in the kitchen. Honestly, I have really enjoyed replacing my phone time with reading the Bible, listening to podcasts, or doing recovery work. That may sound crazy or the cliché Christian answer, but I've replaced old habits with new habits. I have learned so much more about myself and the Bible and now sleep so much better.

2. Has it been hard to completely change certain lifestyle behaviors, such as not having your phone in bed at night or not watching rated "R" movies? Are there any other boundaries that have been noticeably hard to change?

At first, I missed not being on my phone, but now it's not even an issue. The movie boundary has been harder because I love action movies and many of them are rated R for violence, but yet they almost all contain some sexual content. But I try and look at the situation and determine if it is truly beneficial for me. That has helped. Some boundaries are harder than others. Saying no to certain movies has been a hard one for me.

There is one boundary not mentioned that has made a noticeable difference, and I imagine it may surprise some. Music. I have stopped listening to secular music because I now realize it is a place of weakness and vulnerability for me. I listen to a lot of praise

and worship music now. It encourages me and reminds me of where I was, what I was delivered from, and what Christ has done for me.

3. Do you view boundaries as a positive thing in a relationship or a negative thing? In other words, did boundaries help or hurt your relationship with Misty?

It has helped. It's not only helped my relationship with Misty but is has also helped my relationship with God. It has also helped me maintain my sobriety. One thing that I appreciate about Misty's boundaries is that they were not set up as a form of punishment, but truly were set up to establish trust and safety.

4. Misty shared that you actually went to your boss and told him that you would not be able to travel alone on business trips with another woman. Can you share what that was like prior to, during, and after that meeting?

I was nervous beforehand. During, I felt very embarrassed. After, I think there was a sense of relief that I wouldn't have to be put in that situation. Thankfully I had a very understanding boss.

Also keep in mind that boundaries can evolve. Since I have stopped objectifying women, I no longer view them as an object for self-gratification nor do I view them as "dangerous". Our boundaries at the seven-year mark are much different than the boundaries I needed in my first year of recovery.

5. This chapter states that consequences for crossing a boundary should push the husband further into recovery. (i.e. going to extra counseling sessions, attending an extra 12-step meeting, talking to accountability mentor, etc.) Why do you think these kinds of consequences are better than other behavioral modification techniques such as snapping a rubber band on the wrist or picking up trash along the highway?

My personal thought is that we, as addicts, are choosing to medicate with unwanted sexual behavior. We do this as a relief from pain whether we are aware of that pain or not. Behavior modification

may work temporarily, but it won't last. It would never work for me long term. I have had to dig deeper and figure out why I'm feeling what I'm feeling. Behavior modification deals with only the head. It's reprogramming the brain. But I think true recovery is when we can reprogram our hearts and replace all of our "stuff" with who we are in Christ. Setting up consequences that will address the heart seem so much more valuable than snapping a rubber band.

CONQUER

"You can never conquer the mountain.

You can only

conquer yourself."

-Jim Whittaker, mountaineer

Chapter 9: Building Trust

Oh boy, now we're getting to the good stuff! It is truly exciting when we get to this part. I would daresay that you may begin to start seeing yourself conquer parts of your recovery mountain very soon, if you haven't already. Seeing and remembering your victories will keep the fire lit and your feet moving on those tough days of recovery.

At this point in your recovery, you have more than likely:

1. Established safety.
2. Set boundaries.
3. Grieved your losses.
4. Found a good counselor.
5. Found a support group, whether in your area or online.
6. Explored family-of-origin and early attachment/attunement.
7. Learned to listen to your husband's actions, rather than his words.

This chapter will be geared directly towards the woman who has chosen to stay in her marriage OR who has entered another relationship. If neither of those are your current situation, the foundations of this chapter can still apply to your current relationship. All of the previous chapters have been similar to an airplane mechanic and the groundwork he/she does while on the tarmac. Until that plane is cleared, it cannot take flight. If you cannot confidently check off some of the points listed above, I recommend that you determine what it is that is holding you back. Is there an area that you feel stagnant in? Perhaps you are still grieving your losses. Do you still feel emotionally unsafe? Chances are, you are reading this book to give you some guidance as a starting point, and you may have not implemented any of the suggestions yet. That is okay. I've given a lot of information for you to process. The purpose of this chapter is to not only outline trust, but give you hope that it is possible for your heart to trust again, even if you aren't ready to do so quite yet.

You've been so hurt and so traumatized that the brain has told you, "You can't trust anyone." You have your armor on as protection for your traumatized self. This is healthy and necessary for safety, but eventually we want to start taking the steps to remove the guardrails and learn to let safe people back in. It feels very risky, I know. It is accepting that we might get hurt, but because we've done the groundwork already mentioned up to this point, we have an entirely new "first aid kit" ready, and we have done the groundwork necessary to know that even if, we will be okay.

If your spouse is in recovery, and you are ready to work on building trust, the next few paragraphs are for you. If I were to recommend any one book for you and your spouse to read specific to building trust, it would be Worthy of Her Trust by Arterburn and Martinkus. (While I cannot recommend other books by Stephen Arterburn, this book was incredibly helpful for us and primarily written by Jason Martinkus).

Although this book is written for men, I chose to read it first to vet it. While I read, I highlighted excerpts and wrote notes in the margin for Jim to have a better understanding of what stood out to me and what I needed. He loved that I did this. It let Jim know what I struggled with, and also how he could help rebuild those parts of our relationship that were so damaged. Just like a man (or woman) may need a manual to rebuild a new car engine, Jim needed a manual to rebuild trust. This book is a great "trust manual" for you and your husband to read and may give you a good starting point.

Keep in mind that building trust in your relationship may look different than it did in ours, and that is perfectly acceptable. You can "personalize" your trust building process, making it specific to you and your husband's personalities, past, current, and future needs. Let this chapter be your guide, but with loads of flexibility.

My husband is a very "black and white" thinker, and you may be as well. Recovery may be hard for you due to the fact that there is a huge amount of "gray" when it comes to this process. Trust-building won't look the same for everyone, so be intentional about what your trust building process should look like.

When we build safety first, then trust second, it will lead us to our ultimate destination of emotional intimacy. For those black and white thinkers, here is a no-nonsense equation:

Safety + Trust = Emotional Intimacy

I remember asking a mentor early on, "Will I ever be able to trust him again?" She responded with a resounding, "Yes!" It encouraged my heart so much to hear that. What I didn't realize was that rebuilding trust wasn't 100% on Jim's shoulders. At some point along the way, I had to remove the brick walls around my heart and choose to trust Jim, too. That is easier said than done after betrayal.

The book, Worthy of Her Trust refers to trust-building like Lego pieces. My 9-year-old son loves to build with Legos. Each kit comes with a very clear set of step-by-step instructions. Building trust looks the same way. It will be step by step, piece by piece, but absolutely possible. This news should encourage both you and your spouse in recovery, because there will be times when you both feel like giving up. This is a natural part of the "climb" phase of recovery.

But eventually, you begin to reap what you have sown, and it is so exciting to get to this point! I know, I know, you don't feel excited yet. That's okay. I'll feel excited for you because I know how close you are! Receive this encouragement and hear me out: DON'T GIVE UP! You can do this! You are almost to the tree line and healthier days are coming!

Let's take a look back and reflect on why you may not feel excited quite yet. Proverbs 12:22 says, "The Lord detests lying lips, but he delights in people who are trustworthy (NIV)". No wonder your feelings haven't caught up with your progress yet. You are still in that phase of realizing the truth of this verse. The truth of the lies.

When our dog, Ralph, finds a dead animal on our country gravel road, you cannot help but know! He rolls around in the stinky roadkill and when I tell you it's gross, I mean it! Ralph reeks of the filth and I have to take him to our outdoor hose to rid him of the disgusting smell. Betrayal is just like that nasty, dead carcass. The way my dog explores a dead animal is similar to the way you've had to explore betrayal. I get you. I feel you. I smell the stench of what you have had to face, what you've taken on, and what you've had to roll around in. I wish ridding your soul of the stench of betrayal could be as easy as a spray of the hose, but my sweet friend, you are being washed by *Living Water.* Redemptive water that is creating new patterns.

Regardless of what happens to your marriage, *safety, truth, and trust are essential parts of any healthy relationships*. Learning how to trust again is not for the faint of heart.

Before we dive into how to build trust, let us first break down the very concept of trust and trustworthiness.

In her book, Rising Strong, research professor Brené Brown teaches an acronym: BRAVING. She created this acronym to help us remember the elements of trust. She calls it, "The Anatomy of Trust" and uses the word "B-R-A-V-I-N-G" to break down this concept. Let's visit her acronym, as it is truly worth exploring.

"B"- BOUNDARIES: I will say no when I feel I need to and I am willing to respect and accept your "no" when you are employing your boundaries. We hold boundaries for others and expect them held for ourselves.

"R"- RELIABILITY: I can trust you only if you do what you say you are going to do over and over again. This means (at work or play) staying aware of your competencies and limitations so that you don't over-promise and can deliver on commitments and balance competing priorities. Your actions mean more than your words. Trust is built over time with small acts.

"A"- ACCOUNTABILITY: I can trust you only if, when you make a mistake, you are willing to own it, apologize, and make amends. I can only trust and respect you if, when I make a mistake, you are willing to let me own it and apologize, and you will offer true forgiveness.

"V"- VAULT: You don't share information or experiences that are not yours to share. I need to know that my confidences are kept and that you are not sharing information about me with other people that should be confidential. Relationships built on gossip about others are not trusting, they are based on "common enemy intimacy."

"I"- INTEGRITY: Choosing courage over comfort. Choosing what is right over fun, fast, or easy, and practicing your values, not just professing your values.

"N"- NON-JUDGMENT: You and I can both struggle and feel comfortable asking for help. We can freely share holes in our knowledge and skills without fear of judgment. If we judge ourselves for needing and accepting help, we may also be judging others whom we help.

"G"-GENEROSITY: Our relationship is a trusting relationship if you can assume the most generous thing about my words, intentions, and behaviors. I will do the same. When in doubt we seek to understand and be curious before we judge.

Trust of others begins with self-trust. Betrayal causes us to doubt our own self. We doubt our discernment, our ability to decipher truth from lies, and our intuitions. Learn how to come back to trusting yourself. Chances are, your intuition was "right on and bullseye." It still is. Don't ignore your instincts.

Trust toward others is possible when they show with their actions that they are "BRAVING." Then you can find the courage to be brave and take a risk as you re-learn who and how to trust. You don't trust "just because" your husband is your spouse, or "just because" someone is family. Learn how to apply BRAVING to your relationships, and if the other individual fails to bear fruit of trustworthiness, allow yourself permission to employ your boundaries and if necessary, walk away.

Remember, you cannot control your husband's recovery. It is tempting to try many different strategies to force change in your spouse. However, there is no amount of begging, shaming, boundaries, or logistical rationale that can change him. The only thing that will change your spouse, is his own will. Your spouse has to enter into humility and surrender. If you haven't seen these attributes, then trust will be limited.

Building Blocks of Trust (Here come the Legos!)

The ultimate goal in building trust is emotional intimacy and living a life of true authenticity and transparency with yourself, others, and God.

Seeing my husband in a state of true brokenness and repentance was the start of building trust. In humility, he completely owned his choices, his lies, and his abuse, and how his choices affected me. *He wanted to change for himself,* not for me nor anyone else. I think this is absolutely key to our ability to trust in our husbands' recovery process, because they are doing it for themselves. Jim was sick and tired of his secret, deceptive life and he never wanted to go back. He allowed me to see his authentic brokenness, and it drew my heart to his heart. True repentance is the first step to building safety and trust.

So, what does true repentance look like? For starters, repentance is different than confession. You confess yet not always repent, but when you repent, you always confess.

Marty Solomon of the Bema Podcast, explains the difference in one of his episodes. He outlines the Jewish understanding of true repentance as defined by Rabbi Danya Ruttenberg. I'm going to bullet point what Marty Solomon shares, but he does go in more detail on his podcast. (See below for link.)

True Repentance, according to the Jewish teachings, occurs in five steps:

1. To confess the sin to God and any other relevant parties. (or to anyone who has been affected by your sin.). *Many Christians think confession equals repentance, but it is only step one of repentance. In and of itself, repentance is incomplete.
2. Acknowledge how that sin has impacted others.
3. Make any possible and necessary restitution or amends. In the principles of Torah, you go above and beyond by not just paying back for what is broken, but also pay for the repairs. This can apply to relationships, too.
4. Outline and communicate how you are going to behave differently in the future. Speak to the parties you wronged. "I know I did wrong. I know I impacted you negatively. This is my plan so that I never do it again."
5. Actually follow through and change your behavior.

In Jewish minds, only when step number 5 has been completed has true repentance taken place because repentance has to do with the changed behavior, not just the acknowledgement. For the full episode, you can visit www.bemadiscipleship.com, episode 242.

As Jim walked through all five steps, his actions told me that he was changing from the inside out. It was because of his heart of true repentance that I chose to stay. Without it, we would be divorced. For some of you, even with repentance, you might choose to leave the relationship. This is understandable, because sometimes the damage is so great, so massive, and so severe that there is no level of restitution that can be made. When that happens, you are not giving up on your marriage, you are giving *in*. You are giving in to the reality that *his* infidelity and *his* deceit broke the covenant of marriage, not you. On my wedding day, the addiction was already Jim's mistress, and I had no idea. I married a man without full consent, so my wedding felt like one big hoax. Oh, the layers to work through!

Let's assume, though, that you see true repentance, and you have chosen to give this relationship another shot. If there is safety in all areas of your partnership, then yes, it is time to begin thinking about building trust. I am going to share some of the main ideas with the purpose of helping you as you draw out your own map.

When it came to building trust in our relationship, we had non-negotiables and negotiables.

The non-negotiable items should be acknowledged and recommended by your therapist and done with his/her help. These should *not* be attempted without their assistance. If they are, they could be done improperly and cause more harm than good. I will also note that while there isn't really a timetable when it comes to recovery, as every recovery journey is unique to its own, the non-negotiables of recovery should happen fairly early to begin the process. It is a jump-start to get the tide turning in the right direction. Below is a list of my non-negotiables and a brief description of each one. (And once again, remember, this is recommended but not required. You get to choose what you need to build trust.)

1. 90-Day Sex Fast: This 90-day fast is for his recovery, as it rewires his brain. The fast was also for my recovery, so I could have space and time to process without the added expectation of physical intimacy. I found it to be a very positive trust-building step because it showed (through his actions) that he was committed to the recovery process. My husband found it freeing to uncover the myth and lie that he *needed* sex. His body did perfectly fine and the fast helped in future seasons in our recovery where I couldn't stand the thought of having sex. (You'll learn more about that issue in chapter 13.) It was very healing. We both agreed upon a start date, and I circled day 90 in my calendar. *Fasting from sex for 90 days requires a support system.* Your husband will need men to support him through this time. He will need accountability and encouragement. You may want to find the same support for yourself. Use this time to take away the pressure of physical intimacy and turn inward. Insecurities may surface for both of you, and it is a great opportunity to self-reflect and lean into the many range of emotions and become students of yourselves. To clarify, Jim fasted from anything that he turned to for sexual gratification. He didn't watch TV, he didn't listen to secular music, he purposefully stayed away from public swimming pools, and more. He went ALL IN. Now, he does all those things and can do so without any issues. But those first six months of sobriety are brutal, so he chose to go above and beyond to ensure he stayed committed and faithful. You

could say it was very similar to entering a homebound rehab center, where the addict has limited contact with the outside world. But eventually, his goal was to partake in any activities he desired but with self-control. First, he had to unearth his "why's" so he could stop consuming humans.

2. Full Written Therapeutic Disclosure: You deserve a full sexual history from your spouse, as well as any other pertinent information pertaining to his addiction(s). However, *there is a process to doing this properly.* Do not rush into this step. This should be well thought out, planned, and implemented by a CSAT/APSATS who has experience in this area. If you can't find a CSAT/APSATS, then a trauma specialist might do an adequate job, but you may need to educate them on the proper steps. The last bullet point below has a link to a guide you can offer your therapist to ensure it is facilitated properly. Our trauma specialist was aware of the importance of a full written disclosure but was also aware that *offering too much information could potentially cause further trauma.* Below is a recommended "guideline" to follow when creating and implementing a Therapeutic Disclosure, although there will be variation between different therapists: *For clarity purposes, I will refer to the person who betrayed as "betrayer" and the spouse who was betrayed as "betrayed spouse".

    - Betrayer goes to one-on-one counseling sessions to work on getting a full sexual history in written form. This generally takes ten to twelve weeks for complete. The betrayer is very intentional and goes through his entire life's timeline chronologically. The "finished work" should be written out, with copies made for the counselor and the betrayed spouse. You do not want this process to be rushed, because if so, he will omit details and then you could be dealing with "trickle" disclosures, which are dreadful and traumatic.

- The betrayed spouse can meet with the same counselor to express what she wants to know so the counselor can ensure they are on the same page. This is to protect the betrayed spouse from getting more information than is necessary and putting her in further trauma.
- The full disclosure should include not just sexual history, but any other pertinent information pertaining to the sexual betrayal. This could include the betrayer's control over finances, purchases made to feed his addiction, emotional affairs, or women he "groomed," etc. Again, no need for explicit details, just stick to the facts. A CSAT is trained in this and will guide you through what to include.
- I recommend at least a two-hour block for the disclosure session with the counselor (three hours if there is an excessive amount of information).
- During the disclosure session, the betrayed spouse is allowed to take breaks as needed. This could mean taking a short walk around the building, getting a drink, or briefly leaving the room.
- The betrayed spouse can take notes and is allowed to have certain information repeated. She may ask questions to clarify, but mostly she listens and is focused on receiving the information, not verbally responding to it. (Although there will be a separate session scheduled for the sole purpose of responding, this is not the time to talk it out.) This session is very difficult. Expect lots of tears, anger, confusion, and grief.
    - Betrayed Spouse: Consider what you may need to process after the session. An hour or two alone? Do you want to go to a park and process? Consider what you may need/want and be sure to arrange childcare ahead of time, so you are free to do what you need. I

heard of one spouse who booked a hotel room so she had the freedom to grieve and process alone. I thought that was a beautiful idea.

- The betrayed spouse will be given the opportunity to write out an "impact letter". This is a letter in response to the disclosure. A CSAT will have a form you can fill out to guide you on what to include, and questions to think about.
- After the betrayed spouse has written and shared her impact letter in a session, the ball bounces back to the betrayer and he begins working on an "emotional restitution letter". This is his letter to validate all your pain, to verify he takes full ownership, and to formally apologize. Again, a CSAT is trained in how to accomplish this and will have forms with outlined details of how this should look. It is very helpful.
- Once full disclosure-from start to finish- has been completed, both parties can begin the process of moving forward towards making amends, forgiveness, reconciliation, or divorce/separation.
- Disclosures may or may not be followed up by a polygraph to set a baseline of trust. (Polygraphs are considered optional and/or non-negotiable depending on whom you speak with.)
- If the betrayer says he isn't ready to do the full therapeutic disclosure, it can feel extremely disheartening. The hardest part of this process is waiting for it. Sometimes, the unfaithful spouse needs some extra time with his therapist to come to terms with this process and ensure he is bringing everything into the light. Especially if the betrayer was discovered in his addiction, versus the betrayer

how disclosed his addiction. The betrayed spouse can then set a boundary by setting a date she needs the disclosure done by, or she will proceed with whatever consequence she chooses. (Separation, in house separation, meeting with therapist twice a week until it is finished, etc.).

- Once the betrayer begins the process, in general, it takes 10-12 weeks to complete. The betrayed spouse can check in with the therapist just to get a general idea of how things are moving along. It could take less time, or more time, depending on the situation.
- The betrayer has full understanding that his past has now become the betrayed spouse's present. Respect and gentleness should be offered while she processes and grieves.
- For more detailed information, I highly recommend visiting this site, as it is extremely helpful. https://michellemays.com/programs/disclosure-prep-for-couples/

3. Individual and Marital Counseling: **HIS recovery, HER recovery, THEIR recovery. If Jim didn't enter therapy, I was out. Regardless if he was in therapy or not, I was going to stay committed to my own healing. Doing so allowed me to take my power back as I implemented new ways of thinking and developed new patterns of living. We did not incorporate couples therapy until year two, after sobriety was well established and there was a history of safety on all accounts.**

4. Attend Support Groups/12 Step: **Jim got involved in a men's group. This added another layer of safety as I saw him connecting with other men, get some accountability, and learn more about his addiction. I also joined a group, and it we grew a community of support.**

5. Participate in Regular Recovery Homework. This was in addition to Bible reading. I needed to see Jim seeking knowledge and learning about his addiction and abuse.
6. Stay Sober. Obviously, I cannot control Jim's sobriety, no do I want to. I am not his gatekeeper. However, he needed to know my expectations within our relationship, and I was not okay with any of his unwanted sexual behaviors. If I discovered or he disclosed, he knew I would not go through this a second time.
7. No "Addict Mode" Behaviors. Addictions are often, if not always, accompanied with abusive behaviors such as defensiveness, gaslighting, blame-shifting, negativity, etc. If they are sexually sober, but still exhibiting some of these behaviors, they are sometimes referred as a "dry sober." These behaviors were/are potential deal breakers for me if it continues to be a part of our relationship. I value myself enough to be treated with kindness and honesty, and I will not allow mistreatment of myself any longer.
8. Honesty and Transparency in all areas of his life, including finances and relationships. This means going above and beyond, telling me information that I should know before I ask. For instance, let's say Jim forgot to text a co-worker about something work related and remembered it at 10pm, after I had already gone to bed. Breaking one of our boundaries, he turns on his phone, makes the text, and then immediately turns the phone off. But, at the same time, he texts my cell phone and says, "Hey babe. I forgot to text Ted about that document for the meeting, so I'm on my phone after you are asleep to get that out. I'm texting you now so you know, and we can talk about it in the morning if you have questions. I love you!" His showing honesty and transparency in the small areas made big impacts on my heart and built trust.

9. No Victimization. The addict is not the victim. The victim of betrayal is the victim. But because recovery is so very hard for the betrayed, sometimes our husbands like to avoid the shame they feel by reversing the roles by playing victim. This is not okay, and boundaries need to be set in place should this behavior arise.
10. Filters on all Devices. Every phone, tablet, computer and laptop had to have a filter installed. There are several good ones to choose from. Filters are an aid, but a changed heart is what will make the real difference. I'll be honest and say, filters don't really matter when it comes to sobriety, but since Jim brought porn into our home, it greatly increased the risk of our kids being exposed at early ages. I never relied on filters as being the key to Jim's sobriety. It goes much deeper than that, but it is a good tool, and it can help from accidental images popping up.
11. Ending Ties with Affair Partner. There should be no contact whatsoever. I needed him to meet with her in person, with me, to tell her he was sorry and that he would never contact her again. (She was a friend of mine, so this made sense for us.).

What are your non-negotiables? Start thinking about them.

Non-negotiables can be implemented in any order; however, it is recommended that they be in place within six months of D-Day. If you are outside of that parameter, no need to worry. Talk with your counselor or trauma specialist and get a plan of action together.

Once you have a grasp on the non-negotiables, you can begin thinking about the negotiables. Negotiables are unique to your set of circumstances and how the acting out looked like. Some of the items listed below may be considered non-negotiable to you. That is perfectly fine. The points given are just a guide. Create your own list and include your husband in on them. This is a good exercise that can be done with a counselor. Negotiables have a ton of flexibility and will vary greatly from couple to couple. Do keep in mind, you cannot control his behaviors or sobriety, nor his desire to live free. Approach this from the standpoint of what you need to feel safe and communicate that clearly.

Below are a few more examples of negotiable and non-negotiable areas we chose to implement to help build safety, truth, and trust:

1. Accountability: Jim chose two men in his life who made concerted efforts to check in on him. It was not my job to manage his sobriety. Him using me as his accountability was super stressful and traumatizing. I communicated that it was his job to be open and honest about his sobriety and his job to initiate any discussions pertaining to his sobriety. Knowing there were men in his life who asked him those hard questions helped build safety in the relationship.
2. A slip plan: We came up with a plan if Jim were to slip in his sobriety. He was to call his accountability partner first. Next, he was to tell me within 24 hours and then reset his sobriety date. Failure to do so would result in a boundary/consequence until safety was once again established, and my safety included a separation if I so desired.
3. New patterns. Humility goes a long way when building trust. Especially after years of blame-shifting and gaslighting. "Old" patterns should be replaced with new ones. Example: during conflict, he didn't defend and shift blame, but listened, took ownership, and made amends. This falls under "negotiable" because it doesn't happen overnight. The new patterns were introduced in year one, but I didn't see a huge amount of change during conflict. I did see he was much gentler, and extremely empathetic. In year two, I started to really see him mature emotionally, and

the fruits of the spirit really started to show up more often and on a more regular basis. By year three, he was soaring. There are power in the words, "Wait and see."

4. Became students of each other. We learned how to be more intentional in the other's needs, interests, and dreams. To aid us, we did multiple online personality tests, fun date-night questions, and more. Year five, we both did psych evaluations and discovered we are a neurodivergent couple! All of these things helped us understand one another so much better.

5. Spiritual Growth. We both became extremely interested in God's heart in marriage, sexuality, and loved learning about the teachings of Jesus. We included faith into our new ways of operating. It was exciting to see Jim genuinely desire to know God, and I found His new-found love for Jesus so awesome. Especially his heart for the vulnerable, oppressed and the poor. Jim also began having a strong desire to use his male privilege by taking stronger stands for women. That really started to take front and center stage in Jim, and I loved it. I could see he really "got it".

6. He respected my boundaries and followed them. If he crossed them, he didn't argue with me, but followed through with the consequence. There is a great YouTube video by Jake Porter called "Are you on the coaster?" Give it a quick watch with your spouse. It is especially good if they accuse you of being controlling because of your boundary setting.

As you can see from above, building trust requires humility and commitment, and happens over time. Seven years out and we are *still* working on building trust.

During our early months of recovery, one of the things I desired was a formal letter of apology to *me*. My heart needed to hear Jim put purpose and intention to his words.

I waited a long time for that letter. Keep in mind, most of our husbands are not going to know how to do a proper apology. They need guidance and practice. With the help of our counselor, my husband took a significant amount of time composing a letter of apology for me. A letter of apology was just what my heart needed to move in the direction of trusting again. The amazing thing is, it healed his heart, too! With Jim's permission, I'm going to share his apology letter as an example. If your spouse is in true recovery and struggles finding language, it may be helpful for him to read Jim's letter, as well.

"Dear Misty,

I can't begin to comprehend how much I have hurt you. I try to imagine if the roles were reversed and it scares and horrifies me. Unfortunately, for you, it is a reality. My selfishness, pride and foolishness has led me down this path and to my deepest sorrow, I have brought you, the one woman I have truly loved, with me. You did not do this, I did this. You do not deserve to be here. I have hurt you over and over and I am so deeply sorry for that. You are an amazing woman with so much potential for good. I have restricted your potential and removed your spark. Without me and my actions, you bring joy to those around you. You are thoughtful, kind, generous, spunky, loving, fun to be around, friendly, beautiful, endearing, energetic, creative, talented, a good teacher, a good mother, a good friend, have a beautiful smile, a contagious laugh, beautiful eyes, and a gentle touch. That is who you are. Not the sad, angry, fearful, hurt woman that is a result of me and my decisions and actions. I need the Holy Spirit to communicate to you the regret and feelings of how sorry I am because I don't think it can be expressed in words. I don't know how to. I want to be the husband that God wants me to be. I want to be a Godly, sober man. I want to meet your needs and desires like you want and how God intended me for. I am a work in progress. Yes, I have an enormous amount to learn. I have a heart that wants to be free from lust and sexual sin. I want to continue to grow towards Christ-likeness. I pray that you will not give up on me. I know you may not trust me or believe me, but I do love you. I love you so much. I am so ashamed and cannot believe I have done all this to you, the only woman I have truly loved...I will ask you humbly, will you please forgive me? Love, Jim"

When we see a man take full responsibility, and acknowledge our pain, our hearts soften. It doesn't fix everything, nor does it magically give us the ability to trust again, but it is a good step. Remember when we talked about building Legos of trust? This letter added multiple bricks to the trust process, and it also tore down some of the bricks I had built around my heart. But ladies, Jim did not automatically know this letter was important to me. I remember the season in which I had to accept that when it came to knowing and understanding my heart, Jim was admittedly clueless. I actually had to mentally "let go" of this expectation and have learned how to voice my needs. I've also learned how his brain works, and being neurodivergent sometimes means missed non-verbal cues. So yes, I had to ask for this letter. And I'm so glad I did! Hearing the melancholy rhythms of his heart was the music I needed to inspire my soul to sing again! The melody was a beautiful cacophony of different sounds: admiration, respect, hope, tenderness, trust, forgiveness, grace and love, all of which were emerging from what

was once blank sheet music. Like a cello, its fullness reverberated through my body and touched the darkest places of my heart, and low and behold, a teeny, tiny flame lit.

Sweet sister, braving to trust again will be an on-going process over many months. Maybe even years. The Bible says, "By their fruits you shall know them" (Matthew 7:16). Listen to your spouse's actions, then make the choice based on what his actions say. But I'm going to challenge you. If your husband is in active recovery and his actions are showing you that he is trying, at some point you will have to decide if it's time to risk trusting him again. He won't do recovery perfectly. Recovery work is clumsy and messy, so make room for grace and imperfections.

Although taking the plunge of trust feels a lot like jumping off the side of a cliff, by now, you have done the necessary groundwork towards your own healing and have a stronger emotional core. You know that although it may feel like free-falling, you are anchored. The empowerment you have grown in will give you the courage you need to make that move. You'll know when the time is right.

I'm really proud of you. You are doing the tough work, and it requires a great deal of courage and vulnerability to do so.

Heartwork Challenge:

1. Go back to read the acronym "BRAVING." What thoughts come to mind, if any?

2. **Do you feel your spouse is showing fruit of being worthy of your trust? Why or why not?**

3. **Do you have any non-negotiables to add to the list?**

Q & A with Jim
Chapter 9: Building Trust

1. Can a man who has sexually betrayed his wife ever be fully trusted again? Why or why not?

I feel like the answer is yes to that, but I suppose it depends. I think that the only way that it is possible is through humility and honesty. My faith also plays a role. If I try to gain trust on my own, it won't happen. I need supernatural help. I had to become a safe man for Misty, and my faith is what gave me the endurance to keep going on the hard days of recovery. It is definitely possible, but it will take both parties involved to be fully committed to recovery work.

2. What has been the most difficult part of earning Misty's trust?

First of all, I'm not doing all this work just for Misty. I'm doing it for me and for God. My focus in recovery is more about my walk with Christ and becoming a safe human again. Earning Misty's trust is a happy by-product of deepening my relationship with myself and with God. That being said, it was hard when she pushed recovery material at me to read. I would get annoyed, frustrated, and discouraged. But when I dug deeper into those emotions, I realized some core beliefs. I thought that I wasn't doing enough, and it went even deeper, and I believed that *I* was not enough. So those feelings weren't even really about her, but about deep wells of insecurity in my own heart.

If I did feel frustrated or impatient that Misty wasn't trusting me, what helped was for me to step back and tell myself to stay the course in my recovery and relationship with Christ. I couldn't base my recovery on whether or not Misty trusted me. She had things to work through, as did I. I also had to self-reflect that maybe Misty lacked trust because I still had more work on becoming a safe man for her. Her lack of trust became opportunity for me to self reflect.

3. Misty mentions that safety must be established before trust can be built. Why do you think that is important?

Putting myself in her shoes, I don't see how anyone could trust someone without first feeling safe with that person. It seems like common sense to me. Safety is a building block to trust. And the first part of establishing safety was for me to be honest with myself, with God and with her.

4. How did partaking in a Full Therapeutic Disclosure impact you and your relationship with Misty?

It impacted me by bringing it all out into the light, and I had nothing to hide anymore. It was scary and emotionally taxing, but after it was done, it felt like a huge burden lifted. Misty then knew it all, and if she was still willing to love me for who I really was, without me wearing the mask, she was accepting my true self. If she chose to walk away, I would understand.

It was hard on Misty at first, but it was another step in establishing safety and trust because we were living in full honesty for

the first time. We both walked away from it feeling grateful we chose to do it. Our counselor did an amazing job facilitating it.

5. Misty asked you to take a polygraph. How did that make you feel initially? And did that feeling change? Why or why not?

Initially, I was angry. Very angry. In fact, I threw it right back at her and said, "If I have to take one, then you do, too!" I was convinced she had had an affair, too. I didn't trust her, either. I knew myself so well, and had convinced myself that she was the same as me. Misty told me this kind of thinking was "addict-mode" thinking, and I was doing so as a means to justify my behaviors and avoid shame. I totally agree with her. I was projecting onto her what I was actually guilty of.

My thought process changed at some point before actually taking the test. I no longer felt the need for Misty to take one as well, and I felt like I had nothing to hide because we had just done the full therapeutic disclosure.

After the polygraph test, I felt confident and relieved. I passed, of course, and expected Misty to be really happy. It actually triggered her, because she had to accept that this truly was her reality. Instead of having a happy wife, it made her feel very sad. That was unexpected, but both of us were extremely glad we used this tool.

6. Why do you think taking a polygraph is an important part of the trust building process?

It's just another tool for Misty to know I'm being truthful. I think, "Why not?" If I was in Misty's shoes, I would want myself to take one as well! Sex addicts lie. A lot. My entire marriage, I hid behaviors from her and became a master liar. Polygraphs helped give Misty peace of mind that my disclosure was truthful and complete.

Chapter 10: Husbands & Kids

Up until this point, we have been climbing up the mountain of recovery and navigating through our forest of grief. In this chapter, I want you to take a little detour with me as we explore the river of recovery in an aluminum canoe. By the end of the chapter, I hope the words, "Paddle on!" will have new meaning to you. Grab your emotional lifejacket, compass, and oar, because entering the river of recovery is full of unknowns and will require a spirit of adventure, preparation, determination, and support.

A Spirit of Adventure

In 2018, a friend of mine came to me with a crazy idea. She wanted us to enter the MR340, a nationally known race in our home state of Missouri. It took place on the wide Missouri River, 340 miles from Kansas City to St. Louis, MO. All in a canoe. Sounds like a fun adventure, doesn't it? The very idea took me back to my favorite childhood book by Mark Twain and I imagined the two of us going on a grand excursion like Tom Sawyer and Huckleberry Finn! I didn't even have to think about my answer. Like a catfish on the line, I was hooked.

In the MR340, there were check-in points along the way and each point had to be met within a certain time. Failure to check in by the time allotted meant we would get kicked out of the race. That had actually happened to us the year before. We checked in 20 minutes after the first deadline and had to pack it up and go home. That was the year we "winged it." Disorganized, not truly committed, poor equipment, and a half-hearted approach proved to be our doom. We had the adventurous spirit, but greatly lacked in

the area of preparation. The year 2018 was different. We had a much better plan to set us up for success.

I may have agreed to this craziness due to my traumatized brain! After all, our team name in 2017 was, "We Be Trippin'." In 2018, it was "We Be Trippin' Again." But I am also a natural "free spirit." I own a 1974 VW bus named "Miss Betty Blue" and love taking road trips without an agenda. Spontaneity and risk make me come alive. Whatever was the "yes" factor, I was all in. I was ready to tackle four days on the river!

We trained the best we could. We had most of spring and summer to do so, since the race took place during the full moon phase in late July. My favorite summer nights were when my friend would bring the kids over and we would all head across the street to a lake on private property. The kids would swim and kayak while my friend and I paddled, maneuvered, practiced getting in and out of the canoe should it tip over, and timed ourselves as we paddled against head winds. The best part of our training, was, by far, our friendship that grew. We had long talks about life, recovery, God, and kids. As our paddles dipped in and out of the water, our souls were dipped in the beauty of friendship. When the sun would set, we would relish the beauty of God as our canoe chased the final sun's rays stretched out across the water. We would laugh, vent, give counsel, and cry in that canoe. It was like a floating therapy session and it was extremely healing for us both. As our physical muscles got stronger and took on memory, so did our spiritual muscles.

Sometimes during training, we'd have some cute little girls on the dock giving us the "hitch-hiker" thumb. These girls were our daughters, and their giggles and splashes would echo across the water straight into our hearts. We found the extra weight to be a good opportunity to build strength and stamina, so we were happy to paddle up along the dock and let them climb inside. Sometimes my son would grab hold of the rudder, creating a drag, causing us to just inch along, but we didn't complain and went with it. The extra weight made us stronger.

In chapter one, I mentioned how God spoke to me through a soft encounter with a butterfly. In chapter six, God spoke to me about safe people through my loyal dog, Ralph. In chapter nine, we related building Legos to building trust. And this entire book is based on the analogy of climbing a mountain and how it correlates to the recovery process. Let us now consider, more specifically, the parallels between training for the MR340 and the recovery process.

Planning and Preparation

Let's factor in year 2017 when my friend and I entered the race without a true plan. We were only half committed. We had the wrong kind of vessel, no muscle memory, and no itinerary. We were kicked out of the race at the very first check-in. Recovery is the same. If you are half-committed, not fully immersing yourself in education and/or not getting a plan together, your ability to heal will be greatly hindered, if not altogether halted. You may continually get triggered and flooded based on your husband's choices and may base your healing on what he does and doesn't do. This is why, when it comes to recovery, you must be thorough. Be committed. Get a plan.

During training, we prepared for the "what ifs." What if our canoe tipped? How would we get back in? What if it rained? What if a huge barge came upstream? What if we needed to use the restroom? The same degree of preparation goes into the recovery journey. What if he slips? What plan do you have in place? What if he reverts back to old patterns and behaviors? What if he quits going to counseling? All of the what-if scenarios need to be addressed and boundaries set in place. While you can't prepare for all the what-ifs, you most definitely can cover some of the big ones, and a therapist can guide you through the tough scenarios and questions.

During training, we allowed our kids into the canoe. They were a vital part of our race, too. The kids, along with our spouses, were our grounds crew. We couldnl't have finished the race without them.

When it comes to betrayal, I believe it is best to, at some point, invite your children into the canoe of recovery and disclosure. Even at very young ages, kids are intuitive. *Betrayal changes family dynamics drastically, and so does recovery*. There were some days I had a very hard time being nice at all towards my kids. I was in so much emotional pain and grief; it was all I could do to just to get out of bed. Because of their dad's choice to lie, my kids suffered from betrayal, too. We will discuss the proper approach to sharing the betrayal in a bit, but I want you to, even now, start processing that this may be something to plan for or at least consider. I just don't believe there is ever good in keeping family secrets. However, I will always respect that you know what is best for your children/adult children.

Determination

The morning of the MR340 race, I was full of pre-race jitters. I was afraid of the unknowns but I knew we were prepared. We were not in this race to win or medal. We were in the race to simply cross that finish line. Even if we were dead last, our goal was to paddle on. No matter what, paddle on.

Nothing, though, can truly prepare you for every scenario on the Missouri river. We dealt with heavy rains, swarms of bats, paddling in the dark of the night, extreme fatigue, heat, and really awkward bathroom breaks in the canoe! (Don't ask!) Our motto was: "No matter what, don't leave the boat."

Mile after mile, somehow our paddles continued to dip back in the water. The sun beat down on us during the day, and we would dip our hats in the water to keep our bodies cool. We religiously applied sunscreen and chapstick to protect our skin from the harsh elements. Preparation is essential, but even with the best of planning, sometimes it comes down to simply holding on and begging God for the strength to keep going.

The same holds true for you as you climb your mountain of recovery work. The most important aspect is to keep going and trust the process.

Support

Earlier I mentioned the grounds crew. The job of the grounds crew is to track the canoe they are assigned to via GPS and have supplies, water, and food ready when needed. Our grounds crew would meet us at boat ramps all along the route to toss us whatever it was we needed or give us an encouraging cheer. Both of our husbands and our kids acted as our grounds crew. They followed us along the river the entire way, using GPS to pinpoint our location. They would meet us along the riverbank with cheeseburgers, pizza, ice-cold water and anything else our sore bodies needed to keep us going.

One time we made an "SOS" call to our husbands and told them we wanted a radio at the next boat ramp. My friend's husband went to Walmart and bought us the cheapest little radio he could find, and met us at the next boat ramp. We cranked the tunes on that little battery operated radio and sang, "Islands in the Stream" at the top of our lungs as we neared the 60-hour mark. Dolly Parton and Kenny Rogers gave us just the push we needed to not surrender to the harshness of the river.

Without our husbands' and kids support, we maybe could have done it, but having their support made our journey and struggle *so much easier*. They got us singing again when everything in us shouted to quit. Many times, we would be paddling along and would hear shouts and cheers coming from the bank. We looked towards the source of the voices and would recognize our loved ones, cheering us on at different points along the entire 340 miles.

One day in particular, I was so sore and so tired. The paddle felt like it weighed a hundred pounds and my shoulders and back muscles burned. But I looked across the water, and to my delight, I saw both of our families jumping and waving, giving us the "thumbs up." Just seeing them brought us such joy! I remember getting teary eyed, seeing the men on the boat ramp, waving. Our kids were up on a hill playing on the swings. It was truly a precious sight. My friend and I waved our paddles high in the air as a giant "HELLO!" from across the current of the wide Missouri river.

That particular moment in the race was when my entire perspective changed. God spoke to me very plainly and clearly. He brought together the immediate circumstances of the river race and the larger circumstances of our recovery. It was like He opened my eyes and Isaiah 43:19, a verse I had claimed months before, came alive to me. "Misty! Do you not see it? LOOK! I AM doing a new thing! I will make streams in your desert and rivers in your wasteland!" I could clearly see my husband's role in *my* recovery process. Yes, he had his own issues and his own recovery to work through, but in relation to me, his role was to simply offer support.

He learned how to tap into his internal GPS and was intentional about being aware of my "emotional location." He provided support through his actions of love and care, even if from a distance. There were times I didn't want him to touch me, yet it still meant so much when he sat on the floor a few feet away and was present while I cried. When he spoke words of ownership, such as, "I'm so sorry I did this to you," it would ease my struggle, much like that little radio in our canoe. Jim didn't try to rush my grieving process. He didn't try to rush my forgiveness process. He didn't try to rush my recovery process. He exhibited patience and let me be in charge of the timing in my recovery. He learned early on that he couldn't force his way into my canoe. (And he knew that if he tried, he would get an oar between the eyes!) He knew these things because we established these boundaries early on in our recovery process. He was *attuned* to me.

You get to be always in control of your recovery vessel. This is a season where you call all the shots in the timing of things. If you have a history of chronic people pleasing as I did, advocating for yourself may feel unfamiliar to you. You will learn to first hear your own voice, then trust your own voice, then speak your own voice. When you are working with a counselor, their job is to guide you through this process, but not tell you what you should or should not do. I greatly appreciated how our trauma specialist handled this growth process. He most certainly had his own opinions, and at appropriate times offered them, but he always gave me the space to come to my own conclusions. He had a knack for getting me to talk through all the options in different scenarios, and then gave me the personal choice to take ownership based on my conclusions. The freedom I had to grieve, forgive, and recover from betrayal trauma allowed me to grow and heal.

Offering support requires education. Your husband will need to fully understand what is going on in your heart and your brain. This "schooling" can take place through a variety of ways. There are many books, online resources, and twelve step programs that will educate the sex addict on the consequences of his choices and how those choices impacted his loved ones. He needs to become a student of himself and a student of you. Knowledge empowers change.

Offering support also requires emotional intelligence from your spouse. Initially it may be quite difficult for him to offer it because not only is he emotionally immature, but he also feels shame. Addicts do not like the feelings that shame brings. But *a spouse in recovery is learning how to press into the uncomfortable feelings instead of avoiding them.* Although offering support may simultaneously remind him of his choices, it will give him the opportunity to grow and mature. Keep in mind that he may show moments of maturity and then suddenly slip back into old, immature patterns. There may be times when you have to advocate for your needs and restate boundaries and expectations. This "three steps forward, two steps back" process is normal. As mentioned more than once before, you will have to remind yourself that even in the steps backward, you are still moving forward. It can sometimes feel discouraging when you feel yourself rowing against the current of old patterns. New patterns and ways of doing things is hard. Do not despair and remember to breathe. Slow down, regroup, and invite grace.

In summary, in the role of "grounds crew," your spouse will respect that you are in charge of your healing and you may need space and time. A simple, "I'm so sorry," from your husband can offer just what you need to feel supported and loved. Support should look like daily actions of tenderness, humility, gentleness, and patience. Offering support in simple ways can have a powerful impact in your heart which results in the security of knowing that he is, in fact, in true recovery and isn't just checking things off a mental list. If he is unwilling to support you, then you will have some hard decisions to consider.

Navigating the River of Recovery

There were two areas of navigation that we had to be intentional about to ensure we crossed that finish line: the channel and the beacons.

The channel is the most navigable part of the river and where the water moves the fastest. To assist paddlers in finding the channel, and to ensure safety while paddling, markings called "shore-based beacons" or "signposts" have been strategically placed along the riverbank. The U.S. Coast Guard is responsible for maintaining shore-based beacons (signposts), along with in-river buoys, which mark the channel for the entire lower Missouri River. Learning to read this system will allow a paddler to determine where the channel of the river is located. Of special interest to paddlers is the fact that the shore-based beacons also have the river mileage posted on them. By observing them, paddlers generally know their own location at all times. This combined knowledge of both being in the channel and reading mile markings can determine how well the trip is going and allowed us to estimate how long it would take to reach our destination.

Let's relate both the beacons and the channel to the river of recovery.

Shore-based Beacons

While there are markings along the river to give clues as to how to stay in the channel, if you aren't looking for those signs, you can easily miss them due to overgrown weeds and summer time brush. This can greatly hinder your progress in the race. Beacons provided affirmation that we were on course. Beacons guided us and kept us in the channel.

Trying to find a shore-based beacon in the dark of the night was when we felt the most insecure of our placement on the water. One of us would shine a bright flashlight and seek out the markings in the trees while the other person continued to paddle.

On the river of recovery, you need beacons. A beacon can look many different ways. It could look like a fellow recovery warrior, a counselor, a recovery centered book, an online support group, or a trusted friend. But whichever beacon you use, don't paddle through recovery alone on the river. Finding a beacon isn't always easy. You may have to reach for the light and seek it out. You have to be vulnerable and ask for help.

I might have been able to do that river race by myself but doing it with a friend made it so much easier and the burden lighter. Recovery groups make our river of recovery bearable. Community helps us bear one another's burdens and gets us to laugh in the down-pouring rain and sing songs in the struggle. Invite others into your canoe. Together, we can pick up our oars, and face to the wind, paddle on.

The Channel

As mentioned earlier, the channel is the part of the river that is the most navigable and where the water moves the fastest. It is always present, and when our canoe was in it, we could trust that it would nudge us forward as quickly as possible. Although we still had to paddle to finish the course, being in the channel allowed us to take much needed breaks. It meant we had help from mother nature and didn't have to paddle in our own efforts to make the 340 miles.

In the river of recovery, faith was my channel. The Holy Spirit was my guide that powered up my emotional muscles, so I didn't give up. The Channel represents the Higher Power we need and seek for in order to finish the race. In my experience, I prayed a lot and asked the Holy Spirit to give me discernment and endurance. I feel like I experienced the power of the resurrection of Jesus in my life to get me through those really hard days.

There were times on the river that the beacons were covered by tree branches, overgrown vines, or were completely missing. That is why it is important to know your river. Just because a beacon is lost, that doesn't mean the channel is lost, too. The Channel is always at work for you, providing a way out of stagnant water. The invitation to enter it is always open, but the choice is ours.

As we all can testify, the river of recovery will twist and turn, have huge logs of obstacles, have times of pouring rain, and large barges that can disrupt our peace, leaving us feeling sick with nausea and headaches. These disruptions can push us off course, sometimes unintentionally. When my canoe gets off track, Jesus gently beckons me back into the unforced current of grace. He doesn't condemn me for losing my way, but rather delights in my return. Knowing this gave me permission to be kind and gentle towards myself.

Unexpected Obstacles

We were prepared for obvious obstacles on the river. When there was down-pouring rain and violent wind, we pulled over to the riverbank, put on our ponchos and waited for the wind to subside. When the sun was beating down on us, we reapplied our sunscreen and wore our hats for protection. When the huge barge came upstream, we moved to the opposite side, faced our canoe into the wake so we didn't tip, and gave it the right of way. But we knew there would be obstacles we didn't see coming. The fear of the unknown is what kept me in constant prayer for protection and courage.

In one part of the course, we were paddling right at dusk along some beautiful cliffs. One minute we found ourselves admiring the beauty of the sunset and how the golden light bounced off the rocks, and the next minute we found ourselves in the midst of hundreds and hundreds of hungry bats, swarming around us from every direction. I felt like a Scooby Doo character who opened up a closet and the bats swarmed out. I ducked and swatted with my paddle, screaming my lungs out in panic. My friend, who was paddling behind me, was relaxed and found the humor in the chaotic scene that unfolded before her eyes. Her profession is a nurse practitioner and in sheer orneriness, she began telling me awful stories of rabies she saw in patients while she worked ER shifts! I was bat-crap crazy. Literally. I don't think I paddled any harder that entire race than in those few minutes of trying to out-paddle those bats.

Had I been better prepared, I wouldn't have panicked. I would have understood that bats hunt using echolocation, meaning they use echoes of self-produced sounds bouncing off objects to help them navigate. This allows them to move swiftly and to quickly change directions. I thought bats were blind, so my false belief system caused me to panic when the unexpected hit.

During recovery, you will face your own "bats." Bats can represent any unexpected obstacles. They will come, so don't be afraid to call your resources if you need help and/or preventively create a plan of action. You don't have to face things alone.

When and How to Tell the Kids

When is it time, if ever, to invite your children into the canoe of recovery with you?

For us, it was a matter of *when* to tell the kids, not *if*. Our main concern was presenting them with just enough facts that were age appropriate, so as to not cause more trauma in an already potentially traumatizing event. When we asked for professional counsel in this area, we received three different answers from three highly trained professionals. There are many variables to consider when it comes to this topic. You and your husband's recovery process, your children's ages, and your children's dispositions must all be taken into account.

At the time of D-day, my kids were 7 and 9 years old. We waited two and a half years to tell them. Not because that was the magic number for us, but because we were still working our way through recovery and quite frankly, I wasn't one hundred percent sure I would stay in the marriage. To minimize their trauma, it was important for us to be united when we told them, and to have a strong idea of what the plan was. We also didn't know exactly how to tell our children, so we chose to shelve it until we got to a place where we had clarity and then developed a strategy.

I do believe this is a case-by-case situation and is based upon the discernment and wisdom of you, as the parent. If your spouse is in recovery, he has a responsibility to be the one to tell them. If he is not in recovery, then sadly, this will become your responsibility. The timing will vary from situation to situation.

Traumatic, painful, or life-changing secrets can potentially damage an entire family's mental health and well-being for some time. Here are some reasons why we felt it was necessary to share the "family secret:"

- Betrayal affects family dynamics, and kids deserve to know why the dynamics have changed. We discovered that my daughter had picked up on my anger and hurt towards her dad, and because of that she began harboring resentment and anger towards me. This increased my anger towards my husband, because it was his fault that my daughter was mad at me, and round and round we went. Betrayal affects dynamics in the home.
- Kids are very intuitive. After finding out the truth, both of my kids confessed that they knew more than they let on. They picked up on nuances and admitted to having fear. My daughter had noticed a recovery book my husband was reading, and my son came across a book I was reading on sexual betrayal. But even if they hadn't heard our fights or seen our books, the body keeps the score, even in children. They have strong instincts, too.
- Secrets do not build trust. If a child or teen eventually finds the truth and realizes they had been lied to for so many years, it can create a great mistrust and affect their future relationships. They deserve to know the truth.
- Sharing our struggles models a life of authenticity and transparency. It will send a message that they, too, can live a life of humility and transparency. We have had the most open conversations with them about all sorts of topics, but especially sex. We find this to be one of the most beneficial results. They feel completely safe to talk to us and ask questions about sexuality.
- Not sharing about the sexual betrayal and addiction can confuse the child about secrets vs. privacy. There is a big difference between the two. Secrecy is an act of hiding from the pain of disclosing something shameful. Privacy is a

healthy boundary where mutual respect is honored, and trust is built.

- It gives hope. You are modeling the process of healing of both self and in some situations, the relationship.
- Not telling your kids will limit you sharing your story with others in the future. In order for Jim and I to encourage other couples, we knew we had to tell our children first. It would be devastating to us if they found out about addiction and betrayal through other people.

At what age should sexual betrayal and/or a porn addiction be shared with children? Choosing the right time and place to reveal a devastating or painful family secret is a difficult task for most parents and must be carefully done, ideally with the help of a professional.

Since there is no set way to approach this topic, the best option for me in helping you navigate this, is simply sharing what path we chose to take.

When we felt ready to tackle this mountain, we took our kids to a trauma specialist for a family "emotional check-in." He did a lovely job of chatting with the kids and helping them feel safe and comfortable. When we left the first session, our kids knew they had someone they could talk to at any time throughout their growing up years. Initially we were hoping to go back and do the disclosure with the counselor's involvement. One day, however, it naturally came up in conversation while we were all at home, so we went with it.

Prior to telling them, we struggled to find the right words. What wording do you use to tell your children that their dad was a sex addict and had an affair? We chose to follow recommendations found in Mark Laaser's book, L.I.F.E. Recovery Guide. Laaser mentions that "secrecy kills but honesty heals." I am going to highlight some of his main points.

- Preschoolers can be told that Daddy lied to Mommy and hurt her heart very much.
- Elementary children can grasp that Daddy had an inappropriate friendship with another person. To discuss pornography and internet safety, I highly recommend the book, Good Pictures, Bad Pictures by Jenson, Poyner and Fox.
- Teenagers can handle even more information and be told general facts.
- If the spouse who betrayed is in active recovery, I believe he should lead the conversation. His choices affected the entire family. This can also be used as an amazing opportunity to build trust with his wife.
- Our children need reassuring words of security and safety.
- Our children need a chance to express their feelings and any questions they may have. Include professional therapy if desired.

When I heard Jim completely own his choices in front of our children, I felt so much respect towards Jim. I knew that took so much courage and humility, and it greatly impressed me. We had pre-determined what we would share and what we wouldn't. (They were 9 and 11 years old at the time.) They did not yet need to know all the gritty details, but they needed to know enough. If they asked questions that we felt needed to wait, we simply told them we would share more as they got older. We told them that they had some growing up to do before we could answer everything, but we were offering the right amount of information, so we didn't have any family secrets. They were able to see us united, and that eased their insecurities. It opened up their hearts for later conversations and allowed them to be a part of my writing this book. We knew we would never be able to have freedom in ministering to others if our children didn't know. Our own progress in recovery could have stalled if we had let our fear of traumatizing them keep us from being honest with them. Bringing all the family secrets into the light resulted in freedom for all of us. There have been follow-up conversations and more questions, and I love the openness and honesty we are learning to have with one another.

I understand not all of you will have that same experience. Some of you may have to tell your children on your own. Alone. For that, I am sorry. It is unfair and wrong. Women whose spouses are not in recovery may have the notion that divorce will ruin their kids. I want to share with you that yes, divorce is traumatizing for a child. I know, because I remember my single mom telling us about my Dad's betrayal when I was seven years old. I felt very sad. But divorce doesn't necessarily mean ruin. Sometimes it means freedom. Let me offer a different perspective.

Sexual addiction is a form of abuse because it is almost always accompanied by abusive behaviors. It is not enough for your husband to be in sobriety. Sobriety is a start, but as we have noted, it addresses only a part of the addiction. They must also stop the addict-mode behaviors that went along with the addiction. Shedding both the addiction and the addictive behaviors is a sign of true and active recovery. If your husband is not in true recovery, you are not safe. If you are not safe, God does not expect you to stay in an abusive marriage. So, in some cases, divorce is often results in a peace-filled home. Yes, divorce is heartbreaking, and your kids will feel sad. But the toxicity and chaos an addict brings into the home creates an unhealthy environment of massive proportions. Addictions create tension. Addicts lie, shame others, and justify their actions. They are disconnected emotionally from their loved ones. They tend to be rigid and condemning. They abuse. Sadly, not all addicts want to enter recovery. They fall in love with their addiction and refuse to give it up. If this is your story, do not despair. Any story can be a glory story, regardless of the outcome of the marriage. Stay with your recovery plan and keep doing the hard work.

Divorce is like a death. You will grieve. You will be forced to create a "new normal." Although your marriage is dead, you, sweet sister, are not. You cannot celebrate the resurrection if you don't first accept the death. The same is true for you. You cannot enjoy the best views of the mountain without first accepting your reality then enduring the hard climb. Do not believe the lie that you failed if you are, or will be, divorced. Your resurrection day is coming! Soon you will be above tree-line on your mountain of recovery, and God will take your breath away as you emerge out of the dark forest of grief and enter his Light. This is what we call a life-giving divorce! There is a great book on this topic titled *The Life Saving Divorce* by Gretchen Baskerville. I also love the sermon series on. YouTube by Matt Nappier titled "*Biblical Foundations for Divorce and Remarriage*". Both resources are especially good for those of us raised in evangelical churches that taught us "God hates divorce". There is a much deeper context to those words, and the way I learned it growing up is definitely not God's heart.

Divorce affects kids, but is God capable of restoring your children's hearts after divorce? Yes. Will it come easily? Probably not. Will divorce traumatize your kids? Maybe. Will staying married to an abusive addict traumatize your kids? Absolutely. My point is this: staying married isn't always the best decision for you and your kids. Where there is toxicity, there is chaos and dysfunction. And remember, a marriage is worth fighting for only if both the husband and wife have the heart of a warrior. Both of you need to be all-in for the recovery process. Both of you need to be committed to the work it requires. Both of you need to make the sacrifices it takes to save yourselves and save the marriage. One soldier fighting against the enemy of addiction only causes torment and additional trauma for the one who is doing all the fighting. If that is the case for you, talk to your counselor and create a plan of action to keep your body, mind and soul as safe as possible.

Divorcing is not the end. Divorce doesn't equal failure. Every woman I know in this world of recovery who has gotten divorced gave the most valiant of all fights to try and make it work. They exhausted all resources and tried so hard. Find your tribe of other women who get it and support you. And...Paddle on!

Heartwork Challenge:

1. Do you feel like you have a better grasp on what recovery will look like? Why or why not?

2. Do you think your spouse knows his role during your recovery? If not, what do you need to do to help him understand what you need?

3. Music can be healing. Do you have a favorite song or a playlist that speaks to your heart? If not, this week, I'd like for you to start working on that.

4. **Have you or your spouse told your children about his betrayal/addiction? If not, what has prevented you from doing so?**

5. **Do you agree or disagree that telling your children is a good idea? How does your spouse feel about telling the children?**

Q & A with Jim

Chapter 10: Husbands & Kids

1. How do you see your role in regard to Misty's recovery process?

My role is to be her support. I also think it is to stay on the path of recovery for myself, with the byproduct of rebuilding trust with Misty.

2. Has it been hard to be supportive for so long? Why or why not?

Yes, it has been hard because I hate to see her hurting. I wasn't the one who was hurt, so I don't think I can truly comprehend the depth of the hurt and pain I caused Misty. There were times I wanted to go into my "fix it" mode.

To help me work through the turmoil, I turned to my recovery group. My mentor constantly reminded me who I was, through Christ, and not to see myself as a label. He helped me fight the overwhelming feelings of shame. By doing so, I was able to

exhibit patience and love toward my bride as she worked through her grief and anger.

I constantly tried to enter Misty's pain. Having empathy helped me to be supportive and patient.

3. What are specific ways you have supported Misty through recovery?

- I respected her boundaries.
- I had patience with her and didn't rush her recovery process.
- I focused on my own recovery and individual counseling.
- I began to exhibit humility during conflict, something I still work towards. I mutually submit to her now, whereas I didn't before.
- I gave her space when she asked for it.
- I told her, "I'm so sorry for the pain I caused you."
- I had empathy when she was angry or sad.
- Even with all of these things that I have done, I'm not a master at it by any means. I'm still a work in progress.

4. Why do you think it is important for the husband to tell the kids about the betrayal and not the wife?

For starters, because I'm the one who did it. It was my actions that caused our volatile situation. I needed to own what I did. My actions created negative family dynamics. The kids didn't understand my wife's anger towards me and yet they picked up on it. By me explaining it, it took the blame off of her and they were able to see the situation more clearly.

I also think it's important to not only teach our kids about vulnerability, but to show them vulnerability.

However, I do NOT think a husband should tell the kids if he hasn't been in active recovery. The unsafe man will use that opportunity to cause further harm by minimizing his actions, blame his wife, and fight for control.

5. What was the feeling you had when you told them? What about after it was done?

When I told them, I felt embarrassment, sadness, guilt and fear that they would reject me. I also feared that they would follow my shoes. I feared they would not respect me.

I have found since then, that they do, in fact, still respect me. They still love me. Keep in mind, I can only speak for right now, in this moment. I cannot predict what will happen as they grow, but I am very glad I was honest with them.

6. Do you have any regrets about telling your children about your betrayal and addiction?

No, not at all.

REST

Psalm 69:29 (MSG)

I'm hurt and in pain; give me space to heal and mountain air.

Chapter 11: A Return to Rest and Self-Love

Recovery is ***exhausting***. It will be mentally, physically and emotionally draining. If you have children in the home, this exhaustion takes on a whole new level, because you have to "be on" for your children day in and day out in the midst of your recovery. There will be days when you pray yourself to get out of bed. There will be days when you will pray yourself through the afternoons. There will be days when you pray yourself to make it to the kids' bedtime routines. It will look like one hour at a time, tapping into the supernatural to get you through your days. As your life is in upheaval, how can you find rest in the chaos? Is that even possible? My answer is a resounding, "Yes!" But it takes intention.

For some, rest comes easier. For me, busyness kept me distracted so I could avoid my pain. But rest is so important during recovery.

Rest should be an element that is woven in and out of recovery from the very start. The kind of rest I'm referring to is the intentional and prioritized kind of rest. It is purposeful time that is set aside for your body and soul to get the proper care it needs. If you do not intentionally set aside rest, you may not finish the climb. It is too hard, too tiring, and too exhausting, so rest is a necessary factor when it comes to your healing process. This will be a self-discipline. You will utilize intentional rest on an as-needed basis and throughout each phase of recovery. While it is listed as the third word in our recovery phases of "climb, conquer, rest and restore," remember that these words are not sequentially based but rather interconnected and experienced as cyclical throughout the years of recovery.

There are three types of rest: physical, emotional, and spiritual. All are equally important during recovery. What I find ironic is that we have to work to find rest. If you are separated or divorced from your husband, the principles in this chapter still apply. Together, we are going to dissect each area of rest and why rest is so important.

Physical and Emotional Rest

Even if you are not a person of faith, it is helpful to see from God's Word how rest was and is a priority to God. When He created the universe, He chose day seven to rest. Think about it. Do you really believe that God was tired? Did He need to take a break from life? Why did God intentionally take a rest on day seven of creation, and why is it included in the first chapter of Genesis? I believe it is included because He was establishing the model for all of humankind to follow. He knows our human frailty and our need to recover after labor, and we already know by now that recovery is very hard work, both physically and emotionally.

Jesus showed us that He is a fan of rest as well. In Mark 6, we read the account of Jesus feeding the 5,000. Right before, however, it says he addresses His worn-out disciples and sees their compassion fatigue. In protective love, He offers the gift of rest. Mark 6:30-32 reads, "The apostles gathered around Jesus and reported to him all they had done and taught. Then, because so many people were coming and going that they did not even have a chance to eat, he (Jesus) said to them, 'Come with me by yourselves to a quiet place and get some rest.' So they went away by themselves in a boat to a solitary place (NIV)." I can imagine the relief the disciples felt as He gave them permission to rest!

Jesus knew that investing in people is exhausting work. He also knows investing in yourself requires the same amount of energy, attention and intention.

The emotional parts of us are tightly woven with the physical parts of us. That is why traditional Chinese medicine teaches that certain organs correlate with certain emotions. Conventional medicine recognizes stress (an emotion) can affect organs such as the heart, stomach, and adrenals. Recovery is holistic. It will impact the body, soul and mind.

We need to be fully aware of the amount of energy needed as well as the amount of energy used up during the recovery process. As mentioned before, this is a marathon, not a sprint.

In the last chapter, you learned the role of the spouse (who is in recovery) during *your* recovery process. In the spouse who betrayed, effort to build trust and support takes priority and he needs to be sensitive to your needs. Good humans do things like help out with bedtime routines, fix dinner and do laundry. This is no time to be sticking to traditional gender roles. Domestic duties equally fall on both partners.

While you might wish for him to instinctively know when you've hit your "max" and then act upon it, you must remember that he is still a student of you. He is still learning. Because of this, you might need to learn how to advocate for your physical and emotional needs during recovery. If you need more sleep, tell him. If you need time alone, tell him. If you need quality time, tell him. Whatever you need, it is your time to find your voice and speak up. Many of us have developed coping mechanisms that caused us to stuff our feelings and needs. Now that we are in recovery, we speak our needs and emotions in order to heal. Learning how to do this might take time and practice. If you can't speak up to your spouse in recovery yet, try practicing with your counselor or a safe friend. The end goal is for you to be able to become better integrated with yourself and to be able to identify and communicate your needs.

If your spouse is not in recovery, telling him what you need will more than likely fall on deaf ears. Your main job is to create safety through setting up firm boundaries and consequences. Again, if the abuse escalates with boundaries, one consequence may be emotionally detaching yourself from him as you work on creating a safety plan. Sadly, you cannot rely upon him to support your recovery process.

It should seem like an easy task to prioritize self-care and rest, but in my own life I find that it is quite difficult. Many of us have families to feed and care for, houses to manage, jobs to work, extracurricular events to attend to, and more. Life has a way of taking over. Women, in general, have a very hard time creating space for themselves to get a break. There are simply not enough hours in the day. Women are amazing vessels of selflessness as they pour into their people day in and day out for many years. There ain't no tired like momma tired, right?

Betrayal trauma recovery adds on another thick layer of tired upon tired. It's zombie-tired. Our brains are foggy, our bodies feel fatigue, we experience sleep disturbances and headaches. The stress of betrayal trauma can greatly affect our hormones and our adrenal function, so we need to be extra proactive in supporting our tired body and soul as we work out our recovery.

Let's approach this topic from a different perspective. When we love and care about someone, we go out of our way to express that love through a variety of ways. We may do extra things for them, drop off dinner, or schedule quality time with that person. There is thought and planning and work that goes into expressing our love and care to others. Why are we not putting the same effort into loving our own selves, especially during this turbulent time? Find ways to show yourself some self-love. The way you express love towards others is what I'm challenging you to do towards yourself. Go see a movie alone. Take long walks. Go to bed early or sleep in late. Order take-out so you have a night off of cooking. Hire a cleaning service. In other words, when you feel yourself dragging, come up with a plan to love yourself. This plan may need to be clearly communicated with your spouse, so long as he, too, is in recovery. Let go of expectations that he should instinctively know how to support you and then instinctively offer it. You are your own advocate. State your needs and present a solution. If he is not willing to comply, or unable to, then have a backup plan. Hire a babysitter or call a grandparent. Get creative!

For those of you with young children, another idea is a "trade" with a trusted friend or family member. Trades are when you find another couple or mom with young kids and together you come up with a plan to offer one another a free night of babysitting in exchange for a date night or night out alone (or daytime works too!) In other words, you would watch her kids for a day so she can have some self-care, and then she would do the same for you. You could do this once a month or as often as you want. Get it set in stone as part of your schedule and routine, and make it happen! Be sure to use people you know and trust. Entrusting our most precious treasure (our children) with others is a big deal!

If you live near family, that is another added option. Most of them would be happy to plan one night a month to watch your kids, even for just a couple hours. The point is, prioritize self-love and physical rest.

Special Occasions and Self-Love with the Spouse in Recovery

We all wish our spouses remembered every birthday and anniversary and they knew exactly what we wanted or needed to feel loved. For some, that is not a reality. Our husbands' betrayal is proof that our relationships have been void of emotional intimacy. Our husbands are still learning how to respond and connect with us. We may have to tell them what we want and need. Emotional intimacy is an on-going area of growth, and like you, we are still working on it every single day.

When it comes to your special occasion, what do you value? Is it quality time? A special gift? A homemade card or a store-bought card? How do you want to celebrate your birthday? Christmas? Anniversaries? Mother's Day? Have you considered what you value, and then have you shared that with your spouse? If he's anything like my husband, who has the best of intentions but sometimes a terrible memory, it may be best to give him a written list of presents you want. Give him ideas for special outings or time alone. Be very specific about what you want to do. It will feel awkward and strange at first to present your spouse with an actual list of wishes, but you may find he will greatly appreciate it. He might need to develop some new habits to remember, like setting his phone alarm or notifications to remind him your special day is approaching. Be proactive for your desires! It is okay to approach this lightheartedly and even with a bit of humor. Both parties are learning about each other, sometimes for the first time. When we present our spouses with clear-cut communication, they learn about us and our needs and they often appreciate it! They may feel a sense of relief to not have to come up with ideas on their own. Remember, our men have been thinking and acting like boys for many years. When they enter recovery, they are learning how to emotionally grow-up as men of integrity and maturity. I do not say this with condescending undertones, but rather stating the reality in simple terms.

One of my favorite Mother's Day gifts was a weekend all by myself. I told my husband that I wanted to stay in a little cottage near the Ozark mountains. I left the details up to him, but it would have been perfectly fine to do the research myself and offer that as well. My husband loved and supported this idea. He had so much fun finding the perfect place for me. I arranged childcare for a day and together we worked it out. I have done the same for him. Every Father's Day, I send him away for a couple days to go fly-fishing. We respect that both of us need space and time to be alone and get recharged.

Taking a break from life can look a million different ways. It can be in small ways or big ways. It could be going to bed an hour earlier or asking for a night in a hotel. Whatever and however you go about it is up to you but learn the art of giving yourself a break and knowing how to voice your needs!

Spiritual Rest

When we think of "rest" in the English language, it is typically used as a <u>verb</u>. Something we do. "I'm going to rest." That is the physical rest we discussed previously. Take a mental turn with me as we explore rest from the position of a <u>noun</u>.

"Return unto thy rest, O my soul..." (Psalm 116:7 KJV)

The original Hebrew for the word "rest" is manoah. Manoah is a masculine noun and is defined in Strong's Concordance, Hebrew Dictionary as "Quiet, i.e., (concretely) a settled spot, or (figuratively) a home" (QuotesCosmos).

Mentally go back to your 4th grade English class and pull up the definition of a noun. A noun is a person, place, thing or idea. When we are talking about manoah rest, we are talking about not something we do but a place we enter in. We enter quiet, a settled spot, home.

Manoah rest is one of the greatest gifts the Holy Spirit offers to humans. It is synonymous to peace. It is the song, "It Is Well" when your life is anything but "well." This kind of rest is not something humans can put into words. It is deep and profound and not easy to explain to others, especially if they have not themselves experienced manoah. This incredible rest is not rest *from* our recovery work, but rather a rest *in* our recovery work. It is a state of being, not a state of doing.

While that all sounds so amazing, how do we enter into the noun Manoah? Below are some tips for how to enter this supernatural rest.

1. We keep our hearts soft. Stay teachable and tender. Betrayal can turn us hard, and we know this, so we are intentional about keeping our hearts free from hate.
2. We quit judging ourselves and instead, choose to be gentle and kind during this difficult season.
3. We seek help from mental health professionals, and remain open to medication if we find our depression/anxiety debilitating.
4. We prioritize our physical rest, so we can enter spiritual rest.

Grace is our path to find the land of Manoah

Growing up in legalism kept me a slave to people pleasing. Always striving, always working, always doing in order to prove my worth. Of course, I was unaware that this was happening, but then betrayal happened and I had my Day of Awakening.

I had a mental shift and a heart shift of the focus. All of a sudden, I had nothing to prove. Let me say that again, I had nothing to prove! There was nothing I could do or not do to experience grace. All I had to do was accept it.

I didn't have to prove my devotion, my love, my desires, my intention, or my recovery. Do you know how freeing that was to me? It was freeing because I no longer had that need to defend myself to others. This manoah rest I entered gave me freedom to walk out my recovery and not be overly concerned with how others viewed me, viewed my husband, or viewed our recovery process. Not feeling the need to defend my boundaries, my path to recovery, my timing, or my needs, gave me the ability to truly enter in manoah rest during turbulent times and when others I care about expressed their disapproval. I was able to close my mouth when I needed to. I could discern when to speak and when to not. I could stick to boundaries and stay in my lane. It was amazing. It was Bizarro World again as I became "Opposite Misty."

This place (noun) of rest, of being not doing, is a place of quiet. Not acting quiet. But taking up residence in quiet. Healthy isolation, not toxic isolation.

My enneagram seven self just started to twitch a little as I typed that. I have a hard time staying quiet. My mind is always talking, even when my mouth isn't. I think this is why I love to write. It gives me an outlet for my many thoughts. Recovery work has been a strange blessing for me in that it has forced me to slow down and turn in. Seven years of slowing down! My type-A personality has resisted at times, but at some point, I had to learn to become friends with healthy solitude. When I did, I found the land of rest. It has been empowering and invigorating.

One of my favorite calming activities, is to lie down on our large, round tree swing. I love looking up through the tree branches and seeing the sunlight poke through the leaves. I'll breathe deeply and go through my five senses. Name five things I see, four things I hear, three things I feel, two things I smell, and one thing I taste. Doing this calming exercise in nature centers my soul and fills my heart with gratitude. All of which lead me to the Land of Rest.

Heartwork Challenge:

1. On a scale of 1-10 (10 being the highest), how would you rate yourself on self-love?

2. What are some ideas or ways you can show yourself self-love?

3. Have you had times in the past where you felt hurt about getting the "wrong" gift from your spouse? Share.

4. How do you feel about making a list of what you want to give to your spouse for special occasions?

5. **Have you noticed you feel more tired during recovery? How have you been responding to that feeling of fatigue?**

6. **Have you experienced manoah rest yet? If so, share. If you haven't, what is something you could start doing to enter rest?**

Q & A with Jim

Chapter 11: A Return to Rest and Self-Love

1. Misty discusses how recovery work is exhausting. Have you felt the same way? Explain.

Yes, it is exhausting. Partly because it is so hard for me to figure out my feelings. That takes a lot of work for me. Trying to dig deep and press into my emotions doesn't come naturally for me, so it takes a toll on me mentally, which makes me feel physically tired.

When we are trying to work through issues, I get emotionally, mentally, and physically tired.

2. Do you feel that your recovery process is just as exhausting as Misty's? Why or why not?

No, I do not believe so. I didn't have the trauma that Misty has had to experience. We both have had issues to work through, but I didn't have the trauma to deal with on top of everything else.

3. Why do you think it is important for a husband to understand the kind of energy recovery requires for his wife?

If a husband doesn't understand the energy required for recovery, it would be very easy for him to get frustrated and resentful towards his wife. When he has the basic knowledge of what is required, it allows him to be more understanding and patient.

4. Did you ever have to tell Misty that you needed a break or time to rest? How was that request received?

Yes, I have. As we both got more emotionally healthy, we were able to offer grace towards one another, and now we both understand the importance of rest.

5. Did Misty ever tell you she needed extra rest? Was it difficult for you to understand why?

Yes, she has. It has not been difficult for me to understand why because I have an understanding of the trauma I caused.

Chapter 12: Comparison Game

In today's over-sexualized culture, it's no wonder that most women end up on the crazy hamster wheel of body comparison. Without realizing it, we allow the media to teach us what beauty should look like.

Betrayal trauma can actually deepen body image issues that started in childhood and amplify them in adulthood. Betrayal is a full-blown attack against everything we believe we are as women. It attacks us mentally, emotionally, spiritually, and physically.

My kids have a funny tradition on the 4th of July. It started several years ago when my daughter had an old, cheap Barbie™-type doll. The torso and legs were hollow, and one of my kids had the idea that it would be hilarious to put a firecracker inside her torso (possibly not the proudest moment in my years of mothering, but I allowed this to take place and may or may not have even filmed it).

There she was, with her blonde hair, perfectly shaped eyes, her to-die-for figure, and hot pink, high-heeled shoes. We carefully laid her in a patch of grass, lit the firecracker and ran for our lives. A few seconds later, the Barbie was blown to bits as parts of her plastic pieces went flying through the air. The best part? All that was left of her body was one arm, half a face, and the legs, from the hips down. The hot pink heels were still perfectly in place, but her thighs were on fire and the flame was spreading towards her shoes. We watched as the plastic slowly melted what was left of her, until all you could see was a black, charred patch of grass.

Yep, that's what betrayal does to our body image. Rejection causes our self-esteem to blow up to smithereens.

It doesn't matter if you are super-model thin or curvaceous, the body image explosion affects most of us. Did you hear that? Most of us! I'd even be as bold to say it affects all of us, but since I haven't personally been able to interview every single woman, I'll just leave it as "most" of us.

The big question is: how do we find victory over this area? How do we get off the hamster wheel of body shaming and comparison after betrayal?

Let me get real with you: I am not yet living in full victory over this area of my life, although I have noticed significant growth.

I still fight the core belief that "I am ugly" and seem to be very good at highlighting my physical imperfections.

So what about you? Can you embrace your physical attributes? Can you see both your inner beauty and outer beauty? Some days, all I see is how betrayal caused me to gain 10 extra pounds. I see the flaws that stare back at me daily. There is negative self-talk in my head that I'm determined to turn around. But ladies, even though I'm writing this book, in humility and vulnerability I admit, this area of my life still needs work.

When I look at other women, I see their amazing, inward spirit that just radiates beauty from within, but I can't seem to see and recognize that in myself. And in true honesty, I used to view their beauty as a threat and on some days, I still do. This is not who I want to be.

One reason why betrayal has blown up my self-esteem is because it doesn't feel like a rejection of only my body. Betrayal feels like a *complete* rejection of body, mind, and soul. I had to accept that my husband literally risked losing all of me for the sake of his addiction, and he made that choice, deliberately. When I do the digging of the thought, "I am ugly" it can go even deeper into the thought of, "I am rejected." Another very similar thought is "I am abandoned." Or how about this one: "I am not enough." All of these false beliefs mold and shape our thoughts, our choices, and our behaviors, and definitely affect our self-esteem.

Another reason my self-esteem was blown up had to do with my family-of-origin. Sexual parts of my body were made fun of in my early teen years, resulting in a young adolescent girl who felt extremely insecure and flawed.

While family-of-origin and betrayal played a big role in my self-hate, they weren't the only contributing culprits.

Have you ever considered how the church has conditioned you to believe certain things about your gender and how your body works? I had never considered that until sexual betrayal brought it all up to the surface, and like an overflowing, clogged toilet, the toxic sewage began pouring out.

The Menstrual Cycle: Curse or Blessing?

In 7th grade, I found myself, along with the other 7th grade girls, sitting in Bible class at my conservative, Christian school. I yawned as I stared at the clock on the wall, willing my stomach to make it to lunch. With my head leaning on one hand, I looked down at the run in my pantyhose and made a note to add some clear fingernail polish, which I always had in my locker for times such as this, to prevent the run from spreading down my entire leg.

Today our teacher was talking to us about our menstrual cycles. No, this wasn't health class, this was Bible class. But the topic came up naturally because the Scripture focus was Genesis 3, when sin entered the world.

The teacher strayed from the text briefly, looked down at us at our desks, and told the class that our periods were a result of sin and God's curse on Eve.

I really don't remember much from the entire hour, but what I do remember is significant. I remember details of that ten-minute side note, like my stomach growling and the run in my pantyhose. Those ten-minutes seemed to make such an impression, that my brain seemed frozen in time. So much so, here I am, thirty years later, deconstructing what I learned in those ten minutes and having to reframe every second of it.

This lesson sent a strong message to me. So strong, that I believed my body was cursed. "I am bad because I am a woman" and "My body is bad because I'm a woman" were two shame-based beliefs that carried into my adult years.

If you grew up in fundamentalism, were you taught the same things? That our menstrual cycles resulted from sin and Eve's curse? If so, then the next section may be healing for you as we reframe the truth about our unique bodies and God's perfect design.

First, I'd encourage you to go back and read Genesis 3 on your own. While there were consequences for sin, Eve was never cursed. Her body was never cursed. But there were consequences of her choice. One of those consequences was that her body changed.

A body changed is very different from a body cursed.

Prior to sin, God called all He created as "good". After sin, He had to make immediate adjustments to His original design, but we can see that His good plan never changed, and His creation, even today, is still good. 1 Timothy 4:4 says, "For everything God created is good..." (NIV).

Although the female body changed, she is still made in the image of God. She still reflects the goodness of His design. And her body is good. Let's take a short bunny trail and briefly look at menstrual cycles and how they can benefit our bodies (Pawlik, 2020; "Health benefits," 2022).

1. Hormone balance: Regular menstruation tells you that your body is in homeostasis. When hormones are in balance, you feel great, are energetic, sleep well, and take interest in sex. When you're under constant stress, your hormones become out of balance, and when we miss a cycle, that is our body's way of saying we need to be checked out. Our cycles are an excellent barometer to overall hormone health.
2. Bone health. The natural balance between the hormones estrogen, progesterone, and testosterone helps ensure both healthy periods and healthy bone turnover. In fact, your bones are an endocrine-, or hormone-generating organ. If the balance is disrupted, your periods may become irregular — providing a useful clue that bone build-up may not be keeping pace with bone breakdown.
3. Thyroid function. The thyroid acts like a "transfer station," controlling the rate of function for every cell and gland in the body, including growth, repair, and metabolism. If your thyroid is healthy and doing its part, your periods are much more likely to be regular.
4. Healthy weight maintenance. Estrogen dominance and insulin resistance are both types of hormonal imbalance associated with extra body weight and menstrual irregularities. Also, being underweight because of stringent dieting, overtraining, or other extreme physical or emotional

stress, can also cause menstrual irregularities, including amenorrhea (lack of periods).

5. Adrenal function. The adrenals produce the stress hormone, cortisol. Cortisol indirectly affects the balance between sex hormones. As a result, many women will skip or have irregular periods when they're under stress which can be reduced by supporting our adrenals.
6. Natural Body Cleanser. Having a period is a natural cleansing process, which releases bacteria from inside the reproductive system and helps you discharge excess iron. This "cleaning process" can help lower the risk of cardiovascular disease. When you suppress or stop menstruation by using birth control pills, you may interfere with your breast and bone development. Your fertility levels are also affected when you don't get your period for a long time. This is one of those benefits of having a period that isn't visible or observable, but it is powerful.
7. Slows down the aging process. Women age more slowly than men because menstruation causes iron loss. Too much iron feeds free radicals, which increase the risk of heart disease, stroke, and Alzheimer's disease. When you have your period, you lose some iron every month. This can help lengthen your lifespan – and it may be one reason why women live longer than men. A longer life is a definite benefit of menstruation.

There are more I could list but imagine if my teacher had taught these seven benefits of having a period, and how our bodies are a reflection of God's goodness instead of God's curse! What if I had learned that my period was God's internal benchmark made just for women to communicate that our bodies are functioning properly? How would this have affected my overall view of myself as a woman created by God? How would this have affected my relationship with God? How would this have affected my sexuality? Mind you, this is just touching the tip of the iceberg. Entering the purity culture in my teens also did a number on my sexuality and self-esteem, but we will address sexuality more in the following chapter.

In summary, to repair my self-esteem I've had to address my father's abandonment, verbal sexual abuse, identify the false teachings from fundamental Christianity, and unpack sexual betrayal. This was my antidote to seeing myself the way God sees me: beautiful, wonderfully designed and wonderfully made, and perfectly imperfect. Recognizing God's goodness in my womanhood instead of only seeing flaws is easier on some days than others, but I keep leaning in as it comes up. Slowly, I have learned to love myself. All of me.

Have you struggled with self-esteem the way I have? I would guess that most of you reading this can, in fact, relate to this on-going struggle.

Since we are all in the same boat, how about you and I work this out together. I admit, I've had a head start, but I'm still struggling in this area of my life, and sometimes these core beliefs are so stubborn, it takes doing it over and over again to get the results we desire.

If you are in a support group and have chosen this book as your study, do this activity together. Talking through it may help you as you process out loud.

If you are working independently, do item #3 in Exercise One, and then do all of Exercise Two.

Group Heartwork Challenge:

Exercise One : Affirmation

1. **Sit in a circle with your group.**
2. **On a piece of paper, write something about the person to your right that you define as "beautiful" and why.**
3. **On the same piece of paper, write something about yourself that you define as "beautiful" and why.**
4. **Going around the group, read both your answers out loud.**

Exercise Two: Time to name, claim and reframe!

1. **On a separate piece of paper, write out a negative emotion you've had recently. (Use the wheel in Chapter 4 if you need help.) Once you have identified it on the feeling wheel, be sure to look towards the center and see the deeper emotion.**
2. **Next to your feeling word, think back in your life and try and identify your earliest memory of feeling the exact same way. Briefly jot down the memory.**
3. **Now, look at the list of Core Belief statements from Chapter 4. Choose any that jump off at the page in regard to this particular memory. Write it down.**
4. **LERC it. Use Chapter 4 as your guide.**
5. **Last step: journal. In the rest of the space, write a few sentences to yourself from God's perspective. What would God tell you about your body? Your personality?**

Share with your group. I know sharing such personal things is scary, but part of your healing process is to live in vulnerability and authenticity. You got this, girl!

Q & A with Jim
Chapter 12: Comparison Game

1. Misty discusses how her self-esteem has been annihilated from betrayal. What have you said to her to help build her esteem back up? Has it helped?

This is a complex question. My betrayal nullified my words of affirmation, especially when I praised her appearance. Misty even went through a season where she actually hated my compliments. She would respond with a sneer, which made me question why I should even try.

Misty did, however, respond well to compliments about her character, her intelligence and her attributes.

Sadly, Misty had to rebuild her worth due to betrayal trauma. She felt worthless. She had been betrayed by her father, and now me. As she began to see her worth, over time she was able to receive my praise. However, Misty never sought her worth from me. Although it's important for me to affirm her, she got her true worth from Jesus.

2. Many women automatically assume their husbands cheat because they must not be attractive enough. What do you have to say about that assumption?

It is due to our selfishness. It doesn't matter what a woman looks like. When we are acting out, it is never fulfilling. Addicts are never satisfied. There is nothing she can or cannot do or look like to stop us from acting out.

3. How does pornography affect a man's idea of "beauty?"

It deceives the brain. It makes the addict brain think that beauty has to look a certain way, but it is all fake. It is also completely based on the outward appearance, and doesn't consider

the woman's character, desires, needs and safety. Porn is about self-gratification and doesn't even care or consider the other person.

Chapter 13: Emotional Intimacy and Sex

Many people have never been taught how to develop and exhibit healthy emotional intimacy with another human. It's possible it wasn't modeled properly in their family of origin. If your own parents came from dysfunctional family systems, then chances are they too, are unfamiliar with what true emotional intimacy is and what it looks unless they have done the same work you are doing. If emotional intimacy (EI) seems like a foreign concept, or if you are unsure, you are in good company. The good news is, it can be learned!

It is important to first establish that EI should not be addressed in your marriage relationship until safety has been established, well documented and trust is building. We addressed that earlier but it's really important you don't rush this process, and that your radar is up if a therapist, clergy, or others try to push this process before it is safe to do so.

When a husband's actions speak that he is in true recovery, and you are ready to take this step, you can begin working on EI. However, there may be times, even during active recovery, that something will come up and you feel unsafe again. It is acceptable for you to establish safety once more before engaging in any form of intimacy. There needs to be some understanding that with the couple in recovery, engaging in intimacy will ebb and flow.

This is a good time to remind you what "true recovery" looks like. Here are some good signs that your husband is in active, true recovery:

- He is attending recovery meetings.
- He is maintaining his sobriety.

- He is attending individual therapy.
- He is willing to attend marriage therapy, once safety has been established and after attending individual therapy.
- He is reading recovery books or showing interest in learning about his addiction.
- He is getting educated on what his partner is going through during her recovery.
- He has written a full disclosure and has done or is willing to do a therapeutic disclosure with his wife.
- He has set up accountability with a sponsor or mentor.
- His words match his actions and he's showing fruits of the spirit.
- He has exhibited the five steps of repentance and brokenness over his choices and offers you empathy. He no longer fights to be in control and mutually submits to you.

There are different areas that fall under the large umbrella of "emotional intimacy." This is still an area of growth in my marriage. For so many years, I had to take great care to build a wall around my heart for protection from the addiction. I was not cognitively aware of the addiction, yet my spirit knew. I had no choice but to do this in order to maintain safety. My wall served me well, but at some point, I knew it was no longer necessary. That wall doesn't crumble because of confession. It begins to crumble as he makes living amends. As our men continue to build trust, another "chip" of our wall will fall, but it doesn't happen overnight. That wall protected us, and it still can and does if/when he defaults to old patterns. Some of us had to erect walls for protection in our early years, too. My wall is my safety and necessity when I am with someone who isn't safe. It isn't a negative part of me to hold onto when I need it and when it serves me. We must decide if/when it is safe to lower this defense. As we move forward in this conversation, I am assuming that you feel completely safe with your former betrayer.

Sometimes the damage done prior to his repentance is too great to continue into emotional intimacy, even if the husband is showing all signs of being in active recovery and truly repentant. Be honest with yourself to determine if you are ready to be open to growing in emotional intimacy with your spouse. Are you holding back simply because of fear? Are there still areas where you do not feel safe that need to be addressed? Was the damage done before his recovery/repentance just too big to move beyond? There is much to consider. Take your time. Whatever you choose is okay.

Emotional intimacy occurs when there is safety, truth, and enough trust and mutuality between you and your spouse that it allows you both to share your innermost selves. Deep emotional intimacy is when we feel wholly accepted, respected, and admired in the eyes of our mate even when they know our innermost struggles and failures. Emotional intimacy fosters compassion and support, providing a firm foundation for any relationship.

I like to compare emotional intimacy to a large, beautiful tree. In "emotional intimacy," I believe there are 3 specific parts:

- Root system: Spiritual intimacy
- Trunk: Soul-Sharing
- Branches, leaves and fruit: Sexual Intimacy

All these together intertwine into deep, beautiful healthy tree of "emotional intimacy". I don't believe most couples are superheroes in all three parts, but more than likely have strengths and weaknesses in each one. The illustration and description following might shed light on an area that may be lacking in your current relationship and give clues to how you can build a stronger tree. Below is my own synopsis of each part. We'll start from the roots up.

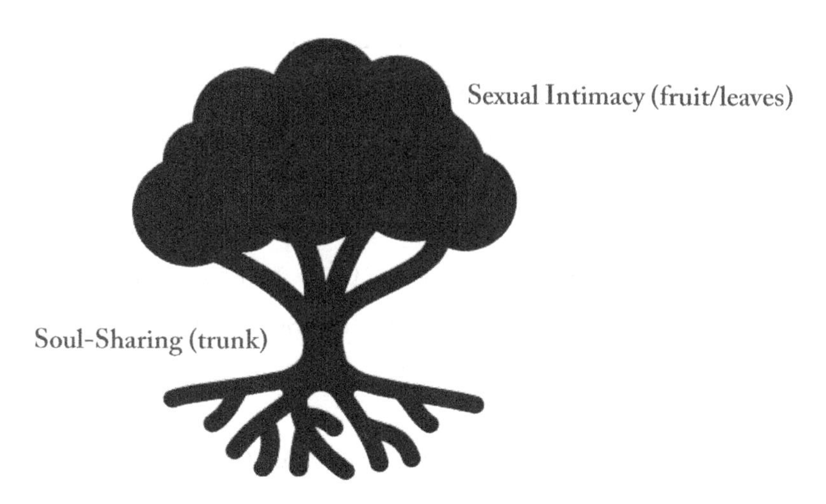

ROOT SYSTEM: Spiritual Intimacy

The foundational type of intimacy is spiritual intimacy. Spiritual intimacy is the entire root system of a healthy marriage. It is the most important facet of all other factors in obtaining emotional intimacy. It can impact all areas of connection between a couple, including sex. If the spiritual intimacy is absent, all other areas of intimacy will be greatly impacted.

I like the way it was described in an article I found online, written by Kiran, titled "The Power of Spiritual Intimacy: Strengthening Relationships and Finding Intimacy."

> "Spiritual intimacy, the deep connection and shared spiritual values between individuals in a

relationship, plays a crucial role in strengthening emotional bonds and providing a sense of purpose and fulfillment.

Exploring spiritual connection allows us to go beyond the surface level and truly understand and support each other on a deeper level. Nurturing our spiritual bond creates a safe space where we can share our fears, hopes, and dreams without judgment. It allows us to be vulnerable and authentic with one another, fostering trust and emotional intimacy.

Through spiritual intimacy, we find solace and strength in our shared beliefs, and it brings a sense of peace and purpose to our relationships. It is through this deep connection that we can truly experience fulfillment and find a higher meaning in our lives together."

While I am keenly aware of the importance of spiritual connection with my spouse, that doesn't mean it comes easy for me. At the time of disclosure, our entire relationship and marriage (17 years) had been completely void of any spiritual intimacy at all, even though we regularly attended church together. Just because you attend the same church and believe in the same theology doesn't mean the two of you are connecting on a deep spiritual level.

What Spiritual Intimacy is NOT

Spiritual intimacy does not mean we have to politically align. We do not have to agree theologically. We do not have to pray together. We do not have to attend the same church or believe the exact same things.

We are two very different people. In fact, we are opposites. If you know the enneagram, Jim is a one. I am a seven. As a neurodivergent one, Jim feels calmest when he follows the rules. He is in the details, is a perfectionist, and loves checking things off his to-do list. He is more serious, frugal, hardworking, and diligent. He tends to lean towards rigidity, especially under stress. He doesn't love traveling, mainly because he hates change. As a neurodivergent (ADHD) seven, I am the free spirit. I never wear a watch because time stresses me out. I'm high energy, busy, and fun-loving. I love spontaneity and can't stand being in my house too long. I have a really loud laugh, and I love laughing. I walk fast, I talk fast, I think fast. I embrace change, and pretty much have a positive outlook on everything, which can be both wonderful and a form of denial. I tend to buck the status quo, because I crave the freedom to be a free thinker. Our differences are such that there is no way we will align on everything. The difference now versus before D-Day, is that we are no longer tied down to patriarchy or a complementarian marriage. We function as egalitarian now. (Complementarians believe men should lead, women should submit. Egalitarians believe in equal partnering, where both parties practice mutual submission.)

Both of us were raised in patriarchy where men in the church were spiritually abusive, entitled and power hungry. We didn't want this dynamic to be a part of our new marriage post D-Day, so we had to reframe what spirituality is/isn't. I didn't want to be a subservient bystander but an equal partner, connecting with God together. Until

Jim could view me (and women in general) as his equal, my wall stayed up.

I also had a lot of fear. It felt so incredibly risky. Creating space for my husband, who betrayed me, into this very sacred space felt threatening. Perhaps even foolish of me.

I had to see a true heart change, true growth, and true humility for me to even think about spiritual intimacy. Once safety was well established and he began building trust, I was able to start rooting our relationship in our new shared values.

What Spiritual Intimacy IS

Spiritual intimacy can look a million different ways. I respect that not everyone reading this book will love following the teachings of Jesus the way we do. But I want to highlight that there are so many other ways humans can connect spiritually. I'll bullet point some of my favorite ways to connect on a spiritual level, but there are many other ways, too.

- Investing in people together through random acts of kindness.
- Talking with other couples in recovery together.
- Being generous together.
- Taking walks in nature, hiking, star gazing together.
- Telling our partner what we like about them, and naming something they did for us that made us feel grateful.
- Stewarding earth together, and being kind to creation, animals, nature.

- Enjoying a glass of wine while we watch a show together, or attending a music concert that we both enjoy.
- Listening to podcasts or reading a book simultaneously that challenges our thinking, then discussing it together.
- Observing religious traditions that are meaningful to us as a couple.
- Seeking guidance from a place of faith to help us navigate life.
- Being sensitive and actively advocating for the vulnerable and oppressed, together.
- Being naturally curious about the way the other thinks about certain topics, including theology, politics, religion, etc. But then, giving one another autonomy and respect when we don't see things the same way.

We took our spirituality out of the evangelical box, and when we did, we found the heart of God.

TRUNK: Soul-Sharing

Learning how to live in vulnerability is hard for many of us. We take the risk of removing the masks we've worn our entire lives and let others in. (That is, safe people. You do not have to allow unsafe people into your innermost places.) Healthy connection with another human is worth the risk. It means being open and honest, and loving without an agenda. If your spouse is exhibiting trustworthiness, if he is in active recovery and if he exhibits humility, then it is possible for you to start practicing soul-sharing. If you are choosing to walk away from your marriage, this section is still a valuable read. It can apply to other relationships, future relationships and maybe offer validation.

Soul-sharing is when we share our feelings, our dreams, our fears and our thoughts. It may look like sharing parts of your past and entrusting your spouse with the deepest parts of yourself. When our spouse reciprocates, we respond with compassion and gratefulness that they opened their heart with us. When one person entrusts another person with personal information, feelings, fears, dreams and hurts, it is such a special gift. What an honor! The worst thing one could do to squelch intimacy is to react in condemnation, judgment, opinions, laughter, or rudeness. This is not the time to "fix" or have opinions. Soul-sharing is when each party practices listening in love and offering words of affirmation and validation. This is something we worked on together in therapy.

LEAVES & FRUIT: Sexual Intimacy

Healthy sexual intimacy is the fruit-bearing branches of a strong root system and healthy trunk. However, the world, and often the church, says otherwise. I want us to approach this from God's original design, and His version of sex is the best version of all!

Sex ought to be celebrated and connected. It is our truest expression of one-ness, love, forgiveness, grace, adoration and hope! And of course, it is all about intimacy. That being said, both genders will have a very hard time being fully present if their emotional needs are not being met, if either feels unsafe in the relationship, and/or if there is no spiritual intimacy or soul-sharing.

After betrayal, women may not desire sex at all. The betrayer might assume his betrayed partner is purposefully withholding sex as a form of punishment, but in reality, she may be in so much emotional pain that her heart cannot even consider sexual intimacy. As part of their recovery, the betrayer can use this time to work on reframing what healthy physical intimacy is. A healthy view of sex is a way to connect in a deep, intimate way where both parties have a spirit of giving and receiving. If it is only for physical release and finishing, bodies become objects. This makes sex merely a transaction.

Talking about sex after betrayal, and when one partner is actively experiencing betrayal trauma, is so complex. There is no way I can address it all in one chapter. So let me highlight what I believe is the most important things to know for those of you starting out the recovery process.

- If you were raised evangelical or Mormon, please read the book *The Great Sex Rescue*. It addresses the dysfunctional and harmful teachings on sexuality that we were raised in.
- The betrayed partner has every right to protect her sexual self until she is ready. She doesn't "owe" him anything sexually at this time. She can take as long as she wants/needs, and isn't required to engage in sex if she doesn't want to. Obligation sex is a form of rape.
- Dissociation is very common during sex after betrayal. This is due to sexual trauma. This is when your body is present, but your mind is not. You wouldn't see a heart doctor for brain surgery, the same applies to our sexuality. When it comes to reclaiming sexuality, I recommend you see an

AASECT certified sex therapist. I am currently seeing two sex therapists, and it has helped me tremendously as I work through my sexual trauma.

- Never use sex as pawn. In other words, don't offer sex to get the results you want in the relationship, and don't withhold sex to get the results you want in the relationship. Withholding to punish is very different from abstaining to work through sexual trauma.
- Check your hormones if you have low libido. Chances are, your lack of libido is not physically related, but it is still good to have them checked. However, understand that lack of desire is very normal after betrayal, and a therapist can help address they "why's" and "how's" of reclaiming your sexuality.

As mentioned earlier, betrayal causes a huge disruption in the marriage relationship and in the victim. It can potentially take a long time for sexual healing to occur in both parties. Sometimes, the betrayer has sexual trauma in his past as well. All of these things need to be worked through in therapy.

Some wives have been terribly abused in the bedroom by their porn-addicted husbands. Abusers may have bullied, coerced, raped, or forced their wives to act in ways she didn't feel comfortable with or that went against her values. Wife rape happens, typically through coercion, a more covert way of having non-consensual sex. Obligation sex is a form of rape because she doesn't feel like she can say no. When it does, wives remain silent in their pain or may not even realize what is happening. Many sex addicts groom their spouses, doing extra things for her or buying her gifts in an attempt to gain her sexual compliance. Sexual abuse within a marriage is devastating.

Some addicts use sex to blame their wives for their addiction. They may say it is her fault for not having enough sex or for not engaging in specific sexual acts that went against her values. Some husbands initiate sex constantly, and some don't initiate sex at all. Because of that, instead of connecting with their wives, they connect with women online, where they are seemingly wanted and aren't forced to emotionally connect and address their insecurities. This is why dissociation is often a result in the spouse who was betrayed.

Dissociation can go away on its own, sometimes immediately and sometimes days, weeks or even months. However, long periods of dissociation may require a therapist to get the proper support and help.

Fantasizing is different than dissociation, although the two can overlap. Both are often used to escape pain, stress, and/or anxiety. Both are used as tools for the user to be separated from real life. But there are very distinct differences between the two that I'd like to briefly highlight.

Dissociation is needed to seek safety in an unsafe situation or relationship. I felt *OUT* of control.

Some women will intentionally dissociate to avoid feelings of severe emotional pain. She may deliberately think about the grocery list, or the meeting at work she had that day, or whatever else she wants to focus on, so long as she doesn't have to focus on her current circumstance. It's used as a survival mechanism.

Fantasizing is deliberate and intentional. The person has *FULL* control of the outcome and the sexual narrative playing in his/her head. The person fantasizing feels powerful and excited. It isn't used to survive, but rather to control and fuel the spirit of entitlement.

Another big difference between the two is the hormones that are released. Dissociation releases the hormones that correlate with trauma, the fight, flight, freeze or fawn response. A rush of cortisol (the stress hormone) is released, and the body goes into a trauma-response state.

When a person fantasizes, the brain releases the hormones responsible for "addict-brain". A neurochemical cocktail of dopamine, oxytocin, adrenaline, endorphins, and serotonin enter the addict's system, which acts as a "hit" to the addict brain.

Dissociation results from a trauma response.

Fantasizing results from an entitled response.

Oh, the layers to work through in recovery! I want to remind my women readers that you have a voice in the bedroom. If you do not feel safe, you can set a boundary of no sexual intimacy until safety is established and he begins building trust. Again, boundaries are not set up as punishment, but as protection for your heart and to establish safety. Let's be open, honest, and real that this area is deeply affected by betrayal and addiction. It is tainted. There is trauma and deep attachment wounds that needs healing.

Sadly, many people will counsel the spouse who was betrayed to go home and have more sex. They push her to engage sexually with a man who has caused so much pain and hurt and where security has been stolen. It's no wonder most women greatly struggle with having sex after betrayal. Telling the victim to "just have more sex" is ignorant, unacceptable, and quite frankly, abusive.

I want to speak hope to the betrayed spouse. If you are sexually struggling, that is to be expected. You are responding *normally* to the trauma you've endured. It only makes sense that you are sexually traumatized from sexual betrayal. Be kind and patient towards yourself. Your brain, body, and heart are capable of healing. Your sexual self is capable of healing. I know, because I am in the midst of that kind of healing work as I type these words. Remember, you don't have to say yes to sex, especially if you are not safe to say no. And if you are not safe to say no to sex, you are in a dangerous situation.

Pornography and Sex

Porn in a marriage is an absolute killer of good sex. This is hard to believe for many who consistently view porn, because they confuse intensity for intimacy. I really like reading Dr. Barry McCarthy's book, *Contemporary Male Sexuality*. In it, he explains how porn follows the male model of sex which is predictable: arousal, erection, intercourse, orgasm. Men and women who view porn have the notion that they love "sex," but what they are engaging in isn't healthy sexuality. It is a male dominant and cheap version of the real thing. Have you ever eaten fake cheese? It may look like cheese, melt like cheese, and maybe even taste like cheese. But when you bite into the *real* thing, you realize what you've been missing all along! Porn addicts, and many of us who have been influenced by porn, are tricked into thinking porn sex is what we want, but we end up feeling void, empty, and/or shameful. When a couple begins to experience healthy sexuality, they experience a deep, fulfilling intimate experience that cannot be replicated.

Too many couples today try to exist without emotional intimacy. Over time, a relationship lacking EI will become empty and lifeless, and the couple will experience distance in their relationship. The sad thing is, they may not even realize it. Our marriage was never intimate to begin with, because porn was blocking us from ever experiencing true intimacy from the very start. I was powerless to stop the slow drift so long as my husband was viewing porn without my consent or knowledge. I mentioned this earlier, but repetition is key to understanding: *It is impossible to be secretly sexually acting out, including the objectification of humans and emotional affairs, and be emotionally intimate with your spouse.*

Why do you think it is hard to develop emotional intimacy? Here are some ideas I came up with:

- Lack of safety. At this point in the book, I hope you've learned you are WISE to avoid EI if your partner is unsafe.
- Fear of rejection. (If I share who I really am, you might criticize or reject the real me.)
- Unfamiliarity with our own feelings, needs, or wants. (If I'm not sure what I feel or need, how can I share it with another human?)
- Lack of vocabulary to communicate our feelings accurately or to verbalize exactly what we want or need. (If I don't know the words to describe what I'm feeling or needing, then it's easier to just keep my thoughts to myself.)
- We expect our spouse to just know. (You can read my mind, can't you?)
- Fear of being hurt again.
- Fear of trust.
- Unresolved resentment in the relationship.
- Attachment disorders from either spouse.
- Unresolved past trauma.

- Lack of sobriety. Your husband is still sexually acting out, even possibly on you. You are not his rehab.
- Neurodivergence/personality disorder/mental health issues. If you suspect any of these things, seek out a psychologist.

I'd like to share our experience with reclaiming our sexuality.

After Jim's disclosure, there were times I voiced my need to fast from sex. I was not purposefully withholding sex to manipulate or control. He was still shedding addict-mode behaviors, and so I felt unsafe. Remember, addicts can compartmentalize. For many years, our spouses were experts at compartmentalizing when they viewed porn or acted out. You may have asked him, "Did you ever think of me when you were partaking in your addiction?" Often, the answer will be a flat out, "No." That is because sex addicts can literally put us in a box on the shelf of their brains and shut the lid. They can do the same with sex. There could be an argument that absolutely torments you, but sex addicts can put that aside and still engage in sex. If my husband is not connecting with me during the day on a consistent basis, I am most often unwilling to have sex. What happens in the course of my day often stays with me well into the night. If I don't feel emotionally connected, I find it extremely difficult to engage during sex. *And that's a good thing.* Your husband must learn how to be emotionally intelligent if he desires to be in a loving, committed, intimate relationship. You do not "owe" him sex.

Jim now has the exact same experience. If we are not emotionally connected, he does not desire sex. He no longer feels entitled to sex and he desires emotionally intimacy just as much as I do.

Offering sex without emotional intimacy allows either party of only wanting to pursue physical release. Healthy sexuality views the other person as a whole human, where both desire connection and fun

At some point, if your husband is working towards sobriety, it is often recommended that he partakes in a 90-day fast from sex. This is three months for his brain to rewire and jumpstart his dopamine and oxytocin levels back to normal. This fast operates similar to how a cocaine addict would stop using drugs. This time of rewiring is very important. Jim chose to dive "all in" and also fasted from all unwanted sexual behaviors, including objectification. For a short season, he didn't watch TV, didn't listen to secular music, and intentionally focused on viewing women as whole people, not as objects. This meant he did some deep soulful work in therapy and together, we deconstructed some pretty awful theology.

Going 90 days without sex did more than just rewire my husband's brain. We were amazed how most things we had been taught by churches, sex education classes and marriage conferences were incorrect. Let me explain.

In our early 20's and in the early 2000's, we attended a marriage conference. It was led by a certified Christian sex therapist. During the conference, she told the entire group that men must have sex every three days and we, as good and faithful wives, should offer our bodies as an act of love to our husbands. That statement empowered abusers and sex addicts. Before we go a moment further, allow me to speak truth: that statement is scientifically *false*. Men do not need sex to stay healthy. To tell women they are "required" to cater to their husband's sex drive is flat out wrong and deeply imbedded in full blown misogyny. Nonetheless, that is what we were taught and what we both used to believe was truth. The 90-day fast showed us that he did not "have" to have sex every three days. We started to understand God's definition of sex and how to connect

during sex in a more intimate, real way. Jim had to acknowledge that, as an addict, sex had been for his own self-gratification. He had to reframe it with a healthy view of sexuality. I asked him to write his own words on the topic.

> "Pornography and the teachings within the church both taught me a distorted and dysfunctional view of sex. That view of sex is selfish, disconnected, and unsatisfying. After viewing porn, I would feel deep wells of shame and self-hate, yet I couldn't stop. Now, to connect with my wife physically, it is no longer just about the sex. It is a physical, emotional, and spiritual richness resulting in the best sex of my life. To view sex from a healthy perspective is so much better than what porn and the church taught me. When I have a sexual encounter with a healthy mindset, and as God truly intended, I feel loved, known, joy, safe and emotionally intimate. It is completely opposite of what I knew before, and I'm sad I wasted so much time on something so superficial. Porn is anti-sex, totally against what real sex is."

Porn and teachings from our fundamentalist church ruined sexuality in our relationship, so Jim and I had to go back, revisit what we had been taught, unlearn, and then seek out good resources that taught us healthy sexuality. What a journey, one we are still on.

First on the list was forgetting sex, and simply focus on becoming friends again. Laughing together. Playing cards after the kids went to bed. Listening to recovery material together and discussing it. Taking personality quizzes and studying one another in natural curiosity. Going on walks together. Watching a movie. Growing as best buddies.

The best thing we did for reclaiming our sexuality was to stop focusing on the fruit (sex) and instead, focus on the roots and the trunk. And that took *time*.

In closing, I want to give you a visual aid on the following page. This poster is yet another great resource for you as you reframe and reclaim your sexuality!

DO YOU KNOW THE DIFFERENCE?

PORN-RELATED SEX	HEALTHY SEX
Sex is using someone	Sex is caring for someone
Sex is "doing to" someone	Sex is sharing with a partner
Sex is a performance for others	Sex is a private experience
Sex is compulsive	Sex is a natural drive
Sex is a public commodity	Sex is a personal treasure
Sex is watching others	Sex is about genuine connection
Sex is separate from love	Sex is an expression of love
Sex can be hurtful	Sex is nurturing
Sex is emotionally distant	Sex is emotionally close
Sex can happen anytime	Sex requires certain conditions
Sex is unsafe	Sex is safe
Sex can be degrading	Sex is always respectful
Sex can be irresponsible	Sex is approached responsibly
Sex is devoid of morality	Sex requires morals and values
Sex lacks healthy communication	Sex requires healthy communication
Sex involves deception	Sex requires honesty
Sex is based on visual imagery	Sex involves all the senses
Sex has no ethical limits	Sex has ethical boundaries
Sex requires a double life	Sex enhances who you really are
Sex compromises your values	Sex reflects your values
Sex feels shameful	Sex enhances self-esteem
Sex is impulse gratification	Sex is lasting satisfaction

Heartwork Challenge:

1. **Which part of the EI Tree do you struggle with the most? Spiritual, Soul-Sharing, or Sexual? Share.**

2. **Has pornography been a part of your marriage? If so, for how long?**

3. **If the answer above was "yes," how does it make you feel to accept that EI is impossible so long as porn is in the marriage?**

4. **Do you think you or your spouse struggles more with EI?**

5. **If you husband is in recovery, are you willing to share with him what you learned in this chapter regarding EI? Why or why not?**

6. **What were your feelings/thoughts on the issue of sex? Have you struggled in this area? Have you had triggers during sex or dissociation during sex (thoughts of low self-esteem, thinking about other things like the grocery list, wondering about the images he saw on the computer, etc.)? Take some time to be honest about this topic. Determine if you need to discuss with a counselor and your spouse.**

Q & A with Jim
Chapter 13: Emotional Intimacy and Sex

1. Why do you think the 90 Day fast from sex is so important?

Multiple reasons.

First, it is so important to re-wire the brain and get the dopamine and oxytocin levels back to normal. Sex addiction affects the brain, just as any other addiction does. When a crack addict goes to rehab, they don't get to use crack. Not even a little bit. That is part of the natural process to beating the addiction. The same holds true for the sex addict brain. There must be a "rehab" mentality of a complete fast to normalize the chemicals in the brain. This applies to not just porn, but any kind of act, thought or behavior that feeds the addiction.

Secondly, it busted the myth I believed that I had to have sex. I didn't think it was possible for me to go that long without sex. It really helped me to find out that yes, I can physically and mentally go that long without sex and survive.

Third, it took that dynamic out of the equation in our marriage and therefore, took away pressure and allowed us to focus on our own healing. Misty really needed that time to establish safety in the relationship. I needed that time to re-wire my brain. It gave us the chance to focus on areas that needed 100% attention.

Lastly, it helped me in future periods of fasting from sex. Yes, there have been multiple seasons without sex. There have been times where Misty was so angry, or so sad, that she couldn't even think about sex. I could offer her the time and space she needed to work through the trauma and it offered me time to continue building trust and making amends. Sometimes I needed a break from sex, too, while working through my own pain or if I felt emotionally disconnected.

2. When you first contemplated partaking in the fast, what feelings came up?

That it would be impossible. This was a part of my sobriety work. However, at that point, I was so desiring change, I was more than willing to do it. Whatever it took, I was "all in." However, I had doubt that it was possible for me to do so.

I also felt grief and general sadness to not have sex. I knew I would miss it. But I knew it was a necessary part of the process.

3. How did you manage the 90 day fast? Did you have tools in place to help?

Yes, having my mentor involved was key to my success. We had almost daily check-ins. He gave me the tools to keep my mind right throughout the process. I didn't rely on Misty to meet my needs, but continually turned to all my resources. I asked God to help me view women through His eyes, as whole people, not as objects. I didn't listen to secular music, which was a trigger for me. I was very intentional about what I watched/didn't watch on TV. If there was any potential at all that there would be temptation, I made the choice to not view it. At stores, I kept my eyes straight ahead and was intentional to not look around. (This was another way that I often acted out.) I was addicted to objectifying women, so I was overly cautious until I was able to view women as humans, not objects. I leaned into my faith, and was in God's Word and followed a protocol outlined in my recovery book. Keep in mind, these tactics were extremely rigid in order to help me reach *stability* in my sobriety. I had to be overly cautious until my brain reset and rewired. Once I gained stability, I worked on changing my *heart* so that I didn't have to focus on behavior modification tactics. Working from the inside-out will ensure long-term success.

4. What fears did you have going into it?

Fear of failure.

5. What did you learn about yourself and/or Misty by doing the 90 Day fast?

That I don't "need" sex. It is possible to live without sex.

Prior to disclosure, pornified sex was always on my mind. I was constantly fantasizing. Pornified sex had literally taken over my life. Now I am able to stay in the present and be more engaged with those around me.

It definitely shed light on how deep I was involved in my addiction. I had fallen so far into the addiction and literally had no clue. I felt like I couldn't live without pornified sex.

I've learned how to be more attentive to Misty's needs. Again, my view of sex was all about my own gratification. Now I can view sex in a healthy way. That it is sacred. Healthy sex is a reflection of the beauty of my relationship with Misty. The fast helped me begin the path to understanding and practicing emotional intimacy.

6. Did Misty experience PTSD symptoms during physical intimacy? If so, what did you do or how did you respond?

Yes, often. My role is to support her, no matter what. Whatever she needs to feel safe, I want to provide that for her, even if that means not engaging in physical intimacy.

7. Do you notice that Misty is more open to physical intimacy when are attune to her? Why or why not?

Yes, absolutely. I have learned that Misty cannot compartmentalize sex, which is a really good thing! If her daily needs

are not being met, her heart will not be open to physical intimacy because our relationship is lacking emotional intimacy. Sex should be the product of a loving, open, honest, kind relationship. I feel the exact same way, and desire emotional intimacy before partaking in physical intimacy.

8. Overall, how has sex changed for you over the past seven years vs. life before disclosure?

I'm having the best sex I've ever had because it is a complete union. It is so fulfilling. I feel fully known and fully loved. I feel connected to another human being and God. I have nothing to hide. It is an expression of wholeness. I stated in detail how sex has changed for me in the previous chapter. Here it is again.

"Pornography and the teachings within the church both taught me a distorted and dysfunctional view of sex. That view of sex is selfish, disconnected, and unsatisfying. After viewing porn, I would feel deep wells of shame and self-hate, yet I couldn't stop. Now, to connect with my wife physically, it is no longer just about the sex. It is a physical, emotional, and spiritual richness resulting in the best sex of my life. To view sex from a healthy perspective is so much better than what porn and the church taught me. When I have a sexual encounter in a healthy mindset, and as God truly intended, I feel loved, known, joy, safe and emotionally intimate. It is completely opposite of what I knew before, and I'm sad I wasted so much time on something so superficial. Porn is anti-sex, totally against what real sex is.

RESTORE

Psalm 71:20 (NIV)

Though you have made me see troubles, many and bitter, you will restore my life again; from the depths of the earth you will again bring me up.

Chapter 14: The Role of Grace, Part 1

In this chapter, we will look practically at the role of grace and how it helps us in our difficult climb. It is one of my favorite chapters in the entire book. But, before we discover how grace can manifest practically in our recovery process, I think it is important to take a little detour to address what grace is and what grace isn't.

Tackling this concept is intimidating to me. I am no theologian; I haven't attended a seminary or had any formal education in Bible philosophy. I have learned about grace through my own studies of the Scriptures, my own experiences, and some very special people in my life who did have the proper training. But what I'm about to share was the game-changer for me.

If you have been raised in Christian circles, the word "grace" is often tossed around in everyday language. "By God's grace, I (fill in the blank) . . ." I cannot help but wonder, do most of us even understand what we are speaking of? I didn't. Oh, trust me, I thought I knew. I learned the definition "unmerited favor of God" before I had entered the first grade. I heard that same definition over and over again throughout the course of my life. But seven years ago, my life changed. I began asking myself all sorts of questions, including questions about grace. What I discovered was startling. I had to unravel and untangle the knots of rule-following and performance-based thinking that were hindering my climb.

I cannot properly describe what this process of unraveling and untangling looked like. I had to work through anger and forgiveness. As I mentioned earlier, in one of the EMDR sessions with my trauma counselor, it came out that I had self-hate for the very fact that I was born a woman! Let that sink in... shame for the very gender God created me to be! It was extremely scary and sad that such awful, horrible shameful thoughts about myself were born out of one word: legalism. As you mature in your faith, you will feel more comfortable asking uncomfortable questions. Daring questions. Controversial questions. You develop the art of weeding through false teachings, especially when it comes to legalism.

The legalism I grew up in had greatly distorted the Gospel message of grace. At the time of disclosure, I questioned everything, including my faith. The foundation of what I thought was right theology collapsed, much like the walls of Jericho. It felt like the carpet got pulled out from under me, and all I could grasp was air. Legalism had given me a false sense of security and my heart was entirely undone.

The thing about legalism that makes it so lethal is the deception. It looks so good and sounds so right. In most cases, it is extremely subtle. While this chapter cannot address every single area of my life that legalism has damaged, I would like to share just one example of the covert deception.

I recently came across a blog regarding God's grace that started out so good. My heart was open, yet discerning. Everything was beautifully written until I got to one sentence. "Salvation is a matter of obedience."

I have a special alarm in my brain that goes off when it detects a legalistic belief. A vintage sounding "A-Woo-Gah!" went off inside my head as I re-read that sentence and began to unravel what the author was implying. But before I unravel that with you, I wonder what you think about that phrase? Would your alarm go off? Or would you simply read it and move on, as if nothing out of the ordinary had been said?

The reason why we are sitting on this topic is because it can be truly the most life-impacting part of your journey, so long as you learn to both recognize the false teaching of legalism that is still so prevalent in today's churches and Christian circles, and then dive into the mystery of grace.

What Grace Is Not

Let's start by briefly discussing what grace is not and how legalism is both dangerous and anti-Jesus.

Go back to the definition mentioned earlier. Many churches teach that grace is "unmerited favor by God." Unmerited means unearned. That means there is nothing that we can do or not do to obtain God's grace. This sounds good, until you hear a preacher tell you something like, "salvation is a matter of obedience." In one breath, a Christian may say we can't earn grace, and in the next breath, a Christian says we must obey in order to obtain salvation. Do you see the conflict? Obedience is a very important part of our walk as we put our trust in God, but is obedience required in order to obtain salvation? Is obedience required to earn God's grace?

In legalism, individuals live under a list of rules in order to pursue a life pleasing to God, and due to their knowledge of the Scriptures, they often have persuasive and smooth talk. They sound so convincing and have so much knowledge of the Bible that to disagree with or question a legalist feels foolish. There is much pressure under legalism to *do*. Grace allows us to just *be*. The focus in legalism is living a life that pleases God (doing) instead of living a life of trusting God (being). Let that last idea sink in.

Any time a person implies by either word or action that you must do something in order to obtain salvation or favor from God, run for the hills. This is false teaching and is most certainly not grace at all. You must be intentional in discerning what you hear from what you see because legalism can be so sneaky and is often covert.

I have observed that legalistic-minded individuals tend to over-spiritualize issues. Rather than entering uncomfortable feelings, they spiritually bypass emotions by quoting Scripture or praying. A legalist will rarely, if ever, show vulnerability. Legalists tend to be critical and condemning towards others, but sometimes only in their own heads. They learn how to hide behind their masks of religion and good works, but their subliminal messages are extremely destructive and can keep themselves and others enslaved to shame and the rat race of constantly trying to earn God's love and favor.

Legalism acknowledges that grace is, in fact, a free gift, but then distorts it by adding a dose of work and expectations on the side. This is not grace. And thank God it isn't!

I want us to look at grace from a fresh, new perspective. I admit from the start that I am still discovering grace. There is mystery in grace. I do not fully comprehend it, except that I know it meets me where I am and leads me to where I need to go, but without a drop of judgment. It finds me no matter my state of mind and in every circumstance. It is involved with every relationship, every decision, and every emotion. Quite frankly, I hope to be on the path of grace for the rest of my days, until I take my last breath here on this earth. I do not think it is humanly possible to "master" grace. There will always be more. How awesome is that? There will always be more grace! Therein lies the mystery.

Let's start with the basics of grace. But remember, let's shed the cliche definitions we grew up on and be open to a fresh

perspective, because this is the most important tool you could possibly yourself in your recovery process.

First, consider exploring the teachings of Jesus. His life was marked by loving others without inserting any kind of agenda. He loved advocated for the marginalized. He knew how to elevate the outliers. He disrupted the status quo. Studying the life of Jesus and applying His teaching to our lives has been a huge part of discovering grace. One of my favorite resources to learn about the teachings of Jesus was to do a deep dive into his most famous sermon: the Sermon on the Mount. I highly recommend listening to the Bible Project podcast, and focus on their series that unpacks all the richness within that sermon. It is incredible! You can find it on www.bibleproject.com, "Kicking Off the Year with Sermon on the Mount, Episode One".

I bet there are other people that may come to your mind when you think of a person full of "grace". Reflect on their attributes, and then determine if you treat yourself the way you saw them treat others in such a loving, kind, compassionate, patient way. We cannot truly offer grace towards others until we can first offer and receive it towards our own selves.

What Grace Is

If I were to summarize what grace means to me, it would be in two words: freedom and power. Grace gives us the freedom and power to face whatever circumstances come our way and helps us deal with our past, present, and future without judgment. My editor put it beautifully when she said, "Grace is found when we are pushed past the limits of our human strength. Grace is what we call it when God supplies our need, whatever that is, when our need exceeds our

resources. When we simply can't. . .I had no other source, within or without, that could give me the comfort to reach my indescribable deep grief. Sure, people and clergy and my dog and books were resources, but not enough. Like the hymn says, "When I've come to the end of my hoarded resources, He giveth, and giveth, and giveth again. Grace is God's inexhaustible willingness and ability to meet us and supply us."

Let's take out our binoculars and get an even closer look at how grace is both freedom and power. You're going to need this foundational lesson for the next chapter, where we will look at how you can apply grace practically in your recovery process.

People who are stuck in the pit of legalism get very edgy when we talk about power and freedom. They start to squirm in their seats a little bit and their hands get fidgety. Legalism may preach grace, but it certainly doesn't practice it. Those who are in bondage to a performance-based faith have the notion that having "too much grace" could potentially put one in a position to sin more often. It is the thought, "Because of grace, I can do whatever I want and just ask for forgiveness later." A legalist's philosophy that too much grace is risky, and therefore leads people into sin, is a philosophy that doesn't at all understand what grace is. I know, because I used to be one of them. I distinctly remember telling a friend after visiting a church, "I'm not so sure about the preacher...he was a little too grace-heavy." Do you know how embarrassed I am to admit I said that? Legalism is downright snotty. There is a reason why Jesus referred to those who practiced the law as a bunch of snakes!

When we invite grace into our lives, our inner-self changes. With this new, we find new freedom (which we will get to subsequently). Grace redeems, not destroys.

Grace is Power

This concept, that grace gives power, is so important in recovery, both for ourselves and for our spouses. Who knew that the gentleness of grace would be so empowering at the same time?

My husband refers to this wonder-working power over and over again as being absolutely key to living in sobriety. For years he tried to "white knuckle it" and he failed time and time again. True recovery is from the inside out, not the other way around. Once Jim faced him shame and invited grace in, he found sobriety and recovery to actually be possible. Grace has not increased his desire to sin more, but rather resulted in his wanting to turn from his old ways and completely embrace the difficult journey ahead so he could become the man he desired to be.

In my healing journey, grace has given me the power to endure the long, slow road of recovery. Without grace, I would have continued to self-hate, judge myself, and possibly stayed in a victim mindset instead of a victor mindset.

Without grace, I would still be seeking approval from others.

Without grace, I would be stuck in the cycle of people-pleasing, feeling exhausted and burnt out.

Without grace, I would still be rooted in shame and beneath the mask of my smile, hurting deeply. I would still feel rejected, unworthy, unloved, and unwanted. With the power of grace, I was free to still experience all those thoughts and emotions, but grace met me *in* those feelings, *through* those feelings, and then pulled me *out* of them.

Grace was the power that boosted me out of my despair.

Grace was the gentle friend that didn't judge me when I cycled back in despair.

Grace gave me the power to let go.

Grace gave me the power to express my anger.

Grace gave me the power to explore the pain from my past.

Grace gave me the power to face "the other woman," and extend forgiveness and love.

Grace gave me the power to set firm boundaries.

Grace gave me the power to state my needs.

Grace gave me the power to firmly say no.

Grace gave me the power to get out of bed and be a good mom.

Grace gave me the power to stand up for myself, even when I was scared.

Grace gave me the power to trust God's provision after spending thousands of dollars we didn't have on counseling.

Grace gave me the power to accept my reality when I wanted to deny it.

Grace is the life-giving energy to accomplish tasks we thought we could never do on our own. I suppose I could keep going on about how many ways grace manifested as power in my life. It is truly the power of God operating through and in us! Following the teachings of Jesus may sound "religious," but it is actually contrary to man-made religion. His followers busted out of the religious traditions of their time and they followed this controversial, radical-thinking, progressive and grace-filled person by the name of Jesus.

Grace is Freedom

Betrayal trauma and sex addiction recovery has a way of surfacing every shameful thought and emotion we've ever had and bring them right up to the surface. Having that vile come out of me all at once was shocking. Hate, vengeance, revenge, revenge-sex, suicidal thoughts, self-loathing, shame, and anger are just a few of the toxic poisons that oozed out of me. While I was pushed into this septic pit by my betrayer, there was a season when I didn't want to get out. I admit that I wanted Jim to feel my hate, my anger, and feel exactly how I felt, so I wanted to sit in that vile just to make it sting as much as possible. I wanted him to see me miserable, so he would feel shame for what he did. I wanted him to feel worthless, as I felt worthless. I wanted him to feel unloved, as I felt unloved. My "hiking boots" had to wade through a swamp of so much filth and sludge. The heaviness made it hard to function on some days. These were the darkest of days, when I definitely did not feel "free." The chains that my husband had worn for almost thirty years fell off him at the time of disclosure and transferred immediately to me. I was wearing his chains because of his choices. But, over time, I started to recognize that some of the shackles were actually my own. I was enslaved to false core beliefs and it was affecting my ability to live. Before I knew it, I was not only knee-deep in thick, muddy, emotional sludge but now had shackles and weight hindering my progress. I was stuck. I was tired. I was lost. I was angry. I was depressed. I was confused. Can you relate? These were the days where I thought it was impossible. There was no way I could make it through this. I told God, "I hate my life!" I had many nights where I literally rolled up in a ball on the floor of my bathroom and I would sob. For hours, I would lie there. And as I would sob, I would talk to Jesus, but with few words. Mostly I would say, "Jesus, help." Sometimes it was, "Jesus, I can't."

It was on the bathroom floor, in between sobs and snot and my body convulsing in dry heaves, that grace found me, again and again. Grace gently whispered, "I see you, and you are so beautiful." Often, I would close my eyes and envision my head lying upon Jesus' lap, His hand stroking my hair. It was grace where I found the freedom to just be me. This made a profound impact on my recovery and healing, because it took off so much pressure that I put on my own self to "snap out of it." I quit trying to please God and others, and allowed myself to just be. Knowing that I could be in whatever state I was in, and still find love and acceptance, changed my entire view of God, of myself, and my relationship with others. Grace offered so much freedom for me to have space, to make mistakes, to grow in maturity, to fail, to need more time, to cuss and throw tantrums, and so much more. I had never in my life experienced that kind of love before. I *fell* into Grace. I emotionally collapsed right in its arms and grace caught me. When I did finally escape from that awful swamp of self-hate and despair, it took some time to figure out how to live on a daily basis with this newfound freedom to just be.

Initially, this was uncomfortable. I felt like I was inconveniencing others. My authenticity felt so foreign. As I began to understand grace and what it really meant, I finally allowed myself to *receive* it. As I did, profound revelations and healing began to stir in my heart. And the more I received it, the more I was able to love myself and then pour that love into others. That resulted in chains being loosened, then completely shaken from my body. Like a bird out of a cage, I was being set free.

I found freedom from my past.

I found freedom from the lies that said I was unworthy, unloved, and unimportant.

I found freedom from legalism.

I found freedom from shame.

I found freedom from rejection.

And, over time, I found freedom from betrayal trauma.

Grace gave me freedom to grieve.

Grace gave me freedom to be real.

Grace gave me freedom to pave my own path to recovery.

Grace gave me the freedom to take my time to forgive.

Grace gave me the freedom to prioritize self-love and self-care.

Grace gave me the freedom to start laughing again.

Grace gave me the freedom and power to begin taking risks. I could jump off the cliff of the unknown and have confidence that if it all goes terribly, disastrously wrong, I would still be okay, because I had grace to power me through it. I could step into the open journey and feel confident that even if I ended up in a place unexpected, I would still be okay, because I had grace to hold me, accept me, empower me. No matter where I was, what I faced, what was in my past, present or even my future, Grace would carry me through.

This confidence was like an emotional protein bar for my weak emotional muscles. Grace nourished my heart as I climbed my mountain of recovery. Grace hydrated my dry and weary soul. The power and freedom I found in grace was like an inviting cup of coffee greeting me each cold morning saying, "I'm here, alive and active on this trail with you...we can do this!"

Heartwork Challenge:

1. **Was there a phrase or word from this chapter that "jumped off the page?" If so, write it down and share why.**

2. **Have you already experienced grace in your recovery process? If so, how? If you answered no, can you put into words why you think that is?**

3. **What would you like to be "set free" from today?**

4. **Take a minute to write a prayer or poem about Grace.**

Chapter 15: The Role of Grace: Part 2

We are going to start this chapter with the story of the woman at the well. Trust me when I tell you, you do not want to skip over this chapter. Why? Because we are going to attempt to jump over a very large boulder hindering your progress: the other woman. Whether the "other woman" was airbrushed online or your best friend, this chapter will boost us over the impossible boulder that is blocking our path to freedom. Jesus, help us.

You may have heard this story a million times before now, or maybe this is your first time. It's possible you are somewhere in the middle, familiar but not overly so. How familiar or not you are with the woman at the well is not relevant. I want you to approach this story as if you have never heard it before. Literally ask God to give you fresh eyes and ears. See if any details jump out at you that maybe you overlooked before. As you read, paint pictures in your head and allow the story to unfold like a movie in your mind.

The following description and analysis of the story, by Jack Zavada, appeared in the Learn Religions website in 2019. This article recaps the significance of the event, as he highlights the context and the details that make this story come alive for the reader. Read with a discerning spirit. Does Jack depict the Woman at the Well the way you remembered her? Did he highlight anything new or interesting? Did he describe her in any way you disagree with? Let's read his narrative, then I will talk about it a bit more about her.

Woman at the Well: A Story of a Loving God

How Jesus Shocked the Woman at the Well with His Love and Acceptance

The story of the woman at the well is one of the most well known in the Bible; many Christians can easily tell a summary of it. On its surface, the story chronicles ethnic prejudice and a woman shunned by her community. But take look deeper, and you'll realize it reveals a great deal about Jesus' character. Above all, the story, which unfolds in John 4:1-40, suggests that Jesus is a loving and accepting God, and we should follow his example.

The story begins as Jesus and his disciples travel from Jerusalem in the south to Galilee in the north. To make their journey shorter, they take the quickest route, through Samaria. Tired and thirsty, Jesus sat by Jacob's well while his disciples went to the village of Sychar, roughly a half-mile away, to buy food. It was about noon, the hottest part of the day, and a Samaritan woman came to the well at this inconvenient time to draw water.

Jesus Meets the Woman at the Well

During his encounter with the woman at the well, Jesus broke three Jewish customs. Firstly, he spoke to her despite the fact that she was a woman. Second, she was a Samaritan woman, and the Jews traditionally despised Samaritans. And third, he asked her to get him a drink of water, although using her cup or jar would have made him ceremonially unclean.

Jesus' behavior shocked the woman at the well. But as if that weren't enough, he told the woman he could give her "living water" so that she would never thirst again. Jesus used the words living water to refer to eternal life, the gift that would satisfy her soul's desire only available through him. At first, the Samaritan woman did not fully understand Jesus' meaning.

Although they had never met before, Jesus revealed that he knew she'd had five husbands and was now living with a man who was not her husband. He had her full attention!

Jesus Reveals Himself to the Woman

As Jesus and the woman discussed their views on worship, the woman voiced her belief that the Messiah was coming. Jesus answered, "I who speak to you am he." (John 4:26, ESV)

As the woman began to grasp the reality of her encounter with Jesus, the disciples returned. They too were shocked to find him speaking to a woman. Leaving behind her water jar, the woman returned to town, inviting the people to "Come, see a man who told me all that I ever did." (John 4:29, ESV)

Meanwhile, Jesus told his disciples the harvest of souls was ready, sown by the prophets, writers of the Old Testament and John the Baptist.

Excited by what the woman told them, the Samaritans came from Sychar and begged Jesus to stay with them.

Jesus stayed two days, teaching the Samaritan people about the Kingdom of God. When he left, the people told the woman, "... we have heard for ourselves, and we know that this is indeed the savior of the world." (John 4:42, ESV)

Points of Interest from the Woman at the Well Story

To fully grasp the story of the woman at the well, it's important to understand who the Samaritans were: a mixed-race people, who had intermarried with the Assyrians centuries before. They were hated by the Jews because of this cultural mixing and because they had their own version of the Bible and their own temple on Mount Gerizim.

The Samaritan woman Jesus met faced prejudice from her own community. She came to draw water at the hottest part of the day, instead of the usual morning or evening times, because she was shunned and rejected by the other women of the area for her immorality. Jesus knew her history but still accepted her and ministered to her.

By reaching out to the Samaritans, Jesus showed that his mission was to all people, not just the Jews. In the book of Acts, after Jesus' ascension into heaven, his apostles carried on his work in Samaria and to the Gentile world. Ironically, while the High Priest and Sanhedrin rejected Jesus as the Messiah, the outcast Samaritans recognized him and accepted him for who he truly was, the Lord and savior.

Question for Reflection

Our human tendency is to judge others because of stereotypes, customs, or prejudices. Jesus treats people as individuals, accepting them with love and compassion. Do you dismiss certain people as lost causes, or do you see them as valuable in their own right, worthy of knowing about the gospel? (Zavada, 2019)

Grace Brings the Unexpected

On May 2, 2020, I found myself driving from house to house in the Kansas City Metro area. I'm an amateur photographer and on that day, I was in desperate need for some extra income. I had scheduled "Covid Captures," something many photographers did as a means to continue working during the Covid19 outbreak of 2020. Photographers would stand from the street or lawn and take pictures of families, allowing them to capture a historical moment with their loved ones while also making some money during a life full of stay-at-home orders and job layoffs.

But this predictable start to my day turned strangely unpredictable during an unexpected change of events.

As I was driving down a country, two-lane highway, I cranked up my favorite music. Nearing the "s" curve just south of town, I took my foot off the accelerator and gave a neighborly "pointer-finger-wave" to an oncoming car. That's how we do it out in the country. I rolled down my windows and with my messy bun coming undone, felt the wisps of hair gently hitting my cheeks and forehead. I plopped my elbow up onto the window frame. I absolutely love country drives. My heart felt peaceful and grateful for the extra $250 I was earning that day.

But out of the clear blue, my state of contentment turned topsy-turvy, and I became more uncertain than I could have ever imagined. I should have known it was coming, but I wasn't prepared. And just like that, I was triggered.

Triggers can be sneaky. One second, you're fine and the next second, you feel like your insides are twitching as you try to keep yourself together. I had just driven past a gravel road that led somewhere I didn't want to remember. It led to hurt and betrayal. It led to rejection and pain. That road led to the home of the affair partner.

I have not spoken much of her up to this point. You weren't ready to go there, and I wasn't ready to introduce her to you. Before "going there," the Holy Spirit wanted us to first remember the woman at the well. Yes, I am included in that reminder, because it is only by His grace that I am able to share with you the unexpected ways Jesus' grace has manifested in my life and the life of my husband's affair partner.

Let's be honest. Women do not like other women who remind us of the Samaritan woman at the well. Not knowing the full story or having a clear picture, we make assumptions about them. We use derogatory names for them. Sluts. Whores. Ho. Man-Eaters. Homewreckers. Cheap. Hoochies. Loose. C'mon ladies. Let's get real with each other. Most of us have had those thoughts about another woman at least once in our lives. But what thoughts come into your mind when you think of the woman or women who seduced *your* husband. Can you even say those thoughts out loud? If they are in there, you might as well tell Jesus exactly what you think of her. He knows anyway. There is nothing that can pull out those nasty labels our self-righteous selves have stamped on other women than when we have been betrayed.

Part of the reason we label other women is because we have been conditioned to do so. Patriarchy and misogyny are deeply imbedded within our culture and has been around for thousands of years. Some might say they've been around since the attack on Adam and Even in the garden, when Adam blamed Eve for his choice. Women have been blamed for men's lust far too long. I'm challenging this notion because it's time for women to be set free from being the scapegoat.

If you study the woman at the well in depth, you might be surprised to find that it is highly probable that she wasn't all the labels the church has plastered her with. There are many scholars who believe that it was highly unlikely she was divorced five times. Rather, her current situation and past relationships could have very well been from other unfortunate, yet common, events. Life events that left many similar women in the same situation. Some of her husbands may have died. Some of her husbands may have divorced her for something as silly as she burned his dinner. She may have been in a polygamous marriage. Women in that culture could not initiate a divorce, and in the patriarchal cultural context, once a woman was divorced twice, it was highly likely that no other man would marry her. It seems far more likely that her story was much more involved that what I was taught growing up.

It is also historically accurate to highlight that in her culture, divorce, remarriage and concubinage were not considered to be promiscuous or immoral. When we focus on slandering her character, we are completely missing out on the most beautiful aspects of this entire story.

For starters, Jesus was extremely progressive by treating her as an equal. He broke all the cultural norms by elevating a woman to this kind of status.

Secondly, Jesus broke racial barriers by inviting conversation with her. Jews hated Samaritans, and that is why Jesus caught her attention rather quickly. She had never been treated like a human before by a Jewish male.

Third, Jesus mentions intimate details about her life to stress to her that she was fully known and fully loved. Jesus never rebukes her.

Fourth, Jesus saw in her a unique partnership as she became one of the first great missionaries and evangelists. A woman paved the way for His coming by declaring the Good News.

It's easy to feel threatened by other women, and to make assumptions about the kind of woman you think she may be. When I feel myself going in that direction, I like to ask myself, "What does my attitude towards her say about me?" Often, it highlights my own insecurities or false core belief systems. We all know what betrayal does to our self-esteem. Annihilation of how we view ourselves and our bodies is wording it kindly. Betrayal is brutal. Because of betrayal, we become experts at comparing ourselves. We are more aware of how we measure up to other women we pass in the store, see at church, see at baseball games, see on TV, or anywhere else we happen to go. It's a mental nightmare to be in our own thoughts. We can't seem to escape the judgment. Whether there was an actual "other woman" in flesh, or "other women" online, our insecurities increase. We don't like how we feel when we are around other women who highlight our insecurities. Is it possible that I have objectified women, too? Is it possible that I have misogyny too? In all honesty, yes. Absolutely.

Having that clearly laid out, I think you know exactly what I was feeling after passing that country gravel road on the two-lane highway. I've experienced years of triggers, so addressing them was nothing new to me. I immediately started talking to Jesus about it. Once I was able to get a few cuss words out of the way, He finally got a break in the conversation to speak back. I typically know when God is speaking to me, because he puts very specific thoughts in my head, usually random, and my heart tends to beat faster. This was no exception. I want to walk you through what can happen when Grace enters in, even during a trigger.

First, I was reminded of the woman at the well. I have always loved her story. I love how Jesus elevated her humanness. Her life had purpose. He spoke to her like a real person! She mattered to Jesus. Even knowing all this, I could feel every muscle in my body tighten as the thought registered with my heart. "Misty, you need to go to the affair partner's home and tell her she matters."

Oh God, no. Absolutely *no*! She and I had been friends prior to D-Day. I trusted her. She betrayed me. I had already worked through my forgiveness towards her. That part of my life was over. Or so I thought.

I continued to argue with God and myself as I kept on driving. I texted my support group and asked for prayer. I was a nervous wreck, yet felt a magnetic pull to drive to her home.

My stomach was full of knots. I did some deep breathing exercises and began to wrap my mind around how this would look.

With my spirit starting to calm, I surrendered my will.

Before we go any further, please hear me out. This was something I felt called to do. This is *not* a good thing for everyone to do. And even though grace covers the negative labels, that doesn't mean we don't need to have firm boundaries (which include never having contact with the affair partner again, etc.). Not every affair partner is repentant. Some are dangerous and/or emotionally unsafe. Please do not apply my story to your story, but simply glean from it what you can.

I turned off the highway and slowly made my way onto the longest mile of gravel road in my entire life. My heart was nearly pounding out of my chest. I was terrified. In a last desperate cry, I thought again, if there was anything else I was supposed to do or say. I then had the thought to give her my entire morning's earnings from my photography sessions. I had an envelope full of cash sitting next to me in the passenger seat. I looked down at it, and shrugged my shoulders as if to say, "I am so confused right now, but for whatever reason, this feels right." And before I knew it, I was pulling into her driveway.

The last time I had pulled into this driveway was on D-Day several years ago. Without my husband's knowledge, I had left our house and drove straight to hers. I needed to hear her side of the story and try to sort out truth from lies. It was an awful experience. I sat on the floor of her barn, begging for truth. I was a heap of a mess. While she smoked a cigarette, my entire body shook with sobs as the details of my new reality struck me like a poisonous dart to the heart. It was a dark day.

But on this day, three years later, I parked the car and grabbed the envelope. By grace alone, my feet moved towards the front door. I took another deep breath and whispered, "Help me, Jesus" and knocked on the door. Her husband answered, and with a protective scowl on his face, asked what I wanted.

Now, just try and imagine how ridiculous I sounded! "Hi there. So yeah, I was driving by your street, and God told me to come here and tell your wife that she matters. Oh, and uh, here's some money for her too." He literally stared at me and just blinked his eyes. I told him I knew how crazy it sounded. He asked me if there was a note or something to give to her. I tried to explain, again, that I had randomly driven by and felt an urgency to stop by. With a facial expression that said, "Are you crazy?", it was plain to see he had a very hard time understanding why I would randomly show up on their porch, after three years, with a wad of money and a message from God. I didn't understand it either! It felts so illogical, so irrational. I started to walk away, but just as I was about to turn my back, she came to the doorway and began to walk out onto the porch where I stood. Her husband threw the envelope of money on the ground and slammed the door shut. He was clearly not on board with this entire fiasco, and I can't say I didn't blame him!

She took my hands in hers and immediately started saying how glad she was that I was there and that she had been wanting to tell me some things but was too scared to reach out. Clarity and understanding began to sink in. Was it possible that I felt led to show up here so *she* could heal, not me? Maybe this crazy situation wasn't even about me, but about her? Really God...*her*? In those few seconds of processing, I saw my judgment towards her. My stinking thinking said this was an exercise for *my* healing, *my* faith, and *my* growth. Let me be totally raw. I did not think she was capable of receiving healing. I had arrived thinking this was all about me. How incredibly self-centered.

She led me through the back door for privacy and we settled in the shade. This already felt different. Last time I was here, we were hiding in the darkness of a barn. This day, we were sitting outside, not afraid to be seen. She wasn't smoking, and I wasn't in a heap of desperation at her feet. Surprisingly, my spirit felt peace. I had no ill intent towards her. In fact, I would say I was supernaturally filled with compassion towards her. The only confusing thought going through my mind was, "What is happening?"

We ended up talking together for about an hour, sharing our regrets, our hurts, and our hearts. The longer I sat there, the more I realized that we weren't that much different from one another. We both had been experienced pain. We both felt broken and flawed. We both had been set free from our past. We had both had discovered Jesus in a new, fresh way. We both felt sad that it took tragedy to steer us into a life of grace, freedom and power.

While we were talking, two teenagers came out of her home and she introduced me as "her friend, Misty." I'll never forget that. Because as I sat there, with the "other woman," I saw her truly as Jesus saw the woman at the well. I saw her potential. I saw her heart. I saw the pain from her past. I simply saw her. The "*other* woman" had become "*another* woman." She was no longer a label, but a lesson. A lesson on Grace. Love. Forgiveness. Kindness. Unity. Courage. We sat there in tears and talked about how none of it made any sense at all. We should hate each other. We should *both* hate Jim. But yet, I felt true, genuine care for her. I knew, of course, that things wouldn't be as they once were. I still needed boundaries in place to keep my heart safe. But I couldn't shake the fact that I was experiencing a truly empowering moment between two women who were more alike than different.

When I left, I felt completely exhausted. I sent her a text a while later and reminded her of the message that drove me to her in the first place. "You matter." Does this sound completely insane? How could the betrayed and the betrayer come together and see one another as equals? Grace met me in the car that day and followed me onto the back porch with the woman who shattered my heart and threatened my family. But there is more.

Later that evening, I was able to sit down privately with my husband and tell him the entire day's events. He sat next to me, his jaw dropped and eyes wide. It shocked him. But the incident also spurred him into another level of healing. I mentioned in an earlier chapter that my husband had already apologized to her, but he had not yet apologized to her husband, and it had always bothered his conscience. At midnight that same evening, my husband sat at his computer and typed out an apology letter to her husband and mailed it the following week. Making amends isn't easy.

When grace enters in, labels move out. This labeling applies to affair partners, porn stars, sexual abusers, dead-beat dads, critical mothers, and sex addicted husbands. But it also applies to you. Your label. Betrayed. Rejected. Unloved. Unwanted. Where we see the broken, Jesus sees the mended. Where we see rubbish, Jesus sees beauty. As we grow in our spiritual and emotional maturity, as we lean in to our triggers and enter recovery, our hearts change, for the better. As mentioned in the previous chapter, grace empowers us to have radical love and acceptance towards ourselves first, and then we can extend it towards others.

Offering grace towards those who have harmed us doesn't mean there are no consequences. There are still boundaries, legal ramifications, destroyed relationships, etc. However, grace gives us the ability to zoom out, get a bird's eye view, and gain healthy perspective.

Invite Grace into Your Journey

Grace transcends all human understanding and brings the heavenly realm down into our lap. It allows us to climb the unthinkable and bear the unimaginable. Grace has the uncanny ability to give us the grit when we need to fight, and the space to enter tranquility. It's friend, Wisdom, helps us discern when to enter

the battle and when to lay our weapons down. But whether we are gearing up for the climb, or in a posture of unloosening our hiking boot laces to rest, grace is there. When we invite grace into the journey, our hearts of stone soften and help us shed the demands of recovery, the critical skepticism, and the angry outbursts. Light will flood into the darkest places of our heart and bring new life. Peace in the midst of chaos.

Grace for Self

How would your life change if you applied grace to yourself? What if you were able to shed the perfectionism and shame-based thinking, and turn them into radical acceptance? What if you learned how to view your body as the masterpiece that it is, imperfections and all? What if you saw yourself as the capable, lovable, but flawed person you are, and be 100% accepting of her? How would showering yourself with grace affect how you parent your kids? Respond to abuse? Set a boundary? Live honestly with others? Do your recovery work? Bringing grace into the hard is what will give you the permission you need to go easy on yourself. To be kind to yourself. To be patient with yourself. To stop expecting perfectionism from yourself. To lose the shameful thinking. Grace in the climb doesn't mean you quit doing the work needed for your healing. You release the pressure you put on yourself to do it perfectly. You quit beating yourself up if you don't read your Bible every day. You stop comparing yourself to others. You advocate for your needs and don't feel guilt for it. Grace is the safest place for us to be fully known and fully loved just as we are. We don't have to do; we can just be.

Inviting grace into your recovery climb is also what will power you up that steep hill of recovery work. You will need to take

breaks to breathe and catch your breath, to rest, grieve, and process. Grace is in the climbing, grace is in the resting, and grace is everywhere in between.

When we can extend this gift of grace towards ourselves, we can then pour that grace on others, even to those who have betrayed us.

Grace for Others

Now let's consider what could change if you were able to let grace enter into your thoughts towards the "other woman." How would your life change if you were able to have compassion towards her? Forgive her? See her as fully human, just like the woman at the well? Shed the label? Have empathy for her? Do you not see how loving your enemy leaves you as the victor? The kind of grace we are inviting in is freeing. Transform your thoughts to see others as Jesus saw others. He was able to see past the behaviors and stigmas, and He can help us do the same, through grace. Because we have extended grace towards ourselves, we can stop demanding perfection towards others. We learn to love others where they are, without inserting our opinions. (And remember, loving others where they are might mean setting boundaries which is still exhibiting love.)

Grace helps us to let go of the pain that keeps us tethered to our abusers and those who have betrayed us.

Grace liberates us. It offers us freedom from the years and years of pain, but we must learn how to invite grace in to do its transformative work. Without grace, the people who have hurt us can continue to do so. They still have power over us as long as we hold on to that hurt. For many years, my fist has been clenched tight around pain inflicted by others, giving me some sense of control. But living a life that can receive and give love means we have to learn how to open our hands, and thus our hearts, to extend grace. That doesn't mean we have to release the need to follow through with appropriate legal processes or setting firm boundaries. It's releasing my desire to vindicate my pain in the way I think is best, and instead, releasing it.

Grace for the Spouse Not in Recovery

How could your life change if you were able to extend grace towards your sexually addicted husband? You see, when we radically love ourselves, we know how to exhibit love towards our enemies. How could your life change if you were able to offer your abuser love? If your husband is acting out, you are not showing love to yourself or to him by allowing him to exert control over you or to continue living in his addict-mode behaviors. If you have learned how to radically love yourself, then you exhibit that love by laying down your sword of constantly trying to defend yourself and move into a position of offense. You show your love by no longer hiding behind the abuse. You rise up into the courageous woman you are and fight for *safety*. If your spouse is exhibiting abuse, it may not be safe for you to be confrontational to your abuser. In such cases, getting a good safety plan together and having appropriate legal support would be a safer version of "rising up."

As a woman of grace, you know that a marriage with no boundaries is not psychologically healthy nor is it spiritually sound. It empowers a repeatedly destructive spouse to continue to believe the lie that the rules of life don't apply to him, and if he does something hurtful or sinful, he shouldn't have to suffer the relational fallout. That kind of thinking is not biblical, healthy, or true.

For the welfare of yourself, your children, and your spouse, there are times we must take a strong stand. To act neutrally in the matter only allows the person's self-deception to grow unchallenged.

The addictive person is a destructive person who desperately needs to experience God's grace and love, but to receive it, he needs to see himself more truthfully so that he can wake up and make the necessary changes. It's true that we are all broken and in desperate need of God's healing grace. The problem for the destructive person is that he has been unwilling to acknowledge his part of the destruction. He's been unwilling to confess or take responsibility or get the help he needs to change his destructive ways. Instead, he's minimized, denied, lied, excused, rationalized, or blamed others. This is why, through grace, we set boundaries. It is primarily for our safety, but in doing so, we hope to invite him into the recovery process.

When we invite grace into our boundary setting, we can firmly and boldly state our expectations in a tone of self-control and without scolding, shaming, condemning or punishing. Although the primary purpose for boundaries is creating safety for you, implementing tough consequences is what can often jolt someone awake with the strong medicine of God's truth and the reality of his choices. We hope that by doing so, they will come to their senses, turn to God, receive His grace, and thereby stop the destructive behaviors for the glory of God, their own welfare, and the possibility of the marriage being restored.

When all hell breaks loose, you can trust that His grace is sufficient when you feel your weakest. Through grace, you accept that you have permission to leave. Through grace, you know you are not condemned by walking away from the destruction. Paul tells believers that we are to distance ourselves from those who claim to be

believers yet live immoral and destructive lives (1 Corinthians 5:11 NIV). You understand that God, in His deep love and affection for you, does not demand that you stay in a relationship where you are abused. His grace means you can be free! You are free from the fear of being alone. Free from the fear of being condemned. Free from the fear that your kids will be ruined. Free from the fear that God will not provide. You are free to enter His peace! Grace is what will catapult you into what seems to be the impossible.

Grace for the Spouse ***In*** Recovery

Sometimes the damage within the marriage is enough to terminate the marriage even if he is fully in recovery. Showing grace doesn't have to mean pursuing an intimate relationship with him. Maybe showing grace means being happy for him that he chose recovery and will better his life.

Should you choose to stay in the marriage, how could your life be changed if you chose to love your husband and radically accept his shortcomings? (To reiterate, we are *not* speaking of an *abusive* spouse, but the spouse who is in active recovery and showing signs of true heart changes.) Take a moment and consider your husband's heart. John Lynch, author of The Cure, says, "Grace is the face love wears when it meets imperfection." Grace meets us where each of us are on the journey, but gently takes us where we need to go.

As you observe his changed behavior, you can trust him enough to be more vulnerable with him, but it's a process. We can extend grace to our husbands during their learning process and give them space to grow. We won't see perfection, but we ought to see progress.

For example, what would happen if, the next time your husband reacted with immaturity and instability, how would grace play out? What would it look like? Rather than give the silent treatment or lash out, you could calmly say, "That was very hurtful to me, and I felt like responding in my old, unhealthy way by shaming you and giving you the silent treatment. But I love you, and I know we are *both* learning how to communicate in a new, loving way. I love myself enough to speak truth in love, and I love you enough to hold you accountable for your approach. How about we rewind what just happened and try to talk this out in a productive, healthy way?" If you feel unsafe, you can table the conversation until you are both with a therapist who can mediate and help direct his reactivity towards productivity.

Grace doesn't mean people get a free pass to continue harming us, and grace invites, never demands.

In closing, I want to offer a paragraph from John Lynch's autobiography, On My Worst Day.

On my worst day I am:

Adored, enjoyed, clean, righteous, absolutely forgiven, new, acceptable, complete, chosen, able, intimately loved, smiled upon, planned for, protected, continually thought about, enjoyed, cared for, comforted, bragged on, defended, valued, esteemed, held, hugged and caressed, kissed, heard, honored, in unity with, favored, enough, on time, lacking nothing, directed, guided continually, never failed, waited for, anticipated, given all grace, all patience, at peace with, pure, shining, precious, cried over, grieved with, strengthened, emboldened, drawn kindly to repentance, relaxed with, never on trial, never frowned at, never hit with a two-by-four, at rest in receiving complete access,

given gifts, given dreams, given new dreams, continually healed, nurtured, carried, never mocked, never punished, most of my humor enjoyed, not behind, not outside, given endless affection.
(Lynch, 2013, p. 76)

That is how Jesus sees you on your worst day. It's time we see ourselves in the same light.

Heartwork Challenge:

1. **In your own words, describe what grace means to you.**

2. **Name a specific way that grace, when invited in, could potentially change your perspective in recovery?**

3. **How has grace manifested in your recovery climb thus far?**

4. **Can you relate to the woman at the well? Explain.**

Q & A WITH JIM

CHAPTER 15: THE ROLE OF GRACE, PART 2

1. How has grace impacted your recovery process?

It's been critical. Not only does understanding grace help me stay sober, but it has helped me in the ability to build emotional intimacy with Misty. Grace is hard to put into words. It is essential, for both the present and the future. I fail all the time, so if it wasn't for grace, I would remain in a constant state of shame and rejection, which would inevitably destroy my sobriety. Grace is the key to recovery, the key to intimacy, the key to peace...it is the key to everything!

2. What has been the hardest thing to understand about grace?

There is nothing I can or cannot do to earn it. It is free.

3. Has it been hard for you to receive grace? Why or why not?

Yes, it has been hard to receive it. Growing up in legalism, I was conditioned to believe that I must be a certain way or do certain behaviors in order to earn God's favor as well as the favor of others. This constant state of trying to prove my worth and perform my way into grace was exhausting and impossible. I've also had to learn how to let go of control and pride and realize that I can't do it on my own. I need God.

4. Has it been hard for you to offer grace towards yourself during recovery? Why or why not?

Yes, it has been very hard. Again, it goes back to legalism and being raised in an environment where I was expected to look good, act good, and perform my way into favor. Legalism kills grace. Misty and I have both had to completely unravel the false theology of legalism and learn what grace means.

5. How can a husband show his wife grace during recovery?

Men, in general, need to stop trying to "fix" their wives. They also need to accept that wives have their own pace in recovery and offer them the space and patience they need in order to heal.

6. What or where would you be without grace?

I'd be addicted and in my filth. I would also still be hurting the people I love.

Chapter 16: Restore

I am not a theologian. I have not taken any courses in original Hebrew or Greek. I could not win a debate with a 5-Point Calvinist or break apart the book of Romans.

Having that confession out of the way, I must approach this chapter delicately. Why? Because I don't have it all figured out. This part of my life hasn't yet been written, and yet, here I am, starting this final chapter, staring at a perfectly blank page both on my laptop and in my life. God's pen still holds ink to be used in my story. Not exactly a "grand finale" finish to a book of a budding new author, right? But maybe, just maybe, this is the point. Maybe there is something to be said for a blank, white page staring back at me. Maybe I shouldn't feel pressured to have and know all the answers when it comes to restoring life after betrayal. Maybe this book has something to do with my own restoration phase. Lies in my head certainly tell me I must have some kind of deep wisdom to share on this topic of "restoring," or else, why am I even attempting to write a book? Isn't restoration the whole point? Then again, maybe I should go back and omit this phase of recovery and not even mention it? Why did I mention it in the first place if I haven't yet personally fully experienced it?

Am I crazy? Or am I on to something? Or is it just too soon yet to know?

I suppose it all boils down to one word: hope.

Restoration sounds hopeful, doesn't it? But what does restoration mean?

It seems to me like this word is tossed around a lot in the Christian community.

People say, "God is in the business of restoring," or "God restored our relationship." But what does that even mean in the context of betrayal and sex addiction? How can God restore the sick, twisted, perverted and demented stories of our lives and turn them into something...well...good?

I've spent considerable time reading up on this topic. My initial thoughts on this final stage of restoration came from the popular verse in Joel 2:25 (NKJV) where God says, "So I will restore to you the years that the swarming locusts has eaten..." God's people had suffered the complete destruction of their entire harvest through swarms of locusts that marched like an insect army through the fields, destroying the crops and multiplying their number as they went.

For four consecutive years, the harvest was completely wiped out. God's people were brought to their knees in more ways than one. But "the Lord became jealous for his land and had pity on his people."

In the coming years, God said, their fields would yield an abundance that would make up for what had been lost: "The threshing floor shall be full of wheat, and the vats shall overflow with new wine and oil. You shall eat in plenty and be satisfied..." (Joel 2:24, 26 NKJV).

This wonderful promise for those people meant that years of abundant harvests would follow the years of desolation brought on by the locusts. The phrase, "the years the locusts have eaten," is a metaphorical phrase to us today. It refers to a season of extreme hardship, pain, and testing.

But could it apply to betrayal? Sexual addiction? Betrayal trauma?

The word "restore" didn't sit right with me. All it took was a simple Webster Dictionary to confirm that my instincts were correct. See if you can see why:

Restore: to bring back to the original condition.

Ummm, Girl. C'mon now, we have come way too far to even think about wanting to go back to our "original condition!" Can I hear an amen? No wonder I'm all caught up on this word! God doesn't want us to go backwards. He's been doing a new work in us and He's not done yet!

I began to think I had completely chosen the wrong wording for my phases of recovery, (climb, conquer, rest, restore) and should start from scratch, and rethink what actually happens when we are on the other side of the mountain of recovery.

The problem with my thinking is that I was looking at this through the English language, and the Old Testament was originally written in Hebrew. My geeky, educator self got super excited. I enjoy looking up Hebrew translations and digging into Strong's Concordance.

I poured myself a cup of organic decaf coffee, sweetened it with fresh, raw honey and a splash of my favorite goat milk, and settled into our cozy couch. Ralph, our Golden Retriever, sat at my feet, warming my toes with his body. Whenever I pull out Strong's Concordance, I know I'll be still for a while. I totally nerd out and the teacher in me loves to study words. Imagine lounging next to me as I pour you your own cup of coffee. Let's sit together on the word "restore" and see if it begins to make more sense to us.

Going back to Joel 2:25 (NKJV): "So I will restore to you the years the swarming locusts have eaten..."

Restore: original Hebrew word Shalam (Sha-LAHM).

My first thought was how closely this word resembles "Shalom," which many know to be the official Hebrew greeting meaning, "Peace." Well, now, if I plugged that word in, that would put an interesting twist on this verse, wouldn't it? "I will give *peace* to you from the years the locusts have eaten." Oh, that sounds so nice. Peace after years of climbing up a gigantic mountain...I can handle that, can't you? But the word isn't SHALOM. The word is SHALAM (pronounced Sha-LAHM). Here's what Strong's Concordance states, as presented in Biblehub:

PART OF SPEECH: verb
USAGE: to make amends, to make an end.
DEFINITION: To be complete or sound.
DETAILED DEFINITION: to be at peace, to be complete, to finish.
USAGE: TO MAKE AMENDS, to make an end.

Oh wow. Now this is starting to come to life for me. Let's definitely start here because I'm starting to get fired up from totally nerding out on all the dictionaries on my lap and word definitions opened up in about 20 browsers! Now we're making some headway.

"To make amends": to compensate for a loss or injury.

Let's say I borrow a pair of earrings from a friend, and I lose them. I cannot give the original earrings back to my friend since they are lost, but I can give her money for what they were worth. I made amends. This makes sense. God will not "restore" us in the sense that He will bring us back to our original condition. He will "restore" us in that some way, somehow, we will be compensated for our losses.

Our losses will never come back. What we have lost will not be "restored" to the original condition. Those losses are why we have felt every stage of grief and cried many, many tears. In the midst of despair, I need to know, hear, believe and have hope that regardless of what happens to my marriage, I am still capable of creating a glory story!

"Restore" is a verb. It is action. Movement in a new direction. It is wreckage to reclamation.

Maybe by the time you read this, I will have a ginormous list of restoration in my life. I definitely have a list going, but it isn't ginormous. It is small, every day things that I observe or feel and think, wow...I've come a long way.

I know not everyone's story will end with a restored marriage. But once again, consider the woman at the well. Jesus didn't restore her marriage(s) or her relationships with others. He restored her to Himself! I love that so much. Once again, we are reminded that God is pro-people before being pro-institution. This restoring process is about <u>you</u>. You are the priority.

I also believe that restoration can be about giving back. I, personally, didn't climb and conquer that mountain to keep it all to myself. I found my voice and I'm learning how to use it for good, for purpose. You will find your voice again, and when you do, you just might have what it takes to toss a rope to help others. You will be a lifeline for other women who are just starting their hard climb. This will look a million different ways, but I know that sharing my experience is what I am called to do, even though it scares me silly.

Climb. Conquer. Rest. Restore. You, my dear friend, are now ready to <u>RISE</u>.

Rise out of abuse.

Rise out of despair.

Rise up to the challenge of recovery.

Rise above the lies that say you are not worth it.

Rise into your new, stronger version of you.

Your "Hallelujah" may get tired, but there is a new song for you to sing.

Clean your wings and soar because you are breathtakingly beautiful.

It has been my greatest sorrow and my greatest reward to write this book for you. Sorrow because I wish I didn't have to. Reward because if it helps just one sister, it was worth it. With these final typed words, I pray God's ink would inscribe healing words upon your wounded heart. Better days *<u>are</u>* coming, so rise. Let's go do some serious rock-climbing.

Dear Woman,

You are beautiful. I am so sorry you are hurting. This was not my plan for you nor your marriage. Feel free to invite me into your pain. I will never put pressure on you. I do not demand your affection. Take all the time you need. In regard to the mountain you are facing, you are capable. Tell me all about the journey. When you do, it makes my heart full to connect with you. I am not intimidated by your anger, insecurities and hate. So, go ahead, get it all out. I won't stop loving you, even on your worst day. Right now, I am beginning a new work in you. I will help you rise again. When you conquer, I will rejoice with you. When you cry, my heart will bleed with yours. When you feel inadequate, I'll let out a ginormous, "You got this, girl!" When you need rest, my lap is ready. When you experience a victory, we will enjoy the breathtaking views of the forest below. Together, we will rise. Together.

I love you, God

Hear my cry, O God; listen to my prayer. From the ends of the earth I call to you. I call as my heart grows faint, lead me to the rock that is higher than I. For you have been my refuge, a strong tower against the foe" Psalm 61:1-3 (NIV).

Heartwork Challenge:

1. **Open-ended question: did anything in this chapter jump out at you?**

2. **Do you have hope? Why or why not? (there's no right/wrong, just observing where you are in this moment).**

3. **Throughout our journey together, what are one or two things that have been pivotal to your healing process?**

4. **What can you be grateful for today?**

5. **Take a minute and proclaim restoration (making amends/make an end) to your mountain of recovery.**

6. **Do you foresee yourself offering a "rope of hope" to other women? How so?**

7. **What has God taught you during this book study?**

Q & A with Jim
Chapter 16: Restore

1. Do you think it is possible for a sex addict to find restoration? How?

Yes. There are tools, such as recovery groups and professional counseling, which help along the way. But again, the key to recovery and restoration for me is grace. But that grace played out many different ways in recovery.

2. Do you think it is possible for a marriage to find restoration after sexual betrayal? How?

Yes, it is absolutely possible! But it is hard work. I think Misty beautifully outlines the process of how to work towards marriage restoration. It is imperative to remember that it takes both partners to be 100% committed to their own recovery work.

3. Does restoration always mean the marriage will work out? Explain.

No. Individual restoration is possible no matter what. That is the hope we have. Individual recovery should be the goal. If the marriage fails, and the marriage was your end goal, then you will not be restored. But when both individuals get healthy and restored, a healthy marriage can be the by-product of two healthy individuals.

4. Misty uses the sentence, "The best views happen after the hardest climb." How do you know when you are seeing "the best views?" What are signs or things to look for?

Misty and I both agree that the best way to know if you are on the right track is to look at how you resolve conflict. The way we resolve conflict now is entirely different than how we resolved it before we did the painful work of recovery.

Another sign is intimacy. Are you able to share feelings, ideas, and dreams with one another? Are you able to have moments of laughter? Are you becoming friends again?

Relationships, in general, start to look different. In a good way. Healthy boundaries are established and if they get crossed, you are able to maintain stability and not get completely flooded with emotions.

I used to say our relationship was like a sine wave. It was up and down all the time. But as we worked on it, the constant highs and lows slowly started spreading out and the valleys weren't as deep. In general, the relationship starts to calm down and show consistency.

5. Do you think you and Misty have fully arrived at the peak of the recovery mountain? If no, are you seeing signs that tell you that the marriage is on the right path? Explain.

No, we have not fully arrived, but we are seeing signs that we have conquered some big hurdles. We have experienced all of the answers in the previous question, and it is very encouraging.

6. How do you think God views the sex addict and does He even want to restore him? Explain.

There is nobody outside of God's love. NOBODY. He loves everyone. He wants everyone to be restored to Him. Jesus says He will leave the 99 to pursue the 1. There are many examples in the Bible of messed-up people that God pursued and transformed. So, how does God view the sex addict? He loves him/her. But the choice is up to him/her to receive His love and turn away from his/her destructive choices.

Resources and References

Books

Anderson, S. (2014). The journey from abandonment to healing. Berkley.

Aterburn, S., & Martinis, J. B. (2014). Worthy of her trust. WaterBrook.

Blythe, A. (2020). Trauma mama husband drama. Self-published.

Brown, B. (2010). The gifts of imperfection: Let go of who you think you're supposed to be and embrace who you are. Hazelden Publishing.

Brown, B. (2015). Daring greatly: How the courage to be vulnerable transforms the way we live, love, parent, and lead. Avery.

Brown, B. (2017). Rising strong: How the ability to reset transforms the way we live, love, parent, and lead. Random House.

Carnes, P. (2019). The betrayal bond: Breaking free of exploitive relationships. Health Communications Inc.

Chapman, G. (2015). The 5 love languages: The secret of love that lasts. Northfield Publishing.

Cloud, H., & Townsend, J. (2016). Safe people: How to find relationships that are good for you and avoid those that aren't. Zodervan.

Fjelstad, M. (2013). Stop caretaking the borderline or narcissist: How to end the drama and get on with life. Rowman & Littlefield Publishers.

Haas, M. (2018). L.I.F.E. recovery guide for spouses. (D. Laaser and M. Laaser, Eds.) Bowker.

Keefer, S. (2018). Intimate deception. Revell.

Laaser, M. (2004). Healing the wounds of sexual addiction. Zondervan.

Laaser, M. (2013). L.I.F.E. recovery guide for men. Bowker.

Lynch, J. (2013). On my worst day: Cheesecake, evil, Sandy Koufax and Jesus. John Lynch Speaks.

Lynch, J., McNicol, B., & Thrall, B. (2016). The cure: What if God isn't who you think He is and neither are you? Trueface.

Maltz, W. (2009). The porn trap: The essential guide to overcoming problems caused by pornography. HarperCollins e-books.

Milligan, I. (2010). Understanding the dreams you dream. Destiny Image Publishers.

Petersen, A., Sweeten, G. R., & Geverdt, D. F. (1990). Rational Christian Thinking: Renewing the Mind. Equipping Ministries International, Inc.

Rubin, J. S. (2013). The maker's diet: The 40-day health experience that will change your life forever. Destiny Image Publishers.

Stringer, J. (2018). Unwanted: How sexual brokenness reveals our way to healing. NavPress.

Tell, B. (2015). Lay it down: Living in the freedom of the gospel. NavPress.

Van der Kolk, B. (2015). The body keeps the score: Brain, mind, and body in the healing of trauma. Penguin Books.

Weiss, D. (1998). The final freedom: Pioneering sexual addiction recovery. Charisma House.

Weiss, D. (2019). Partner betrayal trauma. Discovery Press.

Wilson, G. (2015). Your brain on porn: Internet pornography and the emerging science of addiction. Commonwealth Publishing.

Online Resources and Services

Betrayal Trauma Recovery. BTR. https://www.btr.org

Blythe, A. (2021, January 21). 50 Things You Need to Know about Betrayal Trauma. Betrayal Trauma Recovery. https://www.btr.org/betrayal-trauma-glossary/

Blythe, A. (2016, July 5). How to stay safe when your partner is unfaithful. [Audio podcast episode]. In Betrayal Trauma Recovery. https://www.btr.org/boundaries-in-marriage-2/

Carr, W. (2019, May 21). Pornography Still a Problem for Many. Daily Gate City. http://www.mississippivalleypublishing.com/daily_gate/pornography-still-a-problem-for-many/article_f4d9d722-7c02-11e9-a815-1ffd32bd019a.html

Covenant Eyes. (2020). Pornography Statistics. https://www.covenanteyes.com/pornstats/

Fight the new drug, Inc. (2020). Fight the new drug. https://fightthenewdrug.org

Herfeord, Z. (n.d.) Healthy Personal Boundaries & How to Establish Them. Essential Life Skills. https://www.essentiallifeskills.net/personalboundaries.html

How Porn Affects the Brain like a Drug. (2017, August 23). Fight the New Drug. https://fightthenewdrug.org/how-porn-affects-the-brain-like-a-drug/

Joi. (n.d.) Center for peace. https://cenfp.org

Hull, M. (2020, August 4). Pornography Facts and Statistics. The Recovery Village. https://www.therecoveryvillage.com/process-addiction/porn-addiction/related/pornography-statistics/

King, J. (2020). Narcissistic Politics in Intimate Relationships. Prevent Abusive Relationships. https://www.preventabusiverelationships.com/articles/narcissistic_politics_abuse_signs_524.php

Kinnaman, D. (2016, February 5). The Porn Phenomenon. Barna. https://www.barna.com/the-porn-phenomenon/

McDugal, S. (n.d.) Trade your wilderness for wild. https://sarahmcdugal.com

McDugal, S. (2020, October 31*). Signs of Marital Sexual Abuse.*[Video] Systems of Abuse Series. YouTube. https://www.youtube.com/watch?v=gvcCmNBrKA0&list=PL9WSC9P1z2VeGeak1Id8gsioSdaKnYGBI&index=9

Moore, A. (2014, June 12). Defining and Enforcing Boundaries in Sexual Addiction Recovery. adammmoore. https://adammmoore.com/2014/06/12/defining-and-enforcing-boundaries-in-sexual-addiction-recovery/

QuotesCosmos. (n.d.) Manoah. In Strong's Concordance, Hebrew Dictionary. https://www.quotescosmos.com/bible/bible-concordance/H4494.html

Rennison, C.M. (2003) *Intimate Partner Violence, 1993-2001.* U.S. Department of Justice. https://www.bjs.gov/content/pub/pdf/ipv01.pdf

Shalam. In biblehub. Online Parallel Bible Project. https://biblehub.com/hebrew/strongs_7999.htm

Weiss, D. (2020) Sex Addiction. Break the Chains of Sex Addiction. https://www.sexaddict.com/six-types-of-sex-addicts/

Zavada, Jack. (March 2, 2019). Woman at the Well: A Story of a Loving God. Learn Religions. https://www.learnreligions.com/woman-at-the-well-700205

Appendix A

Learning How to Study the Bible from a RESTORED perspective

Restoration is about building something NEW. For me, that included who and where I turned to study the Bible in a way that included full context from an Eastern perspective.

We found the following sources to help us un-learn false theology and replace it with new truths that changed our lives.

- **The Bema podcast: www.bemadiscipleship.com**
- **Bible Project Podcast: www.bibleproject.com**
- **Text In Us Podcast**
- **Elle Grover Fricks (teaches Hebrew) www.ellegroverfricks.com**
- ***Back to Eden* by Bruce C.E. Fleming- book about Gen. 3:16**
- **Breaking Down Patriarchy- podcast**

Appendix B

Some thoughts from other women who have been in active recovery. (Their names have been changed for confidentiality.)

"Jan"

What I wish I knew then:

- **Betrayal trauma is worse than death! (My mom was the victim of betrayal trauma and then remarried a wonderful Christian man and he died. She said the betrayal was worse than death.) It's real.**
- **Boundaries!**
- **Definition of abuse- yes, lying is one form of emotional abuse and so is leaving out information. Emotional infidelity IS infidelity and hurts just as much. So is pornography use, so is punching a wall...**
- **Know how to recognize gaslighting**
- **Your marriage is not more important to God than your emotional safety**
- **God is not punishing you for your past**
- **Someone who doesn't know what abuse is (or is an abuser themselves), who tells you to love more, pray more, submit more, or anything besides get to safety is not a safe person**
- **Find the right counselor and one who is trauma-informed and knows about sex addiction**
- **You do not need marriage counseling until you're safe**
- **A women's betrayal trauma group is key to healing**
- **Get counseling for yourself**

- **This is not about you, it's never been about you and there's nothing you did to cause betrayal, nor could you have prevented this**
- **You do not need to protect his facade and doing so allows him to continue to not feel the consequences of his behavior including with family, church, children and friends**
- **Ask the right questions. Instead of "how are you doing?" ask "When was the last time you ___?"**
- **A polygraph is a wonderful tool to verify truth**
- **You deserve to be free from abuse/lie/porn/infidelity, etc.**
- **God gave you intuition; don't ignore it**
- **If you do not have a job or your own money, learn a skill, babysit or clean houses and save some money so you can feel like you have a choice**

"Sharon"

What I wish I knew before I started this healing journey of recovery:

- **That everything the enemy had intended for Evil, God intended and used for good.**
- **I wish I knew that in the darkest hours of my life God had a plan.**
- **That He would take every shattered broken piece of my heart and put it back together again, heal me and use me to help other ladies walk and find freedom as well and that I would find great joy in doing so!**
- **That the scariest most vulnerable parts of my life would be used to testify to other women that it is possible to find hope, help, healing and love.**

- That God uses the darkest most painful parts of our story to be a light to others.
- That through the process of being open, honest, vulnerable, and connected to all my brokenness, that my husband and I have discovered true intimacy, pure love and thoughts towards one another the way Christ intended us to walk. Absolutely incredible.
- I wish I had known that Jesus was going to reveal parts of Himself to me in way I could not even ask, think or imagine, and that I would find true fellowship and communion with Him.
- I wish I knew that truth is what sets us free but often the hardest thing to walk in, but if willing, there is an amazing life God has for you, full of ups, downs, aches, pains, grief, sorrow, despair that turns to pure joy and love.
- That all this work--hard, ugly, deep, overwhelming work--is worth doing! It will give you the life you want if you do the work!
- I wish I knew how incredibly thankful I would become because I went through this horrific tragedy.

Appendix C

The 13 Forms of Domestic Abuse

***Taken from www.BTR.org**

1) Child Abuse

- **threatening to take children away**
- **refusing to comply with child support**
- **using children as leverage**
- **belittling you in front of children**
- **using children to keep you silent**
- **abusing your children**

2) Cultural Abuse

- **using culture as an excuse for mistreatment**
- **putting down your culture**
- **forcing you to accept or embrace his culture**
- **isolating you from mainstream cultural practices**
- **using culture to keep you silent**
- **using language barriers to isolate you**
- **not providing translation when you can't understand**

3) Emotional Abuse

- **incessant teasing**
- **invalidating your feelings**
- **using guilt to manipulate you**

- **blame you for everything**
- **acting jealous (calling it protective)**
- **threatening you**
- **withholding affection**
- **waking you up from sleep**
- **stalking your whereabouts**
- **stalking your social media/electronic devices**
- **giving you the silent treatment**
- **lying or omission of truth**

4) Financial Abuse

- **limiting your access to money**
- **not sharing bank accounts**
- **requiring an account of every penny spent**
- **making you ask for spending money**
- **controlling the income and cash flow**
- **making financial decisions without you**
- **closing accounts without telling you**
- **creating debt you didn't agree with or know about**
- **wasting resources**
- **not paying child support**
- **taking care of their own needs but neglecting yours or the children's**
- **calling welfare to interfere with income**
- **confiscating your income or cash**

5) Intellectual Abuse

- saying you're over-sensitive
- saying you're crazy
- manipulating information or facts
- attacking your ideas
- devaluing your opinions
- demanding perfection
- playing head games
- making you prove things
- shaming your tastes
- insulting your education
- dumbing you down

6) Pets & Property Abuse

- destroying property
- breaking or smashing things
- punching walls
- slamming doors
- hurting pets
- damaging your car
- confiscating your car keys
- keeping your identification or Driver's License
- controlling your access to GPS or computers/phones
- selling items w/o telling you
- keeping cash from selling your things
- threatening to do any of the above

7) Physical Abuse

- **driving too fast or recklessly**
- **slapping or hitting**
- **kicking, punching, or biting**
- **pinching or twisting**
- **restraining you**
- **choking you**
- **spitting on you**
- **intimidating you with actions or gestures**
- **throwing things at you**
- **using items other than hands to hurt you**
- **locking you out of the house**
- **making you sleep outside**
- **blocking exits, not letting you leave**

8) Psychological Abuse

- **saying things and then denying it later (gaslighting)**
- **intimidating you with words or gestures or actions**
- **displaying weapons**
- **threatening to commit suicide**
- **threatening to hurt you**
- **threatening to kill you**
- **minimizing actions or threats after the fact**
- **making it sound like you misunderstood or made it up**
- **controlling your access to food**

- dictating what you eat
- using gestures or body language to control you through fear

9) Sexual Abuse

- using pornography
- demanding that you use pornography
- demanding sex as payment
- withholding sex
- criticizing your body sexually
- comparing your sexuality to others
- having an affair/viewing porn/emotional affair
- threatening to have an affair
- forcing sex
- manipulating sex
- sexual put-downs
- sexually abusing others
- withholding medical needs or not allowing spouse to sleep

10) Social Abuse

- isolating you from friends
- isolating you from family
- monitoring your phone calls
- monitoring your emails/social media
- monitoring your mileage
- controlling who you are allowed to see or talk to
- controlling your freedom to work

- controlling your freedom to get education
- keeping you at home
- not allowing equal access to social interaction
- telling you not to talk about your relationship with other people

11) Spiritual Abuse

- using scripture to excuse abusive behavior
- using scripture to manipulate you
- twisting scripture to gain power
- putting down your beliefs
- isolating you from your faith community
- using his church to his advantage over you
- refusing to get counseling
- dictating who you are allowed to see for counseling
- using scripture to keep you silent
- soul-destroying behaviors

12) Verbal Abuse

- calling you names
- swearing at you
- yelling or screaming
- using sarcasm to put you down
- being condescending
- insulting you
- body shaming you
- cutting you off in conversation

- **telling you to be quiet around other people**
- **intimidating you**

13) Power Abuse Lies at the Core of All Abusive Systems

- **creates chaos and conflict by turning people against each other, misrepresenting situations**
- **twists past events to gain control**
- **credit hog — acts like they get everything done, doesn't give healthy credit where it's due**
- **delusions of grandeur, believes they are smarter/wiser/stronger/richer/more powerful than they are**
- **refuses to get counseling, refuses to allow spouse to get counseling**
- **projecting addictions as spouse's fault w/o taking responsibility**
- **racist/elitist — diminishes/ridicules culture, color, gender, age, status —believes own identity is superior**
- **obsessed with being "respected," may get aggressive to peers/children/elderly if perceives they are acting with "disrespect"**
- **entitled, act as if they're better than others, others should give way to their preferences, others should take care of their needs.**

Appendix D
Resources by Topic

Listed below are a few of my favorite books, podcasts and websites I referred to during my recovery and in writing this book. I have grouped them by focus and topic, to help you more easily identify resources that will address your needs. There are many others available, but these are ones I have actually utilized and gained much insight from. I think each author has their own perspective and while I didn't align with all of them 100%, I found enough positive wisdom to feel they are worth mentioning. (Updated 2024)

Disclaimer: **resources recommended have been reviewed, however, I cannot guarantee relevance or success for any individual situation.**

Books on Betrayal Trauma/Abuse for Her

Betrayal Bind by Michelle Mays

Intimate Deception by Dr. Sheri Keefer

Beyond Betrayal by Noni Yates

Worthy of Her Trust by Stephen Aterburn and Jason B. Martinis

The Journey from Abandonment to Healing by Susan Anderson

A L.I.F.E. Recovery Guide for Spouses by Melissa Haas

Not Marked: My Story of Finding Hope and Healing after Sexual Abuse by Mary DeMuth

The Woman They Could Not Silence by Kate Moore

Healing from Hidden Abuse by Shannon Thomas

Books on Sexual Addiction for Him (and for education)

Contemporary Male Sexuality by Dr. Barry McCarthy

Healing Wounds of Sexual Addiction by Mark Laaser

L.I.F.E. Recovery Guide by Mark Laaser

The Sexually Healthy Man by Andrew J Bauman

The Psychology of Porn by Andrew J Bauaen

She Is Not Your Rehab by Matt Brown

Worthy Of Her Trust by Stephen Aterburn and Jason B. Martinis

Unwanted by Jay Stringer

How Not to Be an Ass by Andrew J Bauman

Your Brain on Porn by Gary Wilson

The Heart of Domestic Abuse: Gospel Solutions for Men Who Use Control and Violence in the Home by Chris Moles

Books on Sexuality

Taking Sexy Back by Alexandra H. Solomon

The Sexually Healthy Woman by Christy Bauman

Contemporary Male Sexuality by Dr. Barry McCarthy

Rekindling Desire by Barry McCarthy

Finding Your Sexual Voice by Barry McCarthy

Come As You Are by Emily Nagoski

Better Sex Through Mindfulness by Lori Brotto, PhD

The Great Sex Rescue: The Lies You've Been Taught and How to Recover What God Intended by Gregoire, Lindenbach, and Sawatsky

Theology of the Womb by Christy Bauman

More Than A Body by Lindsay Kite and Lexie Kite

Book on Personal Growth/Relationships

Becoming Egalitarian by Nicki Pappas

Safe People by Cloud and Townsend

The Seven Principles for Making Marriage Work by John Gottman

Stop Caretaking the Borderline Narcissist by Margarita Fjelstad

The Betrayal Bond: Breaking Free of Exploitive Relationships by Patrick Carnes

Daring Greatly by Brené Brown

The Gifts of Imperfectionism by Brené Brown

When Pleasing You is Killing Me by Dr. Les Carter

Adult Children of Emotionally Immature Parents by Lindsay Gibson

Disentangling From Emotionally Immature Parents by Lindsay Gibson

Rejected Shamed and Blamed: the Family Scapegoat by Rebecca Mandeville

Together: Reclaiming Co-Leadership in Marriage by Tim & Anne Evans

The Awakened Family by Shefali Tsabary, PhD

Books on Faith/Religious Trauma

Her Rites by Christy Bauman

When Religion Hurts You by Laura Anderson, PhD

The Making of Biblical Womanhood by Beth Allison Barr

Jesus and John Wayne by Kristen Du Mez

Back to Eden by Bruce C.E. Fleming

Tell Her Story by Nijay K. Gupta and Beth Allison Barr

Pure: Inside the Evangelical Movement That Shamed a Generation of Young Women and How I Broke Free by Linda Kay Klein

Safe Church by Andrew J. Bauman

How God Sees Women by Terran Williams

Lay It Down by Bill Tell

The Cure by John Lynch

The Lord Is My Courage by K.J. Ramsey

Books on Body Health and Wellness

The Makers Diet by Jordan Rubin

The Body Keeps the Score by Bessel Van der Kolk

Books on Biblical Interpretation of Dreams

Understanding the Dreams You Dream by Ira Milligan

Books on Domestic Abuse (for individuals and churches)

The Heart of Domestic Abuse by Chris Moles

Systems of Abuse: A Guide to Recognizing Toxic Behavior Patterns by Sarah McDugal

The Emotionally Destructive Marriage by Leslie Vernick

Why Does He Do That? by Lundy Bancroft

Is It Me? By Natalie Hoffman

Is It Abuse? A Biblical Guide to Identifying Domestic Abuse and Helping Victims By Darby Strickland

The Life Saving Divorce by Gretchen Baskerville

In Sheep's Clothing by Dr. George K. Simon

The Gaslight Effect by Dr. Robin Stern

Favorite Websites/Podcasts:

www.btr.org

www.fightthenewdrug.com

www.michellemays.com

www.wildernesstowild.com

www.leslievernick.com

The Place We Find Ourselves -podcast by Adam Young

Love & Libido -podcast by Dr. Emily Jamea

Jerry Wise: Family Systems Relationship Theory- on YouTube

Surviving Narcissism by Dr. Les Carter- on YouTube

Dr. Ramani -on YouTube

Breaking Down Patriarchy-podcast by Amy Allebest

The Bible Project Podcast with Tim Mackie

Bema Podcast with Marty Solomon

Dr. Jake Porter (for couples in recovery) on social media platforms

Financial Abuse/Financial Trauma/Financial Coach

www.intentionalmoneycoaching.com

321-348-7901

Online Counseling/Coaching Services/Group Therapy/Online Support Groups

www.flourishtherapy.co

www.daringventures.com

www.mountaincitychristiancounseling.com

www.helpfortrauma.com

www.btr.org

www.kcrecoverypartners.com (KC local and online options)

www.michellemays.com

www.cenfp.org (for men only)

www.calledtopeace.org

www.leslievernick.com

www.wildernesstowild.com

Group Leader Tips

If you are using this book in your group, here are a few tips to follow:

1. The group does NOT have to read the same chapters at the same time. Remember, every woman will experience trauma differently, and some will move faster through the material more quickly than others. Have general questions that everyone can answer such as:
    - What did you learn most about yourself this week?
    - What was the hardest part of this week's lesson?
    - What is your recovery goal for this week?
    - What are you feeling today?
    - Where do you feel your emotions in your body?
    - How did you stay grounded this week?
    - What was your greatest strength this week?
    - Answer one question from your homework and share with the group.
2. Set Boundaries by setting a timer for each person so no one monopolizes time.
3. Be respectful of time. Always start and end on time.
4. Remind often that we are to love without inserting our opinion. Feedback can be given when asked for it.

5. When someone is speaking, others should actively listen.
6. Remind women to have their answers written down beforehand. Come to class prepared. There will be times she may show up unprepared. Deal kindly and gently with her. Some days, just showing up is a huge win.
7. Remind women to be sensitive to topics shared. If a topic could potentially be extremely triggering, they may need to use generalized verbiage vs. detailed accounts.
8. Grace, grace, grace! Every woman has unique experiences. Every woman has different forms of trauma that affects her individually. Every woman is on her own journey. This is a support group, not a counseling session. Offer love and support.
9. Validate. A lot. Remind the women that they are seen and heard. Do not reprimand or demand. *Be extremely gentle in all things.*
10. Educate. Pull resources outside of class.
11. Once a week or bi-monthly is recommended for group sessions. You can take summers and holidays off, but I would encourage once/month summer outings or sessions to stay tuned in with one another.
12. Safety, safety, and more safety should be the core basis for traumatized women. They can do all the self-growth in the world, but their abuse can still be happening. Stress safety. Secondly, have loads of resources. A good group leader offers resources (such as counselors in their area, options for different modalities, polygraph practitioners, etc.) Guide the women to learn how to trust their intuition, have their

own thoughts, come to their own conclusions, and educate well on all forms of domestic abuse.

13. Remember your role. It is not your role to rescue, just support and offer resources. Encourage each woman to get into counseling. Create a care team so you are not alone. Creating safety for each woman should be primary focus. I highly recommend you also reading a book about helping victims of domestic abuse: Is It Abuse? By Darby Strickland. It will assist you and give you good insight.

SAFETY PLAN PROTOCOL:

1-800-799-SAFE

https://www.thehotline.org/plan-for-safety/create-a-safety-plan/

Our Family

Us

Ralph

Spike, the Hedgehog

Sunset on the River, 2018

2017 in the MR340 Race

Made in the USA
Monee, IL
20 December 2024